*Routledge Revivals*

# Reflections on Life and Religion

First published in 1952, *Reflections on Life and Religion* is a collection of selected entries made by Sir James Baillie from 1893 to his death. These entries, preserved as MS. Volumes labeled "Privatissima", are a record of the inner mind of a thinker of wide culture who enjoyed extensive contacts with public affairs as well as with worlds of philosophy and education.

The book is divided into three main sections dealing with religion; ethical and social philosophy; and metaphysics and theory of knowledge. Each of these sections is further divided into several shorter subsections, in accordance with the requirements of the subject area. The appendix contains a number of short entries which could not find a suitable place in the main body of the text.

This volume will be a fascinating read for anyone interested in religion, philosophy, and particularly metaphysics.

# Reflections on Life and Religion
Sir James Baillie

*Edited by* Sir Walter Moberly and Oliver de Selincourt

First published in 1952
by George Allen & Unwin Ltd

This edition first published in 2024 by Routledge
4 Park Square, Milton Park, Abingdon, Oxon, OX14 4RN

and by Routledge
605 Third Avenue, New York, NY 10017

*Routledge is an imprint of the Taylor & Francis Group, an informa business*

© 1952 Sir Walter Moberly and Oliver de Selincourt

All rights reserved. No part of this book may be reprinted or reproduced or utilised in any form or by any electronic, mechanical, or other means, now known or hereafter invented, including photocopying and recording, or in any information storage or retrieval system, without permission in writing from the publishers.

Publisher's Note
The publisher has gone to great lengths to ensure the quality of this reprint but points out that some imperfections in the original copies may be apparent.

Disclaimer
The publisher has made every effort to trace copyright holders and welcomes correspondence from those they have been unable to contact.

A Library of Congress record exists under LCCN: 53006561

ISBN: 978-1-032-84245-5 (hbk)
ISBN: 978-1-003-51210-3 (ebk)
ISBN: 978-1-032-84294-3 (pbk)

Book DOI 10.4324/9781003512103

SIR JAMES BAILLIE

# REFLECTIONS ON LIFE
# AND RELIGION

### SIR JAMES BAILLIE
O.B.E., D.PHIL., LL.D.

Formerly Vice-Chancellor of Leeds University
and Professor of Moral Philosophy, Aberdeen University

EDITED BY
SIR WALTER MOBERLY
AND
PROFESSOR OLIVER DE SELINCOURT

LONDON
GEORGE ALLEN & UNWIN LTD
RUSKIN HOUSE  MUSEUM STREET

FIRST PUBLISHED IN 1952

*This book is copyright under the Berne Convention. Apart from any fair dealing for the purposes of private study, research, criticism or review, as permitted under the Copyright Act* 1911, *no portion may be reproduced by any process without written permission. Enquiry should be made to the publisher.*

PRINTED IN GREAT BRITAIN
*in* 12 *pt Fournier type*
BY UNWIN BROTHERS LIMITED
WOKING AND LONDON

*"The final and supreme destiny of the scholar is to unite wisdom with kindness, knowledge with love, care for truth with love of man—and without reverence that is not possible."*
                    J. B.

# INTRODUCTION

THE story of Sir James Baillie's life is a simple record of academic success and domestic happiness. He was born in Angus in 1873 of Scottish parents, and his childhood was spent there and in Haddingtonshire. He seems to have found his vocation very quickly. He became a student of philosophy at Edinburgh University, where his teachers were Professors Campbell Fraser, S. S. Laurie and—later—Pringle Pattison; and in this field his success was immediate and outstanding. A long series of scholarships and fellowships enabled him to prolong his studies at Cambridge, where he had contact with Henry Sidgwick and James Ward, and also at Halle, Strasburg, and Paris. He had thus an unusually varied equipment when he took up his first teaching post in 1900 at St. Andrew's under Professor Ritchie; and he was still under thirty when he was promoted in 1902 to the Chair of Moral Philosophy at Aberdeen, a post which he continued to hold for the next twenty-two years. In 1906 there followed the central event of his personal life, his marriage to Miss Helena James, a niece of Lord James of Hereford.

Among philosophers Sir James Baillie first made his name as an interpreter of Hegel. His early books were *Hegel's Logic* published in 1901 and *The Idealistic Construction of Experience* published in 1906. These were followed in 1910 by a two-volume translation, with elaborate introduction and notes, of Hegel's *Phenomenology of Mind*, which has quite recently been reprinted. His next book, *Studies in Human Nature*, published in 1921, was also his last; for though he had many years of active life before him, his attitude towards academic philosophy in general, and the Hegelian school in particular, had by this time become somewhat detached and critical and his energies were becoming more and more absorbed in practical affairs.

In the first instance this diversion of interest was due to the service which, like so many other University teachers, he was called upon to render in the first World War. During its earlier years he served in the Intelligence Division of the Admiralty. Later he was drawn into the work of conciliation and arbitration in industrial disputes under the Ministry of Labour. In this work his lucidity of mind and urbanity of manner made him markedly successful; and during the years immediately following the war, when he had returned to his Chair in Aberdeen, he was much in request as a Chairman of Trade Boards.

Then in 1924 he was appointed Vice-Chancellor of the University of Leeds; and in this office the remainder of his active life was spent. His tenure came at a time when the University was committed to an almost complete rebuilding programme. He threw himself with energy into this task, and he was notably successful in gaining the confidence and enlisting the support of leading representatives of the business community in the West Riding. But his services to the University and its neighbourhood were by no means exhausted by his administrative activities. Many public ceremonies, in the University and outside, were lifted out of the commonplace by the striking elevation of thought and distinction of style which characterized his addresses and were matched by an unfailing dignity of bearing.

Sir James retired from the Vice-Chancellorship in 1938, and settled in Weybridge, where he and Lady Baillie looked forward to a life of quiet and studious leisure. But this was not granted him for long. He gave up a great part of the following year to an important arbitration in Trinidad, undertaken at the request of the Colonial Office; and he died suddenly in June 1940.

\* \* \* \* \*

Throughout his working life, and not least in the years when he was busily occupied with the cares and concerns of University Administration, Sir James contrived to find opportunities for private meditation; and it was his habit to record on paper, as and when they occurred to him, his reflections on the general topics of human nature and life. These are preserved in twelve large

INTRODUCTION

MS. volumes, labelled "Privatissima," covering the period from 1893 to his death: indeed the last entry (p. 54) was made only a few days before he died. There are over three thousand entries altogether, amounting in all to about half a million words. As these figures suggest, the entries are mostly short: they vary in length from eight or ten words to about two thousand, but most of them approximate much more nearly to the lower limit. Few of them are dated, though each complete volume has a clear indication of the years in which its contents were composed.

As a title, the word "Privatissima" might convey to the world a misleading impression of the contents of these volumes. They are neither diary nor autobiography. They contain no personalities and no intimate "confessions." They are not concerned with academic politics, and they bear no trace of day-to-day controversies. They consist of reflections, mostly grave but sometimes of a lighter character, dealing with questions of wide human interest and illustrating from a number of different angles the meditations of a deeply reflective mind. Though written *currente calamo*, they constantly show the distinction of style with which Sir James's friends had become familiar in his public utterances.

It is from these volumes that the contents of the present work have been selected. By Sir James's will they were left to the University of Leeds, with the condition that no action should be taken about them for ten years after his death, but with discretion to publish parts of them if that were thought desirable. In 1950, when this period had elapsed, we were invited by Lady Baillie, acting in conjunction with the University authorities, to look at the material with a view to making a book of selections.[1] In spite of the obvious difficulties, we have felt it incumbent on ourselves to make the attempt. Quite apart from any interest which the MS. may have as the expression of Sir James's deepest convictions, we feel that much of it is of high value on its own

[1] We had both, at different times, worked on Sir James's staff at Aberdeen and had consequently enjoyed some opportunity of getting to know his mind, as well as his kindness and generosity as a chief.

account, rich in suggestive matter and often felicitously expressed. At the very least it provides a record of the inner mind of a thinker of wide culture, who, for much of the fateful half-century which culminated in the second World War, enjoyed extensive contacts with public affairs as well as with the worlds of philosophy and education.

The reader is perhaps entitled to a word about the principles on which we have made our selection and arrangement. Our aim has been to make a selection which is fairly representative of the complete MS. and at the same time likely to be of interest to the general reader; and there is only one respect in which we have consciously departed from these principles. Many of the entries, particularly in the earlier volumes, deal with philosophical topics in a more or less technical manner; and since Sir James was a philosopher by training and vocation we have naturally included some entries of this kind. But we have made the choice much smaller than considerations of merit would require, not only because the entries in question are technical, but also because changes of philosophical fashion have made them less immediately relevant than when they were composed, and because Sir James's philosophy has after all received full expression in his published work. With this exception, we believe that our selection offers a fair sample of the complete MS. and that none of Sir James's special interests have been neglected. For the rest, we have not withheld any entries which we thought characteristic and of general interest merely because they might seem inconsistent with other entries which we had included or are concerned with controversial topics and therefore of necessity open to criticism. Still less of course have we taken into account the degree in which we ourselves might happen to be in agreement with any particular item. Occasionally we have even retained, because of its considerable intrinsic interest, an entry which we felt sure that Sir James would have revised or reworded in the light of later events.

Our arrangement of the selected material is something of a

INTRODUCTION

compromise. In the original MS. the order of items is purely chronological; Sir James evidently passed from topic to topic as day by day new reflections occurred to him. But for the convenience of the reader we have felt bound to attempt some kind of arrangement according to subject-matter. We are of course aware that any such arrangement is inevitably somewhat arbitrary: however careful and detailed it may be, there are bound to be some entries which do not easily fit into it and others which seem to fit into it in more than one place. Accordingly we have deliberately kept it to a minimum. In particular we have not sought to make the book more readable by introducing contrasts and juxtapositions which are not to be found in the MS. Our aim has been only to provide it with such form and structure as are necessary to enable the author to speak effectively for himself. To this end we have divided it into three main sections, and each of these in its turn into a number of shorter subsections, in accordance with the requirements of subject-matter; and we have added an appendix containing a number of short entries for which a suitable place could not be found in the main body of the book. But within each subsection, and also of course in the appendix, we have printed the individual entries in a purely chronological order.

The topic which bulks largest in the MS. is undoubtedly religion. By professional training of course Sir James was a philosopher rather than a theologian. His status in theology is that of a widely read and profoundly reflective layman of independent mind; and the reader should remember that most of the entries were composed at a time when what are now the latest trends in theology could hardly be taken into account. But the subject was always of absorbing interest to him, and in later years he found in it his complete satisfaction: certainly it provides the occasion for many of his most characteristic, carefully studied, and deeply felt utterances. The first and longest of our three main sections is accordingly devoted to it. The contents of the other two cannot, however, be so simply described. So long as "philosophy" is given a reasonably broad interpretation, we can perhaps say that their topics are mainly philosophical. The second, in which the entries are for the most part of a non-technical character, deals with topics of ethical and social philosophy. The third deals with topics of metaphysics and theory of knowledge; and since it naturally contains more technical entries, we have made it correspondingly shorter. We should perhaps add that Sir James himself described his MS. as "the record of my reflections on life, philosophy and religion;" and we have borne this in mind in subdividing the material as well as in choosing our title.

About the shorter subsections and the appendix not much need be said. The appendix has in the nature of the case no special subject-matter; and though each subsection is concerned with a special topic or collection of topics, the distinctions between them are inevitably somewhat rough and ready, and their contents cannot always be so simply described as those of the main sections. We should, however, like to claim on behalf of the appendix that Sir James's characteristic gifts are often displayed at their happiest in short entries like those of which it is composed. Even though some of the best short entries are to be found, interspersed with longer ones, in the main body of the book, we feel that a fair picture of the special quality of the complete MS. could hardly be conveyed unless a reasonable number of them were grouped together in a separate and distinct place.

In addition to selecting and arranging the material we have also occasionally felt obliged to make small editorial alterations and corrections. In the nature of the case the entries were written somewhat hurriedly and on the inspiration of the moment: it is indeed their spontaneity that gives them their special interest. Had Sir James himself been preparing them for publication, he would no doubt have carried out a careful revision; and we have felt that we should not be true to his wishes if we printed all the entries exactly as we found them in the MS. We have accordingly repunctuated freely; and in a few passages where the meaning did not seem transparent at first sight, we have slightly varied the wording in order to bring it out more clearly.

INTRODUCTION

But here as elsewhere our aim has been to do as little as possible: in fact no more than we believe that Sir James would himself have done in order to present his material in an acceptable form.

\*     \*     \*     \*     \*

A book of this kind obviously does not lend itself, like a systematic treatise, to being read consecutively or at length. It is rather an anthology into which the reader may dip with profit and pleasure as opportunity serves. He will find in it a store of passages which embody sustained thought, expressed in language which is often graceful and often pungent, of shrewd and pithy maxims mingled with the meditative reflections of a resolute seeker after truth. He will make contact with a mind wide-ranging and finely trained; the mind of one who, beneath the involvements and distractions of a public career, consistently devoted much of his time and attention to contemplation of the deep things of eternity and, in that perspective, to the effort to see human life steadily and to see it whole.

We should like to express our gratitude to the library authorities of the University of Leeds and the University College of South Wales and Monmouthshire for their helpfulness and courtesy in making the material available to us; to Miss Elizabeth Sheppard-Jones for invaluable assistance in the difficult business of making a typescript and in reading proofs; and above all to Lady Baillie herself for unfailing sympathy and encouragement throughout.

W. H. M.
O. DE S.

# CONTENTS

INTRODUCTION *page* 7

## I

RELIGION *page* 17

## II

HUMAN NATURE AND CONDUCT *page* 145

## III

THE WORLD AND OUR KNOWLEDGE OF IT *page* 237

APPENDIX *page* 275

INDEX *page* 287

# I
# RELIGION

## I

**1** Wonder is reverent ignorance while superstition is ignorant reverence; and that is a great difference.

**2** It is curious to notice how religious minds have differed in their ways of expressing the relation between man and God. All of them emphasize the unity, but they express it from different points of view. Thus the Jews expressed man's relation to God as if what they said were the deliverance of God Himself; so complete was their sense of unity that man was interpreted from the point of view of God: "God said," etc., "Thus saith the Lord," "when thou passest through the waters I will be with thee," etc. etc. The unity led them to speak as if from the inner mind of the eternal. God was so real to them that they assumed His position and spoke for Him, spoke as if He were speaking; hence their view of prophecy; hence also the impression made by them on later religious minds as being "inspired." But this outlook was really only the expression of a peculiar type of mind, a mind which inverted the ordinary logic of experience and, instead of starting from man's reality and speaking of God from the express basis of man's life, spoke of man from the point of view of God. This psychological peculiarity seems to have misled the ordinary reader, and he has come to look on the Jews as in a unique relation to the religious life of humanity.

We, on the other hand, more conscious of man's limitations,

more conscious of the vastness and majesty of God's life—look at the religious life rather from the point of view of man. Individual man means more to us and seems to mean less to God, and hence we do not venture to speak in God's place in the same way.

But the relationship is exactly the same in both cases; and the limitations are present in both cases whether expressed or implied. We are no less inspired than the Jews; we are only more modest.

**3**   It is fatuous to assert that we cannot know all, cannot know God, etc., because to know all we should have to be all, to know God we should have to be God. Why, a man surely knows his neighbour without *being* his neighbour, or a turnip without *being* a turnip.

**4**   The true meaning of the phrase "religion is a man's own individual concern" is not that it can be left to himself to do as he likes about it, but that religion compels a man to take up a distinctive attitude to ultimate things, and that this is of supreme importance to him as an individual. The phrase certainly does not mean that a man is isolated in his religion; for religion is just the destruction of isolated existence and abandonment to what is absolutely universal.

**5**   The general features for the most part common to all forms of religion can be traced to three distinct sources: the intellect, the will, and the desire of the worshipper. Thus communion between man's spirit and God's in the element of intellect gives rise to "inspiration," "oracles," "voices," etc.: in the element of will, communion gives rise to sacrifice, submission, reconciliation, atonement, etc.: in the element of desire, it is expressed through prayer and praise.

**6** We hear much talk of the religious life of the Eastern peoples, as if each tribe and race had religious ideas which are deserving of respect because held with apparent conviction, and which are even regarded as valid because acted on with sincerity. This is the kind of toleration which arises from the absence of any standard of judgment for the subject in hand, a toleration which arises less from regard for the truth than from ignorance of it or indifference to it. It is ridiculous to suppose that the religious ideas or beliefs of people are deserving of respect merely because they are held with conviction and sincerity. Conviction or sincerity is not a test of truth nor a guarantee of validity; it should accompany the truth but it may very well accompany error; it may be a measure of the value of ideas to the individual, but is not measure of their validity in themselves. It is surely absurd to suppose that people who are brutally ignorant or even careless of the plainest truths of ordinary life should be considered capable of having true ideas about the most difficult aspects of experience such as the relation of God to man. Orientals seem to make a practice of telling lies and mutually deceiving one another: a state of mind like this is constitutionally incapable of having true ideas regarding God's relation to man.

**7** It does not much matter whether we say God forgives sins and, therefore, must be transcendent, or is transcendent and, therefore, must forgive sins: and the same holds of the idea of immanence.

We can see how it is natural that some religions emphasize the aspect of transcendence, and others that of immanence. But, in principle, it is evident that transcendence implies immanence and that immanence implies transcendence: they are both aspects of the divine reality in its relation to human finitude.

**8** There is a curious tendency amongst many or most people to communicate with God in one way exclusively—some by words, others by desires, others by thoughts, others by acts. These all forget that the whole spirit must be in communion if communion is to be effective, and that communion cannot be confined to one kind any more than it can be limited to certain times or places. It must be always, at all places, and in all forms of spiritual life if it is to be sincere and complete. To realize this is just the difficulty of the religious life, and to attain it is the consummation of the religious attitude.

**9** The religious life cannot require the effort of the moral or scientific attitude; for in religion God's Reality must be accomplished in us and through us: we rather accept and acquiesce in the process. It is a relief not to be always in the strain and tension of finitude.

**10** It is remarkable that the closer God comes to man, the more there is of joy in man's life. When God is far off, terror, or at least fear and awe, are the companions of man's soul. Thus, in polytheistic Greece, outside the perils and bitterness of society, life was full of joy; the gods were close at hand, responding to every special need, one god to each purpose or mood of man. On the other hand, the Hebrew God is far off, is one and supreme and remote on that account: as a consequence, life is full of the "fear of the Lord" which is at best but the "beginning of wisdom": God is full of wrath, great in majesty, so far away that He requires mediators, etc. The conception of a divine mediator (or a human-divine mediator) is really implied or required by the very nature of the Hebrew God, in order to destroy the aloofness and bring God near to man, as God should be.

It is doubtless a matter of some importance *how* God comes close to man: not all ways are equally valuable or valid. But that He should be near to man in some way seems evident. For the only creature on the globe who can appreciate His very existence is man; nor can He Himself be both *outside* the world and its bearer and creator at the same time. He must be *in* it, and so *in* man.

Whether we realize this nearness in fulfilling the moral life, in fulfilling sense-life (beauty) or in fulfilling rational activity (truth), in any and every case its realization must, if duly appreciated, bring joy: and this is found in the perfect artist, the perfectly good ("kind") man, the perfect scientist and philosopher.

**11** It is curious how the religious mind at its highest levels retains the characteristics of the lowest—in a dilute form, but still in an unmistakable form. Early nature religions connect God with a place, a hill, a stream, a range of mountains: this same principle reappears in Christianity, where we find that, for thousands, God is peculiarly associated with Jerusalem or Rome. People want a kind of local telephone exchange between man and the Almighty.

**12** Mysticism seems to depend mainly on visual sensation and imagery; rarely on auditory, and never on tactual, sensation.

This is remarkable. Touch in sense-experience is ordinarily looked on as the primary test of external sense and reality: in mysticism (the inner sense) the reality is what is intangible, the opposite, and even the contrary, of sense reality. If mysticism claims tangible significance for its reality, it becomes illusion. Sight is the most important sense for mysticism: auditory sensations are considered mainly illusory in character.

Why should one sense be considered more suited than another to the mystical outlook?

**13** If man is continuous with the inorganic and the organic world, his body part of its substance, the laws of the physical and organic system controlling and containing his natural existence for the most part quite unconsciously to himself: why should there not be a continuity between his mental life and that of the mentality of the cosmic whole? Why should his mind not be in union with all minds, wherever found? Why should his mind not find itself supported by the system of things? At the mental level, he claims and asserts this consciously: at the physical and organic, it goes on unconsciously; and though that is certainly a great difference between the two kinds of dependence and communion, it is the only difference that need be recognized.

The complete confidence that there is this thorough unity between individual life and Reality is the highest achievement of the religious life. It consists in attaining at the level of consciousness to that complete continuity between our mind and the whole of Reality which exists as a fact between our organic life and the life of nature.

**14** A fundamental mistake of mere intellectualism is to suppose that because God is of no value for knowledge, cannot be known, etc., therefore the idea of God may be dismissed from human experience. Even if knowledge has no use for the idea of God, the fullness of man's spiritual nature demands communion with His reality. It is, perhaps, because knowledge is only a partial expression of man's nature that knowledge *can* dispense with God, or confess its incompetence to grasp God's reality. The same is true of sensibility or action: these are inadequate to reach God's reality because they are partial expressions of man's nature, and they do not "need" God because they cannot reach God. But the whole of man's nature demands satisfaction as well as each part of it; and this satisfaction can only be found in a whole which fills out and satisfies all man's life.

**15** It is so difficult to understand why, if God is the great Reality caring for His creatures, even "loving" them as some men have said, He should still seem so far away, so uncompanionable, should leave His human creatures so much in the dark and solitary. What is above all wanted is that the sense of God's presence should be as intimate to the human spirit as body is to soul; yet we seem always seeking, seeking, and hardly ever finding. Why should people always be calling upon God as if He were a Baal or a Jupiter out of sight and out of touch with man? Man clings to the frailest things of earth for comfort and security just because he cannot do any better. It is unaccountable to him that God should mean so much and apparently be so little in his life.

Or is it, after all, that man's fears and cravings, his sense of solitude and his "crying in the night," are precisely the indication that God is calling him to communion and fellowship, just as the sense of error somewhere is due to the implied presence of the truth, or as the disgust with ugliness is due to the love of beauty, or the misery of evil due to the craving for good?

If so, then the very sense of desertion, the sense of God as "far away," is the negative sign of the intimate unity between God and man; a sort of communion actually taking place between God and man, and thus cancelling the very solitude which man feels so oppressive. What is wanted is to change this negative attitude into a positive sense of conscious relationship, by accepting the reality that underlies it and affirming as completely true the half truth revealed in the sense of estrangement. This changes fear into trust, despair into hope, restlessness into peace, solitude into completed union.

**16** The difficulty men have always had in dealing with religion is that God never, so to say, speaks to man in His own person. God only communicates with man intelligibly through the workings of man's own mind. All else in the universe is silent and inarticulate. If man could trust himself to inarticulate communings, doubtless he might have a large domain in which God's presence could be found. But to man, articulation, intelligible expression, "Logos," has been the highest and purest form in which truth is conveyed. Hence the inevitable consequence—that, in expressing what "God thinks," he cannot distinguish God's thought from his own, his religious communications are purely anthropomorphic, and they vary from race to race.

Perhaps after all this is not merely inevitable, but actually to man's advantage; and it may be possible to get over the apparent difficulty or even absurdity of it by distinguishing a certain quality in man's thoughts which marks them as "not his own" but "given" to him, impressed upon him, revealed to him. This quality is the necessity in his thought, a compulsion in his way of thinking, which resembles the compulsion of the world of objects without him when they impress his senses. If a man's thoughts are so linked and held together that he cannot regard his own particular mind as capable of forging the system or responsible for the "force" of the truth, he may rightly ascribe the nexus of his ideas to the reality without him.

**17** It is easy for man to relegate the conscious communion with God to selected moments, days and hours and minutes: that is the reason for the isolation of the religious attitude from the rest of his experience: man merely renews it at stated and separate intervals; he lays in a kind of stock for the day or the week, as he might take in a meal and think no more about his food.

But the effective sense of the presence of God in the life of man is not to be sustained in this fashion. It must be as constant as the breath he draws, as continuous as the beat of his heart. It has to be not a "background" but a permeating influence: God is not a "refuge" or a "retreat," but the All-pervading. Perhaps the constant reminding of ourselves that this is the essential character of our relation to Him may help to break the habit many so easily fall into of relegating Him to an allotted spot, an allotted time in the day's experience.

It is this segregation of God to a separate quarter of life's routine that is the source of "places of worship," "times of prayer" and the like: in its most extreme form it appears as polytheism, or again Deism.

**18** It is often a matter of surprise to religious people that their sense of security in the Divine Life should be disturbed by circumstance, that they are not simply swept along in unbroken mental union with God. But clearly if such was the nature of union with God, the individual would either have no sense of individuality in God's life at all (i.e. no real religious life) or else the only sense he would have would be that of being carried away by force, and against this he would (if he were self-conscious) feel inclined to rebel!

The maintenance of the union must involve an act on our side, otherwise the religious attitude—union through communion, support by expansion—is lost. What is required is a conscious devotion of mind and will in the forms of faith, love or hope according to the situation or difficulty in which we find ourselves.

The only way in which God reveals His continual presence in the religious man's life is through the felt pain of alienation and separation from Him. This is a sign of life, not of loss or destruction; it is a call to re-establish the union which is peace and gladness of spirit.

**19** It has been held by most thoughtful men for at least the generation ending the nineteenth century, perhaps for the greater part of the nineteenth century, that God was a kind of limiting condition of man's finitude, a "negative conception," an infinite beyond the finite, the unknown into which all knowledge receded or proceeded, a spiritual *dernier ressort* or *pis aller*. Religion, in consequence, was in the main the last help of human weakness; little more than a device for giving the appearance of completeness to an incomplete existence. Like the conception of God, religion was in essence a negative condition of mind, or a negation of a negation! To counterbalance all this, man held that he did, or could, or must, find all the positive substance of his being, all that would really satisfy, in his relations of union with nature on the one hand, and with his fellows in society on the other. Knowledge (science) provided the one, social life (economics, ethics, politics) the other. These are the chief interests and tendencies of the nineteenth century.

It is possible, however, and it seems indeed correct, to hold that all this is wrong and must end in failure. It seems truer to say that man never can give or find the whole of himself in knowledge of nature or in his life with his fellows. He has to keep back much from his fellow-men, and keep back the more the less they are in touch with him; and he has to keep back more of himself still from nature; indeed, he can do little with nature except use it or know it. Moreover, unless he does keep detached from both nature and society, he cannot achieve so much in relation to either as he feels bound to try to achieve: by giving himself or trying to give himself wholly to either or both, he both dissipates and loses himself in a flux of finitude. What of the remainder of his life unless somehow and somewhere this, too, has a security and a sanctuary where its aims are warranted and sustained? What if it be that in the life of God alone man finds himself, completely, both in his weakness and in his strength? What if, after all, man's communion with God be the way in which his reality is most fully felt and attained? What if his relation to God be the way to be himself chiefly or wholly, and his relation to nature and man be at best but partial manifestations of what his being means? What if God be first in man's life, and man and nature second, instead of man and nature first and God second? Much of nature is contemptible, and vast numbers of men are not worth "identifying ourselves" with.

If these things be so, if Spinoza's view of man is sounder than Spencer's or Comte's, most of our present day social philosophy has been a blunder, and the aspirations built on it an illusion. And how it has misled us all to the very verge of individual and social destruction.

**20**  It is a mistake to imagine that all men can or should occupy the same religious plane, any more than they can occupy the same intellectual, moral or artistic level. The effort to standardize religious life and to compel all and each to accept this one standard—whether in doctrine or otherwise—has led, and will always lead, to bitter conflict on the one hand or to sheer insincerity and hypocrisy on the other. This is seen as much in the history of Protestantism as in Catholicism, or in Mohammedanism. Forceful acquiescence leads to insincerity and hypocrisy—the pretence of accepting as formulæ for one's own religious life terms which do not reflect its actual processes.

Conciliation on such lines can only be had at the price of sacrificing the highest forms of religious experience to the average—i.e., eliminating the attainments of developed religious life in order to obtain "practical" agreement on the essentials. This sacrifice is too great. It is like giving up the study of the calculus and laying exclusive emphasis on the multiplication table, which "all can understand," like setting aside Shakespeare's sonnets for Tennyson.

There is only one form of conciliation that is worth adopting; and that is the admission that the religious life can be lived and is lived at different levels or degrees of completeness and spirituality.

**21** Men are really rather afraid to find or to look for the Divine Spirit in the very centre of their own lives, in the very springs of their will, their thought and their emotion. They prefer to look for God outside themselves, to put God outside, and keep the Divine Reality external to their mental life. Perhaps it is because God in this way seems easier to deal with: perhaps because in this way men seem to retain a measure of independence. The result is, however, always disastrous. A God that is to begin with outside, remains outside: man's religion becomes a contract of some sort and not a communion: God becomes an object of terror instead of a companionable spirit: human beings tend to cringe before God instead of clinging to God: religion tends to degrade rather than to dignify human life.

**22** When we remember how the Providence which controls the life of mankind has turned to good the immense and even untold evil in the history of nations, the transformation of the little ills in the life of the individual for the purpose of his ultimate welfare may be taken for granted.

**23** Some men need more religion than others, need to cultivate the mood more continuously and completely: just as some men need to keep up more continuous communion with things of beauty, or to cultivate science more thoroughly. In these differences each must follow his own temperament and the cravings of his individuality. There is no compulsion in such things. Compulsory religion is as unreasonable as compulsory art, or compulsory science.

**24** We have to learn by experience that we are not dependent on words for the maintenance of the religious attitude. Words may assist, if we find the right words to express the spirit's frame of mind. But with or without words, it is the spirit's full consciousness of the pervading presence of the Divine Spirit which constitutes the substance and the state of religion. If this is real, in whatever degree, religion is there; if it is not, words are not a substitute for it and cannot create it.

It is the same with the surrounding reality of the physical world: we have this in all sorts of ways, through touch and pressure, through physical support, as well as through our spoken expression of what the outer world is for us. But words are not the essence of, or a necessity of, our sense of the external world.

**25** Religion is effective participation in the life of God, acting by His strength and thinking by His thought.

**26** The great perplexity in the religious life is the impenetrable silence of God.

**27** We talk of man seeking after God in order to find God: the most painful of experiences is to discover that God seems less anxious to find us than we are to find God.

**28** Men complain that they do not know God, and yet they do not complain that their knowledge of anything in the world about them is incomplete. They seem to suppose that knowledge of God can only be knowledge if it is complete knowledge, since God is assumed to be complete Reality. But it seems evident that, if our knowledge of finite things is imperfect, we cannot expect our knowledge of infinite Reality to be other than imperfect.

Perhaps the kind of knowledge that we can have of God is enough for our needs. What we need above all is quietness of mind. We have enough knowledge of God to secure this, if we are conscious of an order controlling our lives at each moment, enabling us to meet each occasion with the appropriate adjustment, and giving us a sense of stability when face to face with changing events in experience. We have such knowledge; it is direct and as close to our necessities as breathing is to life. A more comprehensive knowledge would be of less value to us.

**29** The three main types of architecture which are found in places of religious worship—the vaulted or the curved, the pointed, and the rectilinear—seem to have more than a formal or structural significance. They seem at once to represent and to foster different religious attitudes of mind. The vaulted style seems to be an imitation or representation of the dome-shaped sky, and to symbolize the protecting presence of God, dwelling with man in his temple, God coming down to earth from heaven and tabernacling with man. Men are awed or overawed in such an environment: they are also sustained in calm security of spirit: they feel sheltered and surrounded by the presence of God. This is the characteristic note of the Basilica, the Byzantine, the Eastern type of religious building.

The pointed style represents and fosters the mood of aspiration. Resting on the foundations of the earth, the mind rises and soars with the flight of the columns which gradually meet like the hands in prayer, expressing at once the limits of aspiration, the need for completion, and the modesty of belief in the Divine, *Levavi oculos meos in montes. In manus tuas, Domine.* This style appeals to the mind which would lift up its heart to God in hope and trust rather than to the mind which is certain of the brooding protection of the divine love and mercy. It fosters the attitude of reverence rather than of awe, of elevation rather than of serenity, of belief rather than of confidence, of wonder rather than of conviction. It is earth rising to heaven, rather than heaven descending upon and residing on earth; spirit seeking satisfaction beyond the temporal, the earthly and the visible, rather than spirit satisfied to find the divine everywhere in such wise as to cancel the separateness of earth and heaven, the temporal and the eternal, and transform the earthly almost to a shadowy appearance.

This pointed style is the characteristic note, and perhaps the characteristic contribution, of the Western religious mind—the Gothic (whatever "Gothic" may mean) is, at any rate, in its developed form, peculiarly Western and European. And the Western religious mind is for the most part a mind in aspiration and striving to believe, rather than a mind of assured and unquestioning conviction.

The rectilinear—horizontal, flat ceiling, etc.—represents the purely earthly or naturalistic religious frame of mind, finding the gods in earthly places, gods of streams and rocks and woods, gods of the home and hearth. There is neither the divine coming down from above, nor the human reaching after the divine to regions immeasurably beyond man's finite limitations. We have men of the earth living on friendly terms with spirits, ghosts and deities of the earth, and together forming a common family. There is no need to rise higher than man's height; the gods keep company with their worshippers. The domestic house is, therefore, the suitable tabernacle and style of temple for such gods of nature or human-gods and goddesses. The flat ceiling, the straight horizontal beam, seem to correspond to just such a view of the religious life.

This seems the characteristic feature of pagan religions everywhere, from the crudest fetishism to the sublimated Greek pantheon. It is the note of the Greek temple as of the hut of the primitive tribe (or the Chinese temple?).

**30**   There are two views of religion corresponding to the two most widely accepted views of the "relation of body and mind": that which looks on the mind as a kind of accompaniment of bodily processes, a resonance of which we happen to be aware but which we do not make or influence; and that which regards the mind as the consummate directing agency which can both initiate, control, judge and appreciate effectively, and in the long run alone realize consciously, the full potencies of organic life. In the one view, the mind is passive, in the other, active; in the one, it adds nothing to organic life, in the other, it reacts upon, transforms and raises organic life to a new level.

So in religion: some look on the religious life as merely accompanying the natural and not altering it; the accompaniment is "another" nature, a "supernatural," a spiritual level of being, generally divorced from the "natural" (organic nature) and sometimes hostile to it. Here the religious attitude tends to be that of alienation from the world, men seek through religion "another country," they look for the "life to come" and "quietly wait for the salvation of God." Others, however, look on the religious life as giving man such a consciousness of the Divine as enables him to take up and transmute the natural, making its processes and its laws a means of expressing and realizing an orderly unity of goodness, beauty and truth. In this case the consciousness of the Divine reacts upon the natural and does not merely accept it; for even in acquiescence there is a sense of dominance and triumph; the "supernatural" becomes the consciously transformed "natural"; the natural realizes the spiritual in the sense of embodying the spiritual, the spiritual realizes the natural in the sense of fulfilling all its potencies, giving them their place and meaning in the unity of the whole and thus enabling us to find in the whole love and beauty and truth in one, and the fulfilment of all our desires.

**31** It is not surprising that people in earnest with the deeper life of religion find it necessary to withdraw from the world altogether to attain their end. It is very difficult to maintain a continuous consciousness of the Divine while engaged in the daily affairs of the "world": still more difficult to keep up an intensive communion with the Divine life under such conditions, and experience the peace, joy and love which belong to it.

Hence we find that the vast majority of religious people make a choice in the interests of mental quietude: they cannot face this difficulty and successfully overcome it, and they cannot endure a constant sense of defeat. They cultivate the religious life specifically at stated times or seasons, days of the week or hours of the day; and they leave the influences felt at these times to operate as best they can during the business of the world in a more or less subconscious way: this is the attitude taken up by most people. Or, again, they adopt a superficial type of religion which does not call for any special concentration on divine things, which is sufficient for the day's needs whatever the day, and which for the most part comes to be indistinguishable from the moral life at its best—doing justly, loving mercy, loving mankind, doing their duty and leaving the rest, etc. This is fairly common with certain healthy-minded, good-hearted individuals not endowed with much mystical insight. Or there is the third attitude adopted by the strenuously religious who are determined at all costs to possess a continuous sense of the Divine, and who decide to give up contact with the world as far as possible in order to secure the peace which passes understanding, the realized experience of the love of God: they decide to live a life of religious devotion in seclusion, or in retreat, to flee from the world to the cloister, in other words to abandon the struggle by escaping from the enemy altogether.

All these attitudes are but a confession of limitation and

incapacity to attain the supreme accomplishment of the truest religious life. This can only be the consciousness in human life of the actual life of the Divine as the Divine life is in fact realized. The Divine life is actually realized in and through the earthly life, the life of the world. It is manifested there, because God does control and subdue to His will the realm of nature and human nature which He has created in order to express His activity. To be conscious of the whole in the details of the world's affairs is to be divine: to share this consciousness with God is precisely to realize the religious life in its truest form. This, and nothing less than this, is spiritual religion at its highest.

**32** The coming of God into the life of man, as a fact and as a consciously operative Presence, is surely one of the most wonderful, indeed the most wonderful of all man's experiences. The reality of God is not a deduction from data like the discovery of a planet: it has been expressed almost invariably as a "vision" and, though this represents at best but one side of the experience, it is significant enough of its peculiar character. The strangest part, however, of the whole experience is the intrusion, so to say, of God as an operative Presence into the life of man in such a way that God actively, and to man consciously, communicates His will and purpose to man's mind. There is the same kind of compelling acceptance of this reality as there is in our acceptance of the objects of nature around us: we have to acquiesce in their existence and their presence in our lives: we do not create them, we find them, and try to find them out. We become aware of God, not because we go to seek the reality of God, but because God Himself invades our experience and imposes His Presence within it. The kind of experience in which we become aware of and accept this reality is what we call Religion. God thus creates the religious attitude of mind within us; the religious attitude does not create God: it *begins* by accepting God as a reality in human life and that means that we cannot escape from Him, we can only lay our account with Him and enter into conscious relations with Him. God is the God of the living, and the living God: and is not in the first instance a conclusion of logic at all. All thinking about God begins after the reality of God is accepted by the mind of man: and God Himself, therefore, shows man how to think about Him, and acts upon man whether he can and does think about Him accurately or not.

This on the face of it seems the most natural and obvious way in which God should enter man's experience; for how could so frail a creature as man, left to his own limited powers of thought and desire, ever expect to discover such a reality or even to desire it. It is quite outside the domain of the finite creatures with which man is normally associated. Unless God asserted Himself, man could not even imagine Him or think such a being possible. And God asserts Himself because man is unequal to the attempt to find Him, and in order to relieve man of the need to make the attempt.

Hence it is by no means unreasonable, it is supremely reasonable and inevitable, that the way in which God communicates His presence to man should be through a revelation or manifestation of Himself in and through thought, in and through acts, and in and through feelings, stimulated by and appropriate to His reality. This is the form which religious experience proper has always taken. It is quite *sui generis* in its procedure, its method, its language—just as our consciousness of things of sense is peculiar to the use of our organs of sense and varies with our senses. Hence, for example, we have the emphasis on "faith" as an attitude in the religious life, apart from and distinct from all knowledge—faith not in the sense of trust or confidence, but as a way of communing with the spirit of God.

Everything in the religious life follows from this first step, and every other element in religious experience, e.g. immortality, takes its colour and position from this fundamental origin of religion in man's life. It is remarkable how the highest kinds of religion emphasize most of all this peculiar character of the religious life, and continually insist on its prime importance.

If this be granted, it does not seem specially wonderful or incongruous with the character of religion that, in supremely religious minds, there should be "miracles," "visions," personal revelations and individual communications from God to man. On the contrary, this all seems in the nature of the case. Nor is there anything astonishing in the affirmation of St. Paul: "I am persuaded that nothing shall separate us from the love of God." It is what God Himself might say to man.

**33** Men from earliest days have wished to "see" God, to "feel after" God, to communicate with God by their senses. It is not surprising, seeing the confidence they place and must place in their senses for ordinary dealings with the world. In their despair of satisfying their craving in this way, they are apt to turn aside from God, especially in an emergency. They forget that even physically they have other ways of being conscious of the world in which they live, and that their powers of brain are not restricted to the operation of the senses.

God can be with us and is with us in all ways and in all parts of our personality at once, present to us in our "hearts," our "minds," our "will," and can make Himself realized to us in all or any one of these ways. And that is essential in the case of One in whom we live and move and have our being, and who will never leave or forsake those whom He has made for Himself.

**34** We must leave the past to God: it is impossible for us to change it. We may with equal confidence leave the future also to God to make of it what He will; and we may do so with cheerfulness since we can co-operate in shaping its course.

**35** It is very difficult for grown men to realize that in the eyes of the Divine Father they are at best but children in intelligence and in will. It is hard for the rich in mental as well as material endowment to enter the Kingdom of Heaven.

**36** Religion is not a discovery of the Divine so much as a recovery of it.

**37** Secrecy seems always to have been associated with religion, possibly because all religion involves mystery which is only half revealed and thus partly concealed. The priests have kept something to themselves; they have kept themselves to themselves; the individual keeps much of his religious life within his own heart, which he fails to, or does not wish to, communicate; God speaks in secret and in silence to the spirit. This secrecy is at once the strength and the weakness of the religious life. It also brings religion into sharp contrast with science and art, which are in the nature of the case open and expose their results to the full light of day; otherwise their achievements are not appreciated or understood, and their claims to be universal cannot be established. This is one of the sources of the "conflict" between science and religion, which can hardly be removed; the scientist cannot tolerate or accept mystery as a final element of experience, and he will never believe he is mistaken as long as he maintains the purely scientific frame of mind.

**38** We so often suppose that God is only concerned with the big things of our life, and we tend to appeal to God mainly in what seem to us the larger issues. But the big things of our life may certainly be assumed to appear small things to an infinite Power and an infinite wisdom. And probably Providence is shown most in the management of the smaller concerns of our daily life, and especially in their cumulative effect. It is the small touches which perfect a work of art; the small deeds and transitory acts of life which are most difficult to handle and which minister most intimately to the welfare of men and women.

**39** Men are apt to suppose that the details of life are too small to be a concern of the Divine. But there is a providence even for the sparrow. Love is perhaps shown more in the purposeful ordering of small details for the ampler good of the person loved, than in the control of the great issues of life whose fulfilment is a constant care.

**40** It is said that man is by nature religious. It might be truer to say man is by instinct an atheist, and only acquires the consciousness of God by experience of life.

**41** All the natural processes which minister to the enduring purposes of life are transformed by religion into sacraments of the Divine Spirit. It is not difficult to see how this applies to the sustenance of the body by food, and the continuance of human life through reproduction. These have always been recognized as having a sacramental character. It is more difficult to see that the same applies to physical toil. And it is most difficult of all to recognize that the surrender of the whole of natural life into the hands of the Divine Spirit is no less a sacrament in that it appears to take the form of extinction. Men are more able to treat a part of natural life as sacramental than to regard the whole of it in that way. But there is no reason why the whole of finite individuality—the unity as well as the parts—should not manifest a Divine Presence. From this point of view Death is the final sacrament of human life.

**42** There is a close analogy between the spiritualization of the senses (e.g. sight and sound) by art and the spiritualization of man's life as a whole by religion. In the former, we have painting and music, which utilize sense material and sublimate it to spiritual ends. In the latter, the whole material embodiment of personal life is transformed to spiritual issues by communion with the Divine Spirit. Even the taking of food and the love of gain may be transmuted into elements of a divine life, may be made sacramental: a family meal becomes a sacrament, so does marriage: work for gain becomes a divine service. And all this without loss of the human interest in the processes of man's physical life: indeed, the result is to intensify interest in them by the added distinction given to them through lifting them into a higher plane of experience. Thus the whole of "civilization" may be spiritualized without diminishing the essentially human quality of civilized life.

**43** The object of religion is to enjoy the eternal without anxiety regarding things of time and sense: it does not consist in enjoying the temporal without anxiety about the eternal.

**44** The search for God ceases when worship begins. Worship is devoted communion with the Divine Spirit: it is incompatible with the search for God, since worship believes in God whereas the search for God assumes that God is not believed in. This is an old distinction; but its full significance is rarely realized.

## II

**1** It seems much easier to learn what the Fear of God means than the Love of Him. And it would seem that, in both, there is the greatest need for wisdom as a modifying and controlling factor. When fear brings with it trembling and quivering helplessness, or any degree of moral paralysis (which means the wreck of courage and the ruin of hope), then there seems to be some mistake. Fear is no longer the subdued attitude of reverent *conscious* dependence and self-negating, confident, hesitant trust, but the hopelessness and nervous anxiety of uncontrollable terror. This can be *demanded* by no belief in God.

**2** Most people make the life of religion difficult because they do not clearly recognize that it consists primarily and essentially in acknowledging a reality and not in constructing it; in practically confessing a truth, not in seeking for it; in carrying out a law, not in verifying a hypothesis; in manifesting what is, apart from our acknowledgment, an actual fact, not in trying to attain a far off ideal. The living of it in all its details is, no doubt, for us in a sense the ideal; but we admit all the while that it is actual in so far as it is operative in us; we simply submit to it, it does not depend on us. In this sense it is both ideal and actual at once, much as in science a rational system is both ideal and actual.

It is in this way that the notion of the "Love of God" gets its meaning. It is simply the concrete expression for the actual union of man with God which is of the essence of the religious life. We cannot create love; it must be there or not there, and that is all that is to be said of its actuality. We do not strive to obtain this Love of God; it is actual already without our effort at all. A religious man surely acknowledges this, submits to it, and acts from it and on it, never goes back upon it to doubt it, but makes the full conscious expression of it in his own life his aim as a religious man. We have not to find it out, but to realize it; not to strive to obtain it, but to do what it already implies. It is not something to be tested or discussed, but something to be acted on absolutely and with confidence. Neglect of this truth is responsible for the mistake some religious people make when face to face with evils; they think these cast doubt on the fact on which their religious life rests, as if that life were an intellectual experiment. Evils must be dealt with in the light of the fundamental truth of religion, and cannot cast doubt on it because they are part of the scheme through which it is to be acknowledged and realized.

How far this aspect of religious life is consciously realized is largely a matter of temperament. It is naturally much insisted on by the religions of the East. But some Europeans, e.g. the British, find its realization difficult because of their intense individualism. This makes their consciousness of separation from God keener than their acknowledgment of their essential unity with Him; hence their consciousness of Sin is keener than that of some other nations.

**3** Remember that the important matter is not how little you can believe, but how much.

**4** Is religion a matter of *what* you believe and not rather, as some think, of *how* you believe?

**5** It is an elementary condition of the religious life that we should, so to say, assume that God has His own work to do, and does it. We get into the habit of isolating ourselves from God, and of thinking that the religious life depends wholly on ourselves: so much so that in modern times men go the length of supposing that God is an ideal of their own creation! The real truth for religion is rather that man is God's creature, produced and sustained by God as part of His creation. This should be the underlying idea of the religious life, its ground and essence, without which religion is a purely imaginative experience, at best something "hoped for," not something actual. It cannot be derived from man's mental processes; it must be accepted directly, and remain the same throughout all his experience. The apprehension of it and the living in it are acts of faith; they are the beginning of the religious life and remain an essential condition throughout the religious experience. For those who recognize this, there *is* something to "hope for," namely, a fuller conscious realization of what religion is or will become for us in the future: "faith" provides the "substance of things hoped for," the evidence of things not yet seen. Because, however, faith implies the absence of full realization, and holds often when the realization is very difficult to "see" or "feel," it is not a complete expression of the religious attitude. When faith and full vision meet, and God is felt and realized as so completely one with our spirit that there is and can be no sense of contrast or obscurity, when God is fully one with us and we with God, then the experience of faith and hope passes into the perfect spiritual union which is only expressible as Love.

**6** The element of fear which enters so largely into the religious consciousness arises from the feeling, inevitable to a finite mind, that the individual may come to the end of his resources, and be unable to meet the demands of circumstances and secure himself in the midst of them. What the individual in such a case fails to realize, and what, through religious experience, he seeks to obtain, is the sense that the circumstances, along with himself, are part of one and the same plan, one and the same Reality. When he feels this in all its bearings, fear disappears; for then he feels that he cannot really come to an end of his resources at all since that would mean the failure of the whole scheme of the universe. If the individual felt the whole scheme of the universe to be a failure, he would not feel fear, he would feel despair. The truth is that religion restores and sustains the sense that the individual never is at the end of his resources, for it gives him the feeling that God is his first and last resource, his first and last possibility, and this cannot be exhausted. But to enjoy this feeling continuously he must learn to trust as well as act, to wait as well as to do. No doubt if he seeks to maintain all his security by his own active endeavour, he may readily find himself at the end of his resources; and the sense of fear which will arise is the only means of teaching him his mistake in putting all his life into his own hands, and so leading him to the truer appreciation of his place in a vaster whole than he alone can establish. This truer appreciation is the higher wisdom: hence, as it has been said, the fear of the Lord is the beginning of wisdom. Thus it is that so many religions, and the religious experience of so many human beings, arise out of fear. The fear is just felt estrangement combined with the sense of weakness. Remove the estrangement by realizing oneness with the one source of all strength, and the fear at once disappears.

**7**  The real blessedness of love is in loving, not in being loved; or perhaps best of all, in loving and finding love responded to on equal terms. That is why it is difficult completely to love a being stronger and greater than ourselves: such a being hardly needs us, it tends rather to pity us, more especially if it can dispense with our love. The weaker and smaller being may trust and confide and revere and honour, but it can hardly feel its love is sufficiently important to be worth giving; and the more it is conscious of its own weakness and insignificance the less value does it attach to the love it can give. But the depreciation of love is the destruction of love. The love that clings is the love that is half afraid; and in seeking something else besides the love it gives, it is seeking safety and security or strength.

Hence the difficulty human beings instinctively feel about "loving God." To love God truly seems to lower God to the human level; it is to believe that God "needs" man's love, and misses it if He does not have it.

This difficulty people get over in Christianity by extending their love to a person, the person of Christ or of the Virgin Mary, or of some Saint or, in some cases, straightway identifying love of God with love of man. But these are unsatisfactory makeshifts.

**8**  There are some people who identify a rollicking confidence in the universe with faith in God. This is crude. It confuses good-natured animal spirits with unfaltering spiritual insight. There is no room in religious experience for such an irreverent attitude of mind.

**9**  It is remarkable that some of the chief religions have identified the highest quality of the God of the whole earth with the highest quality of the life of humanity, and called that quality "Love." It is, indeed, strange to see the Almighty Lord and Cupid joined together in a common enterprise; the Father of All hand in hand with the most fickle saint in the secular calendar.

**10**  Gratitude is one of the highest of all virtues, and one of the rarest. The sense of gratitude rests on the feeling of love of a receiver towards a giver: it is impossible where there is either jealousy or a mere sense of justice, or where there is envy or distrust or dislike. That is why it is so difficult.

One of the deepest notes of religious life is the sense of gratitude of man towards the Supreme Being as the fountain of all particular good; even mere existence, from this point of view, becomes a good calling forth gratitude of mind. No higher religious attitude can be attained and, in all the highest moods of religion, it is present—for example, in the sense of forgiveness.

**11**  A great part of religion is experimental. For example, "faith" requires to be "exercised," and its actual strength can only be found by experiment. A vast number of religious people are afraid to "try their faith" too much; they know it is actually feeble, and they shrink from the ordeal with fear and misgiving.

**12**  "The fear of the Lord is the beginning of wisdom": but wisdom only begins when fear ends: there is no wisdom in fear itself: only folly can result from fear, and wisdom begins with the hope which has left fear behind.

**13**  A human being must always be puzzled by the injunction to "love God." It seems almost absurd as a "command," and impossible as a state of mind. The best way, perhaps the only way, in which the individual can realize what is implied in such an idea is to rejoice that his life is in God and is one with God's spirit. To enjoy God's life as our own is certainly the highest achievement of religious experience.

**14**  The silence of God is the most trying and terrible of all God's qualities (if God can be said to have "qualities"). That is why so many men, in despair of knowing what the love of God is or how to find God anywhere, try to accept the love of man as a substitute for the love of God. It is not a substitute that will stand criticism, if it is really supposed to contain the essence of the religious life.

**15** It may be better in the long run that God should be unknown —better for the religious life, better for man. God could only be known at the cost of reducing Him to finite terms, i.e. terms lower than His nature requires. If we really knew God, we should know how to manage Him, know how to deal with Him, lay our account with Him. God would thus cease to be a supreme object of worship and adoration.

If God remains unknown, this makes possible the elements of risk and adventure which are characteristics of the religious life, as of all life. Life without adventure is not life; it is a closed mechanical system of operations. Religion is a form of life, a way of living. Those who take the risk, who make the venture of faith, realize the potencies of life better than those who do not venture their all for what seems most worth while. They cannot really fail, even if they do not gain all they seek or desire; for they gain more by venturing their utmost than by husbanding their resources and so leaving their resources unused, keeping their capital in a safe or their "talent in a napkin." If they succeed in their venture, they gain the whole universe. Moreover, by venturing their utmost, they are on the side of the world, and the world is on their side; for the world is at its best a process of life and is ever on the move, ever energizing forwards, ever realizing new possibilities. God, whatever else He be, is life; and to live fully is to live with God and in God. To live forward is to live upward. This is only possible if we make the venture; and we could not do so, or we should not do so, if all were known, completed and closed once for all.

Faith, therefore, is not a defect, either a defect of knowledge or a defect of man's nature: it is a positive merit, a gift, a power for achievement of what otherwise could not be attained at all—the fullness of life.

**16**   It is good to be a fatalist if your fate is the Divine love, but only then.

**17**   Faith may no doubt create confidence in God: but the confidence in God born of the experience of God's support in difficulty and danger is an enormous aid to faith.

**18**   People speak of the necessity of faith as if faith were a confession of weakness, and as if it were regrettable that we should exercise faith because we cannot possess knowledge instead of faith. Faith is not a condition of helplessness, nor a consequence of blindness. It is a right claimed by the human spirit in order to compass the control of more than we need to know. No human brain could carry or sustain the complexity of the complete knowledge of all things: the excess of light would be blinding and bewildering. The burden of reality is more easily borne by faith in its reasonableness, than by knowledge of its connected rationality. Faith is thus the supreme privilege, the chief strength, and the security for the enduring peace of the human spirit. It proceeds from the joy and not from the distress of the mind; for it is the "evidence of things unseen," and not of our blindness to the invisible. In a manner it is more certain and reliable than knowledge, for it is unchangeable and undisturbed by criticism of things seen and temporal.

**19**   If we were to name the one primary conviction which would provide a sure and permanent basis for personal happiness, for the sense of blessedness in life, it would be the conviction that the Divine Spirit loves each individual. Any person who believes that this is really so in his own particular case, and lives in the light of this belief, cannot but be happy to the fullest extent of which he is capable, cannot but be blessed. It is not enough to try to love God, or even to succeed in loving Him, but to believe with a conviction amounting to knowledge that God loves him—that is the secret of lasting happiness. It is not enough to believe that "God loves all men," or that God loves all His creatures. The point is to believe that God loves particular human beings. Not till an individual realizes that God loves him in particular does this belief achieve its full effect in the individual soul.

It is safe to say that very few people have reached this level of the religious life.

**20** "I glory in mine infirmities—in my weakness" ($\dot{\alpha}\sigma\theta\acute{\epsilon}\nu\epsilon\iota\alpha$). This is indeed a hard saying. Yet how true from the point of view of spiritual religion at its best! The power and love of God (or perhaps the power which is the love of God) can be seen and realized most clearly when it sustains the individual in the midst of, and in spite of, his weakness, when it manifests itself triumphantly in the presence of infirmities, and overrules the devious tendencies of imperfection so as to bring order out of apparent confusion, success out of apparent disaster, real good out of apparent evil. We could not become conscious of the love of God, nor feel gratitude and love so vividly, but for the existence of imperfections or "infirmities." They are, so to say, the opportunities for God's display of His love towards us, a display which we can fully appreciate because we are keenly aware of our own infirmities: indeed all the more acutely aware the larger is our sense of what perfection means, and the stronger our desire for it. And, again, the more we realize our infirmities, the more we feel dependent on the love and power of God for help in the midst of them; so that our infirmities form the reason for our need of God's love and the circumstances by which it is made manifest to us.

Moreover, to view infirmities in this light is to regard them not as disasters, or fatal defects, or regrettable hindrances to the spiritual life, but as an invaluable part or condition of the divine plan for our spiritual life. We can "glory" in them because they serve this purpose; we can glory over them because they can never triumph over us, and because they are the means for the manifestation of love; we can have glory of them, can boast in them, because we have triumphed in them and are confident in the power which will enable us to triumph again; we can even gain glory through them in a way which would be impossible without them, for the glory which we achieve is our share in the glory of the divine power by which alone our glory and our triumph are possible.

But the "infirmities" or "weaknesses" over which we glory in their ways must be genuine infirmities; the infirmities of our finite constitution, our limitations of nature, our constitutional imperfections of individuality. They can have nothing to do with evil; and our glory in them must be quite different from any delight in or acceptance of evil. Evil results from or consists in using our imperfections as excuses for going astray, for self-indulgence, for self-will, for following our imperfections for the sake of being imperfect, submitting to our infirmities for the sake of temporary advantage, indulging our weakness so as to remain weaklings in the satisfaction of self-pity or self-pride. In all these forms there is no glory attained over our weakness, no triumph in our infirmity; we remain infirm and infirmer than we were before. We sacrifice the glory of the whole spirit to the claims of a part, and that the weaker part, of our nature. This leads nowhere and we see nothing thereby of the glory of the divine love, gain nothing of divine power in our lives.

Our imperfections, our infirmities are of many kinds— infirmities of temper, of character, of feeling, of impulse; defects of mind, of will, of intellect; imperfections of body; limitations of circumstance; weakness in the face of nature, timidity and shyness and sensitiveness in the face of our fellow-creatures; sickness, ill-health, pains and sufferings of a physical kind. They are many and vary from man to man in form and type.

We may then glory in our infirmities. Moreover, the glory will be shown in various ways, and not only in cheerfulness and buoyant ascendancy over our weakness, but also, and not least, in the sense of humour which can jest and smile at the incongruities of our situation, and laugh in gladness of heart at our own entanglement in difficulties. For laughter itself is a sudden sense of glory over apparent defeat arising from the imperfections and incongruities of life. And there is no greater incongruity than that in which we find ourselves when, with our infirmities before us, we are conscious at the same time that they cannot triumph over us, and that they are as nothing and can be nothing in the presence of the Divine love, with whose power they appear contrasted and by whose power they are confronted, and over against which their claim to exist cannot prevail.

Yes, we can glory in our infirmities in this way; and not only in our own. We can likewise glory in the infirmities of others; for these, in virtue of our common humanity, partly increase and partly add to our own infirmities. Because they are not directly our infirmities, they present in some respects an easier, in other respects a harder, situation to overcome. We can only triumph in them and over them if we meet them and even welcome them with sympathy because they are our common lot, and with a charity which anticipates that they can and will be overcome. This can only be done by the power of divine love which overcomes all evil by converting it to good and which by surmounting infirmities not our own, proves its all-embracing goodness to us and to all men. On this account, we can even feel grateful for the infirmities of others and to others for the infirmities which they contribute to our common lot. And, by so doing, we are prevented from glorying over others because of their infirmities, and taking pleasure in their infirmities at their expense—the crudest and most cruel form of rejoicing in evil, because the evil is one which we do *not* desire to overcome and from which we have ourselves escaped.

**21** It seems that many confuse the fear of God with the fear of hell, and that some have little interest in the first beyond its bearing on the second.

Probably the confusion has been responsible for more misery and even atheism than any other religious idea.

**22**  It is extraordinarily difficult for the individual to conceive himself as under the protecting care of the Divine Spirit and as helpless in himself; as necessary to the plan of things and needy at the same time; as exalted by the love of God and as humble in heart; as divinely rich and as "poor in spirit." And the difficulty is increased not lessened the more spiritual a religion is.

**23**  It is to be noted that the first command in the spiritual life is to love God, not to have faith in God.

**24**  The Divine love seems never in a hurry but it is always up to time.

**25**  Better make your peace with God: you have to spend a longer time with Him than with anyone else.

**26**  The essential sanity of spiritual religion is seen in the insistence on the parallelism of man's attitude to the Divine and the human spirit. If man is to expect mercy from God, he must show mercy to his fellows—he cannot understand mercy otherwise. If man is to be forgiven by God, he must forgive his fellows. So if man is to have and know and show and believe in the love of God, he must love his fellow-men.

**27**  To love God is perhaps the most difficult of all states of mind to attain, impossible in fact unless the Divine love supplies and inspires the love by which man is to love God. It may be that the gift to humanity of an incarnated Divine Person was the means adopted not only to reveal the Divine love to man in concrete finite form but to provide man with an embodiment of the Divine accessible to his love and within his power to love, since by loving the incarnated Divine person he is in fact loving God.

## III

**1** "The will of God be done" is an excellent confession and prayer, after you have done what you can to bring it about. Often, however, it seems to be said as if it gave a free pass to idleness and indifference, or a consolation certificate for bad work, or even a ticket-of-leave from a bad business.

**2** Sane, wise, human ambitions of whatsoever kind are the best form of prayers.

**3** Good people forget that it is a kind of indirect blasphemy to pray to be good. We pray to be better; and amongst other things for forgiveness of sins committed in the attempt to be good.

**4** If you don't get what you pray for, you had better pray for what you can get.

**5** Prayer expresses as human aspiration and desire what is accepted to be the nature of absolute Reality: hence it is that all true prayers are answered as soon as they are expressed.

**6** It is notable that the only positive request for a positive personal good contained in the "Lord's Prayer" is a request for something to eat, which seems the last thing that a spiritual being would think about, seeing that the beasts of the field get their food as a matter of the course of nature, and man is even "better than they."

No doubt the difficulty in the religious life is to know what to pray for in the way of positive benefits. We are driven to pray by weakness, and naturally our prayers take on a negative character—the removal of sources of weakness in all forms. In consequence some people seem to think we should pray for nothing positive at all: that prayer should be merely communion. This, however, is indefinite and too vague, as we want something concrete and definite to sustain and focus religious life. Prayer should concern the central needs of our spiritual life, our individual necessities for the maintenance of the dominant purposes of our particular circumstances and situation. What we want in religion is the sense of security for the continuance and the strenuous pursuit of these purposes; otherwise religion is not a crying demand, but only an outlook on the world. These purposes are the objects of our strength; and it is when our strength is inadequate to attain them that we call for help and need it. Hence what we should pray for, and are entitled to pray for, is security for the ends that make our individual life precious, sacred and valuable and an attitude of mind and will attuned to them.

**7** Prayer is often looked upon as a method of bringing an alien God into sympathy with our needs and getting assistance from Him. Prayer really has its source in the Divine Spirit dwelling, sometimes very darkly and obscurely, within our lives: that Divine Spirit seeks to become completely conscious in our lives, and the need to pray is thus due to the call of the Divine Spirit itself. Hence prayer is more truly regarded as our way of consciously removing the barriers that prevent the Divine life filling ours completely: it is a way of lifting the films that insulate us from the Divine energy: it is a method of becoming consciously charged or recharged with the Divine power working in the world, the power in which, in spite of ourselves if not with our own desire, we must live and move and have our being.

There are thus only two kinds of prayer—the request for power and the grateful acknowledgment of the gift of it.

**8** It is very difficult to eradicate the egoistic element even from religion. The individual's entreaties for "support," "strength," "comfort," etc., emphasize it: his "fears" and "doubts" accentuate it: he seeks the resources of the Whole for his own sake, and that aggravates it. Only in certain moods is it lost, for example the moods of peace and resignation.

**9** Most people seem to imagine that the attitude of humiliation assumed by the religious devotee in prayer is due to slavish submission, the servility of the subordinate to the overlord. This may be true in many cases. But there is also a humiliation which is produced by an overwhelming sense of gratitude. This cannot be entirely absent from even the ordinary religious mind. It leads to expressions of humility closely resembling in outer form those assumed by servility—so nearly do these extremes of gratitude and entreaty come to one another.

An overwhelming sense of gratitude to the divine is more humbling to the spirit than disaster or death.

**10** It is extremely improbable that there can be any such experience as that of a "special providence." The demand for it is due to an exaggeration of the importance of the individual in the world: he thinks so much of his wants and his needs, forming expectations, making requests and praying for special things, that he comes to think of himself as of special interest to the Divine Power. This is really a kind of vanity. No man can compel the Divine Power to do anything. We cannot make use of Omnipotence for our ends, and we are not in a position to find fault or accuse Omnipotence if we fail to achieve what we want or strive for. The most and the best a man can do is to worship, and that assumes that the Divine Power has its own arrangements to make whatever we may think or desire. It seems almost childish to imagine that Omnipotence can be "good" to us or favour us, when Omnipotence can do without us altogether. So it becomes absurd to ask for anything or expect anything in a world where misery and wrongdoing, evil and good, cruelty and kindness seem equally permitted; and where we cannot foresee or anticipate any consecutive course of events.

Omnipotence which "cares for all" cares for nothing and no one in particular. And if that is so, there is no reason to suppose that there is a conservation of the individual in any future existence: such a conservation may not be in the least necessary.

**11** Even in dealing with God, we might say *especially* in dealing with God, man must proceed in a way consistent with the best in himself and the best for himself. God requires dignity in man; man must conduct himself with dignity before God. To cringe or grovel, to whine or petition, to posture and plead, in the presence of God is to make man so contemptible in his own eyes that the very granting of the requests made, if they be granted under such conditions, lowers the whole conception of his personality, and takes away the whole value of the gift conferred. There are favours which one does not accept from men without loss of self-respect; there are favours one cannot ask for from God without demeaning personality. Probably that is why God so rarely seems to grant requests of a temporary, mundane and circumstantial character. To ask for them seems to imply that God does not know His own business in the management of the world; and if this were so, the request really takes the form of giving God advice how to act in the matter. But a God who claims to be supreme, and yet does not know how to govern, is not a person on whom man can implicitly rely nor a person so transcendently higher than man's personality as to compel spontaneous reverence. The very petition in such a case both lowers the personality of God and lowers the personality of man in making the petition or accepting what is asked.

**12** People are so ready to answer their own prayers that they come to think their own replies are the revelation of God and the direct divine response to their petitions.

**13** The fact that men find their prayers for spiritual help answered only in terms of spiritual experience—peace, confidence, hope, faith, etc.—and not in terms of material bequests or temporal gifts, seems to follow from the very nature of spiritual life. If men ask for temporal things, they are, strictly speaking, not living an eternal life; and the grant of such things would imperil and not sustain spiritual experience, for it would imply that spiritual life depended on temporal events which may or may not happen, and would be overthrown if they did not. But the significance of the life of the spirit is to control or be independent of events in time.

**14** Prayer which takes the form of beseeching is least likely to find its answer according to its desire, for it implies, and indeed affirms, an opposition between the supplicant and the giver which it is the purpose of prayer to remove.

**15** God is not strictly speaking found in prayer but in the answer to prayer; and it is His to give the answer.

**16** It is a mercy that God does *not* answer all our prayers. He answers according to capacity as well as according to need.

**17** People in the British Empire held a day of prayer (May 26, 1940) for help against the most terrible enemy Europe has known. On the night following that day there took place the most shattering blow the Allied cause had received up to that time—the surrender of King Leopold and his army. *Ça donne à penser.*

## IV

**1** "If they believe not Moses and the prophets neither will they believe tho' one rose from the dead"—this is directly and conclusively an argument *against* miracles, or rather against their apologetic efficacy.

**2** Is there anything more striking or unique in the apparent assertiveness of Christ, in His supreme confidence in Himself, than there is in the entire confidence in themselves and their knowledge which, e.g., scientists show? When the latter assert any truth which they fully believe to be true they do not assert it with a reservation, they declare it to be absolutely true.

Is there then not as much ground for the absolute assertion of moral truth? Is a moral or religious genius less to be believed in than an intellectual genius?

**3** One of the reasons why the facts or doctrines of the Christian religion must be interpreted spiritually is that if some of them were accepted and acted on in their veriest literalness, their adherents would become fools completely. Take, for instance, that belief which seems necessary to the life of the Church, the belief in the presence of Christ in His church. If believers took this to refer to—and acted sincerely in the belief that it did refer to—the actual, embodied, existent, individual person who was the historical Christ (and the historical Christ has no other meaning), quite clearly we should have unutterable confusions and delusions of all kinds. From these the general good sense of men delivers them; reality and practical life would not tolerate such aberrations. But if the doctrine does not mean this, then there is nothing left but a "spiritual" interpretation of it, the identification of the "spirit of Christ" with God's presence, or with the spirit of the Christian Church itself, the "spirit of Christ" coming, in this sense, to mean the moral and religious purposes and aims which He embodied. This is indeed implied by the position of Christ as one of the Persons in the Trinity. And it should be obvious that an interpretation of this kind, however we may formulate it in detail, must inevitably lift the life of the Church, its beliefs, its realities, out of any absolute dependence on "historical facts" whatsoever.

Men have to observe that religion would have existed in some form no matter what "historical facts" did or did not appear, but that the form in which it does in fact exist is determined by the needs and aspirations of the community in which it exists, e.g. commercial, military, cultural. Indeed, we see that the form in which Christianity is accepted is determined by, and does not itself and alone determine, the life and requirements of different nations. And the principle that different nations and different men can only accept and live such truths as their general capacity will admit or will grasp argues the same line of consideration.

4   It seems impossible to regard the idea of atonement as adequately exemplified in the mere fact of forgiveness; for forgiveness is a purely negative process, and one which is not likely to be of much efficacy in itself. Suppose, for instance, the ordinary doctrine of Christ's atonement were true, that His whole life's work was summed up in His death and that His death meant forgiveness for those "who believed in Him"—what is to be done with such a view? A man is not a whit a better man because his past badness has been overlooked and "forgiven." (The man does not feel himself a good man; he only feels himself a helpless man whose goodness, such as it is, is not even his own, has not been realized by himself. But no man can be good by proxy; goodness must be personal if it is to be real.)

What is wanted for men struggling with evil is not mere forgiveness for the past but some hope for the attainment of goodness in the future. And that is the real point about atonement; men wish to acquire something of the mind and spirit of Christ. Indeed, it is the main ground of the value attached to His life by men; and without it forgiveness is of hardly any moment, almost a mockery.

5   Undoubtedly one of the greatest arguments for Christianity is the degree of goodness which can be obtained by following its maxims; for the question to be answered in practical life is not

what is the ultimate meaning, the essential truth, but what is the highest possible life that can be attained? What will bring the securest character and noblest spiritual activity?

**6** Remarkable how men will regard themselves as understanding the theological significance of "Christ's life and death," as knowing their own relation to Him, and consequently God's purpose with them and indeed all that can be known about these matters—and yet are each and all as unlike one another, and unlike Christ, as if the whole "sum of Christian knowledge" were a mere stage trick or superfluous excrescence on the surface of their lives. A crank remains a crank after his conversion much as before it; a stubborn man remains stubborn; a mild man mild; a stupid man stupid.

Why will men pretend that their knowledge about God and His ways, in their experience, is actually God's knowledge in them, God's truth in their minds? Better acknowledge at once that all this so-called Christian theology is the attempted explanation on our part of our experience as religious beings, with the civilization, culture and insight we have inherited and are bound up with, and give up attempting to believe impossible assertions. But men are much wiser, and experience is much securer than all their theologies; and their safety lies in that fact.

Individuality and the richness of personality are not exhausted by the life of one individual, and men can no more become like Christ, or be Christs, than they can become like, or be, one another. They must each develop their own lives and be the highest that is in store for them, with the help of Christ's life or without it.

**7** The "divinity of Christ" appeals to the worldly religious minds of Christendom, to the worldly-minded servants of the Church, and the worldly-spirited adherents to its doctrines. The "divinity of Christ" satisfies a natural snobbery of temperament which can hardly be eliminated even in religion. People who would not "know" Christ as a son of man will readily "know" Him as a son of God.

**8** It is remarkable how the idealization of human passion found satisfaction in the worship of mediaeval (and modern Catholic) Christianity—the worship of fulfilled but untarnished womanhood in Mary, and of unfulfilled and untarnished manhood in Christ. The former appeals to men, the latter to women.

**9** Historical Christianity is perhaps little more than a float to be used by beginners in the experience of spiritual religion, and serving to buoy them up till they can, by their own activity and self-control, move about easily in the ocean of spiritual life.

**10** One of the aims of a spiritual religion like Christianity, perhaps indeed its chief aim, is to create a frame of mind in which the individual realizes, at the highest level of his being (in his relation to God), the unbroken continuity with environment found in the life of nature. Just as in the case of mere nature, in the life of the plant or again in the life of the established types of animals, the individual is so harmoniously united with its environing world as to seem to the observer to be but a part of it, taking on its very colour, unaware of any alienation, so when the environing realm is the spiritual Life of God it seems reasonable to expect that the spirit of man may reach a level where he is unaware of any alienation between his spirit and God's, when even the self-sacrifice of abandonment to God's life is unconscious, when the blending of spirit with spirit is so complete that the very shadow of opposition would seem "unnatural" because hostile to man's super-nature. It is this attitude of mind which Christianity seeks to establish. Properly understood it implies or sums up all other aspects of the religion of Christ.

**11** The external relation of doctrines and formulae to the religious life, which is so characteristic of Christianity, is due to the fact that the historical life and work of its Founder are in strictness external to the inner spiritual life of the religious individual. They are events that took place at a remote time in another individual. Being external, they can only be expressed by doctrines that *prima facie* are external to the central religious experience of the individual. They are stated to be "accepted," "believed in" as something given from without and not arising from within the religious mind.

It was inevitable, therefore, that this belief in doctrines concerning what took place elsewhere should come to be taken as the essence of Christian life: and this attitude reached its logical culmination in the method of salvation by formulae adopted in the mediaeval church. The mere acceptance of formulae was in large measure taken to be equivalent to possession of the religious mind of a Christian. Many people still hold this view; many others revolt from it, as did the genuinely sincere religious minds in the mediaeval days. It is felt that more is required than this external acceptance of external formulae. The inner experience must be considered the essence, the doctrines the formal expression. When this is emphasized we have a recoil from the external doctrines to the primal source of religion in the inner personal experience of the religious mind. This is a recoil to the fundamental fact in all religion, the direct relation of the individual to God. It is not the creation of a new religion, nor even a reform of the old one; it is the direct realization of what religion is. But when this direct experience is acquired, the old formulae come to have a new meaning, and are seen to be expressions of the nature of religious experience as felt and realized by the individual. From this point of view Luther's "reformation" was nothing more than a personal rediscovery of what really lay behind mediaeval religion all the while, and of what some others before him, and the best religious minds of the Church always, were quite aware of. His reformation of himself was little more than a personal realization of what it is to be a good Christian as distinct from a good churchman. It was the experience that every good Catholic Christian before him went through (and still goes through)—

Athanasius, Augustine, Bernard, etc. This is proved by the fact that his experience left untouched the value of the doctrines of the Church, which for the most part he accepted after his reformation as he did before it—only in the one state he realized their meaning and in the other he did not.

And this is the universal process of the religious life in the individual. Religion has to be perpetually re-born, re-created, in the individual. There is no religion by proxy. The consciousness of the eternal must be a new and continually renewable experience for human individuals, if it is to be vivid and real. That is as it should be. And no wonder the experience is fresh and refreshening: for to be eternal is to be for ever young. No wonder the experience fills the discoverer with gladness and the sense of enrichment, for it is the source of all joy in life, and of all wealth of mind and spirit.

But how the great Mother Church must feel surprised and pained to find that the discovery of this elemental fact of religious experience, for which the Church is established and to sustain which she exists, should be turned against herself, instead of being brought to her feet as a grateful acknowledgment to herself as the agency which made the discovery possible! If we put ourselves at the point of view of the Catholic Church, this must have been the source of her attitude towards the "reformers." Their hostility to the Church seemed due to ingratitude, for the Church had made them what they were, and given them the possibility of this new experience. The reformers were like poor men who come into a fortune which the laws of the State allow them to possess absolutely, and who then use their fortune to create a revolution or betray the State into the hands of its enemies. This is the dramatic pathos of the Reformation movement.

**12** If the Christian life is to be realized in the world before it can be considered a reality, if the "Kingdom of God" is to be an earthly Kingdom;—if in a word the value of Christianity lies in its historical embodiment amongst mankind—then unquestionably Christianity must be pronounced a complete failure. The nations are no nearer Christianity to-day than they were at its inauguration as a religion. Two thousand years is a long enough time to make an experiment with any idea or scheme of ideas; if it fails after such a prolonged trial it may safely be said to fail utterly. Any political or scientific principle which was still unverified and unrealized after such a period would be abandoned at once.

There is only one conclusion to draw from the facts—that Christianity does not depend for its truth or its value on any historical events that have occurred or will ever occur. Its value lies just in the experience it makes possible of the union of man's spirit with the eternal Spirit as an abiding and an everlasting Presence through all the changes of time and in spite of all the changes of history. The experience of this union is found in the consciousness of an enduring imperturbable peace of spirit, rising to the level of joy, in the midst of all the transitory events of the world, and held firm by an assured trust in the supreme Spirit which sustains and pervades the world of things. The historical origin of Christianity, and the events in the life of its founder, have no more to do with its truth, its truth no more depends on them, than the value of Christianity could be tested by the historical success or failure of Christianity amongst the nations. It is indeed more than probable that the actual failure of Christianity to become an historical reality amongst the nations is just due to the attempt made by so many of its exponents to find its whole meaning in the history and life of its founder.

But perhaps it would be more correct to say that there has been no failure of Christianity at all. For it could be maintained that the attempt to find the essence of Christianity in the events of the life of its Founder must itself fail; and that consequently the religion which has been spread abroad by these methods is not Christianity at all, but a revised Judaism. The Apostle Paul has been mainly responsible for this. He was too much of a Jew to let the spirit of Christianity escape from the historical life of

Judaism. His strenuous attempt to link it up with the past history of the Jewish religion has been the chief obstacle in the way of the acceptance of it as a truly universal religion for mankind. The Apostle misconceived its essence from the start. His passionate racial feeling could only accept it if it were shown to be based upon, and the fulfilment of, Jewish racial aspirations. But if Christianity is to be, as it is, a supremely universal religion, such a procedure is a contradiction in terms: for if it is the outcome of Judaism, it is not universal for mankind; if it is universal, it has no more to do with Judaism than with Mohammedanism or Buddhism. The Apostle pretends to treat it as univeral by passing it on to the "Gentiles," but this is only another way of saying that the Gentiles are to become an extended "Israel of God." The Apostle can hardly be said to have got within sight of Christianity, so tenaciously does his racial emotion connect him with his historical past. His efforts to explain Christianity historically in terms of the past are of a piece with the efforts made by the Church to embody Christianity historically in the present and the future. This is as foolish as to tie up Christianity with the historical events of the life of its founder. These are past and gone and done with: but it does not follow that Christianity has failed. Its Founder may be dead; but He lived in that consciousness of the union of His spirit with the eternal spirit: even if the historical expression of His life had been entirely different, His religious experience would have been precisely the same. In particular His death has no more to do with the truth of Christianity than His birth. If He had died in His bed, Christianity would have been entirely unaffected by this normal event, just as it is by the abnormal event brought about by the mob in Jerusalem.

Along this line we must seek the re-inspiration of mankind by Christianity.

13 Nothing has done more harm to Christianity than the materialization of its controlling ideas: hence, whenever it has prospered from the worldly point of view, it has collapsed a

short time afterwards. It is the very greatness of its principles which has thus led to failure: so few see their meaning and it is easier to misapply than to understand them. Its "Power" has been identified with ecclesiastical and secular and even physical force; its "Charity" has been interpreted as "almsgiving"; its "Rewards" as a bonus of goods in the next world; its "Sacrifice" as the nailing of its founder's body on a tree by a crowd of Jewish ruffians; its "Atonement" as the satisfaction of an angry God by the primitive process of shedding one man's blood to let all others escape; its "poverty of spirit" as the cult of the economically destitute: and so on through all its elements. All this has led to disgrace, folly and ruin. Perhaps the last has done as much harm as any other distortion. "Poverty of spirit" has little to do with surrendering material possessions: it is in essence the recognition that the dignity of our spirit owes everything to the riches of the Divine Thought, and the maintenance of that dignity by this resource alone.

**14** When the nature and value of Christianity are to be determined by historical investigation—which is now the accepted method of interpretation—the fate of Christianity as a universal religion is sealed. There must always be more than one conclusion to be drawn from the facts of history, because history is constantly illuminated not merely by the discovery of new facts and new ways of interpreting the facts, but by changing views of the nature of man and his ideals. But a universal religion, if really universal, must be above all dispute, above all changes of opinion, above all variations in the life of man: it must be the same for all time and for all men. A religion whose character is purely historical does not fulfil these conditions.

**15** Dissatisfaction with Hebraic religion or with Christianity as currently cultivated is usually taken as an indication of want of religious feeling. This is begging the question: it assumes that Hebraic religion or common Christianity is a standard or a *ne plus* *ultra.* The dissatisfaction in many cases is an indication of the presence of deeper religious needs than current religious views satisfy, and is a demand for a newer and a better religion.

**16** The exponents and advocates of Christianity have from the first put its claims in a wrong light; and this has seriously affected its acceptance by mankind. They made it appear as if Christianity were intended solely for the weak and the inefficient: and they have appealed, therefore, to the lowest interests of man and to men moved mainly by the lowest motives—those of fear and infirmity. Those who have done wrong are invited to take the offer of salvation from the consequences of their own guilt—hell and punishment: those who are conscious of their own insufficiency are invited to take advantage of the "all-sufficiency" of Christ. It need cause little surprise that men with a sense of the dignity of humanity and with a sense of honour in paying for their own guilt should have looked askance at such a type of religion; and that those who have availed themselves of it should have been the mean, the destitute and the degraded of mankind. It is because this presentation of Christianity has been the most common that men have always to some extent shrunk from frankly acknowledging themselves as devoted and loyal believers in the doctrines of Christ: if they do so at all, it is not as individuals but as members of a Church where their individual interest and feeling becomes merged in a general social consciousness. Men do not care to proclaim themselves individually as belonging to the degraded and the mean amongst mankind.

This view of Christianity is at best but very partial and inadequate. It is a degraded view of Christianity, in fact, to say that Christianity is primarily intended for the degraded.

**17** It is rather childish to think of God as appearing in the person of one man in Galilee, and incarnating His being in one person in order to appreciate the sensations (pain, joys, etc.) of being a man on earth. God, by creating or expressing Himself in man, from the very first always incarnated Himself in man and in humanity. That alone is atonement; not substitution for man but union with him, rising above man's sufferings because triumphing over pain and death itself. So to triumph is to be divine.

**18** The "incarnation" is perhaps the most extreme and consummate expression of anthropomorphism, and has all the defects as well as the merits of anthropomorphism. There seems no doubt that in some sense it is true: the question is how true. Literally and entirely true, it cannot be. When exaggerated, it is merely another illustration of man's demand for a "sign" from heaven. Man is always asking for "signs" from God; for man is bound up with material conditions, and so steeped in them that he probably understands them better than anything else. But God is much more than human, and no human life can express the Divine nature fully; so that God can never "become" man, any more than man can "become" God.

**19** The difference between paganism or natural religion and Christianity or spiritual religion is that in the first men make gods in their own image, in the second God is said to make men in His image.

**20** The peculiarity of Christ's religion is that Christ asks for belief in Himself as God, as coming from the Father; nothing less and nothing more. It is not enough simply to believe in His works, or in His statements as propositions conveying religious ideas. Many have stated principles of religion similar to or identical with those He enunciated. But no other human person has stated not in effect but in fact that he was God manifest in human form; that those "who have seen Him truly have actually seen the Father." That is the special note of Christianity.

**21** The greater the responsibility the greater the burden of servitude. This is inevitable, for the only way to justify and express responsibility, or power to control, is by convincing others that it is used for their benefit, i.e. by serving their welfare. This is the essence of *noblesse oblige*, and also, on a higher level, of the Christian belief. God is necessarily at the call of man, willing and ready to help in all time of need. God is the supreme minister of all His creatures. Hence the truth of Christ's statement: he that is the greatest among you shall be your minister. This was one of His most penetrating inspirations.

**22**  If there is to be in human experience a religion of the spirit, it does seem essential that at some time there should be an historical revelation of God's mind and purpose as a whole to mankind; not simply to a particular man here and there, but to humanity and, therefore, a revelation once and for all historical time. Left to their own devices men could not invent or construct a scheme of communion with God: they are too blind and stupid to guide their own footsteps into the way of perfect peace: if anyone made the attempt someone else would propose another way and no one could give final decision on such a point. There have been many messages and deliverances, unconnected and sustained by individual conviction. What, however, seems wanted is a continuous revelation in an historically continuous people culminating in a point beyond which it seems impossible to require more for the attainment of complete communion with God and complete peace of spirit.

The claim of Christianity is that no one except the Christ has embodied and expressed the mind of the Divine Spirit for mankind, and that it is impossible to surpass, or to demand, more than what He stands for and conveys in His life and in His message.

**23**  It seems simple and superficially true to dismiss the death of Christ by saying it was a stupid blunder, an act of fanatical fury on the part of the Jews, an act of injustice and cowardly expediency on the part of the Romans, in either case an unjustifiable wrong and, therefore, something that should not have happened and might have been avoided. This all seems plausible from the moral point of view. But from the religious and dramatic point of view, the tragedy lay in the subjection of a great personality and its supreme purposes to the chances and accidents of human passion; or rather in the necessity for a completely divine life to pass through the ordeal of all nature's conditions, and to do this in the very worst form possible, so as to prove the entire dominion of spirit over nature, to show the exaltation of spirit in and through its very humiliation.

All men must die, and the spirit must yield in time to the conditions of time, i.e. it must pass out of the chances and changes of mortality. How this is done at any time and in any case seems more or less accidental; and yet it is in the long run (or short run) inevitable and necessary. Therein lies the drama of every human life, however small the life may be. Its death is a necessity focused in a contingency of nature. The greater the spirit, the higher the significance. Merely to state that the death of Christ was a blunder and an accident is, therefore, to state too little or too much: too little if we mean that it merely took place as one of the events of human history, which is a sequence of contingencies, for this merely says it happened, and that tells us nothing at all about it, finds no meaning in it; too much if we mean that it should not have happened, for that implies that it had *no* meaning at all, which we are certainly not entitled to say.

It is bad enough for most men to face and go through death at all. But to go through it under the worst possible conditions, that is indeed terrible; and the worst conditions are those in which the destruction of the individual life is brought about, not by nature's processes alone, but by the instrumentality of our own fellow creatures, especially by fellow creatures belonging to our own race and kindred, by those of our own household. The tragedy is accentuated when the extinction of life is carried out in the name and with the ritual of justice. Its horror reaches its maximum when the person who goes through this ordeal is all that a person can be, with a consummate vision of justice and goodness, and capable with complete assurance of challenging his judge and his enemies to point out a flaw in his own innocence.

It is only in a divine tragedy that a personality could be overthrown, not for any real particular wrong, but for the apparent wrong of claiming to be innocent of all wrong whatever, for the wrong apparently done to all men in not sharing with them the common infirmity of doing wrong, the common capacity to sin.

Yet one who could not be condemned for sins of His own must, like all mortal human beings, be condemned somehow, since He shares a common life with them. Hence the condemnation Christ submitted to was not condemnation for Himself, but condemnation for the common lot of humanity which He shared. He suffered with them though innocent and, therefore, suffered for them to justify their innocence. Hence in His case the earthly tragedy of the crucifixion became a "divine comedy" of atonement; the transitory satisfaction of human hate became a sacrifice of divine love; the destruction of human life became the achievement of divine life; the enslavement of mortality to death became the liberation of immortality to life; the burial of the body in the earth, the last step of incarnation, became the transition of the spirit to the heavenly regions, the first step to the resurrection of the spirit.

**24** The incarnation and the resurrection seem complementary phases of the same reality. It is small surprise that the creed of Christendom has held firmly by both, as indeed do the writers of the New Testament.

**25** In the Christian view of the world, it is not enough to say that God has revealed Himself on earth in the life-history of Christ. This was of short duration and came to an end. That is merely the historical incarnation of God in the life of man. It is of immense importance, but it is not all, and not the whole truth. Paul and the other apostles maintained, and rightly maintained, that Christ by overcoming death continues His work and God's purpose for man by active participation in the affairs of men, and by controlling the lives of those who believe in Him and His continuing work. In this capacity Christ is the eternal "Mediator" on behalf of man and intervenes between the Supreme Being as Father of all and His earthly children. Incarnation and Mediation are complementary aspects of the life of Christ; the one disclosing His mission on earth, the other disclosing His mission after leaving it; the one the revelation of God to man at a particular historical time, the other the continuing revelation of God to man through all eternity: the one God "manifest in the flesh," the other man manifest in the spirit by communion with God through Christ's perpetual presence with those believing on Him. So the whole is complete, a perfected system of spiritual life.

**26** The irony of the Protestant defence of Christianity is that in support of a religion essentially historical in character it attempts to rely exclusively on reason at the expense of tradition. This is indeed the natural consequence of the endeavour to be "scientific," for scientific thought cannot recognize tradition as a source of conviction. But in the case of an historical religion, tradition is itself a reason, and an essential reason, for belief and for faith. This is the strength of the Roman Catholic position.

**27** It is vain to imagine that opposition to Christianity is wholly, or even mainly, intellectual. In many cases objections based on reason are brought forward to cover up deeper or more genuine objections of an entirely different kind—objections of a spiritual or moral order in the wide sense. Men resent being told to do something better than custom or convention expects them to do. They dislike the self-discipline which purity of motive demands. They turn away with regret and impatience from an ideal apparently beyond their reach, and having its source and inspiration in another world, another order of life.

They will not tolerate, or are reluctant to believe in, the direct personal interference of God in the affairs of the world: they seem to think that this world belongs to man and is to be managed by him; that God should become incarnate in human form is looked upon as an intrusion!

None of these "objections" are really intellectual.

**28** Most people confuse the belief that certain events happened in the life history of Christ with faith in the power by which such events are brought to pass. The latter alone has any religious significance: the former is merely a confession of an historical conviction, or rather of a conviction concerning statements purporting to be historically true.

From the religious point of view the important point is to have faith in a Divine Spirit which can restore the finite spirit to newness of life after the stage of death has been passed. It is not enough to believe that Christ "rose from the dead": that is merely one event in one man's life history, and would have little religious interest if restricted to that alone. Its religious value lies in its being a manifestation of Divine power over death—the natural forces of destruction in their extreme form—a power, therefore, which can be and (so the religious mind believes) will be manifested in those who trust that what happened in Christ's case is thereby guaranteed to happen in their own when they reach the stage of death.

**29** It is difficult to understand how the substitutionary view of the death of Christ as a "punishment suffered on behalf of and in the stead of sinners" should have been accepted by any section of the Church. It is a doctrine that could only appeal to mean people, cowards at heart and contemptible in spirit.

**30** Perhaps no religion has produced such a variety of personality or such a variety of sects as Christianity. This is not a ground of objection: it is a proof of the vitality of its principles.

It is doubtful, too, if any religion has ever been able to guarantee peace and joy in the way Christianity professes to do and does do. These are important points which are often forgotten.

**31**   Christianity is a religion not dependent on a place or even a people. "Not in this place nor yet in Jerusalem": "God is a spirit, and they that worship Him must worship Him in spirit and in truth." It is, therefore, universal. Judaism is a religion with a place and dependent on a "peculiar people." It is, therefore, a particular religion, not for all.

**32**   It is often said that much has been lost to Christianity by our not possessing more of the discourses of Christ, and a fuller exposition by Him of His doctrine of life and conduct in detail. But what more would we have? The main ideas and guiding principles are clearly enunciated. The application of these to the details of life are rightly left to the individual. That is part of the discipline of life: it would have produced a new pharisaism if all situations were prescribed and nothing left for individual judgment and responsibility.

**33**   Supreme power does not need to exaggerate because it never requires to be wholly put forth against anything which can defeat it. Exaggeration, or going to excess in any form, is always a sign of weakness of some sort, and to the extent of the excess defeats its own end. Hence it is that a mind conscious of complete power is incapable of tyranny, and is so constrained in its exercise as to be capable of great humility. It is curious to note how this is expressed in the Christian religion by the conception of the incarnation as the "humiliation" of the Divine.

**34**   It seems foolish to question the reality of the miraculous if we accept the reality of Christ as portrayed in the Gospels; and if we do not, the question of the miraculous does not arise. Christ's life is the main miracle that ever occurred, and may well be the source of many lesser miracles.

**35** The unspiritual man cannot be induced to accept Christianity except with reluctance: he would prefer *not* to believe it to be true. This accounts for most of the objections men raise to Christianity: they are not really theoretical, they are emotional.

**36** Much has been said against the claims of Christianity, and criticism of them has no doubt rendered good service directly and indirectly to truth. But it is curious to observe how continuous reflection only strengthens the claim that, in all the essentials of a spiritual religion, Christianity is able to satisfy the highest aspirations and to fulfil the greatest demands of the human spirit at its best. One illustration of this is the way in which it claims to do justice both to the supremacy of the Divine Spirit and to the freedom of the individual spirit. Not the least important of its doctrines is that the Supreme Divine Spirit wills nothing but love to man, and wills that love in such a way that man has only to share that love in order to find his own highest satisfaction and partake in the Divine Life at the same time. And what more can man ask? It ensures even the permanence of the individual finite spirit, since God's love is eternal.

**37** It is possible that Jesus could not have been so confident of His peculiarly divine mission had He not felt His power to do exceptional things out of the ordinary course of nature. He may have required extraordinary works to justify to Himself His extraordinary faith. His consciousness of Himself as divine would be confirmed by the unusual acts which He did with complete success. A unique personality could after all never discover its uniqueness by living and acting in an ordinary way. In consequence, He cannot be said to have been divine because He worked "miracles": we must rather say that He worked miracles because He was divine, and that He both disclosed and discovered His own divinity by doing so.

Hence He rightly said to His followers "believe in me at any rate for the works' sake"; they could appreciate "works," because these appeal to the senses, and His works, being exceptional, betrayed the presence of exceptional, i.e. non-natural, power. Such an unusual power is identified, and easily identified by the ordinary mind, with spiritual power. And it was reasonable for Jesus to ask His followers to believe in Him for the works' sake if He had believed in Himself for that reason, because of the works He had done and could do.

**38** It is suggestive that Jesus seemed disinclined or was unable to exercise His exceptional spiritual power over nature unless those on behalf of whom He exercised it showed their belief in Him.

**39** "Prophecy fails" and always will fail because it is a mere message; and it can never make such an impression or do so much for the world as a person. That is the difference between the work of the mere prophet and the work of the Founder of Christianity. Jesus did not claim belief merely in what He said, but for what he did; and that is a deeper realization of personality. He and His works were original, not so much His words. This is ignored by some critics of Christianity.

**40** One of the great difficulties, perhaps indeed the most fundamental, presented by Christianity is that the Divine personality of its founder is held to be at once a manifestation of an eternal process (He "proceeds" from the "Father") and also an historical individual coming into being and passing away in a process of time. In the former sense, the process has the quality of necessity, it is part of the order of the Universe as the realization of the Divine Life: in the latter sense, the appearance is a contingency, an event in the history of the world, and like all events it has the quality of a happening, something that might or might not have taken place and is presumably dependent for its occurrence on what is looked on as the free or arbitrary will of God. Anthropomorphism tends to emphasize the second alternative, and many statements in the New Testament support this: it is perhaps the way most people take Christianity. But it is not easy to reconcile a contingent event, however brought about, with an eternal process of the Divine Spirit. Yet somehow the Divine and the human aspects must be reconciled if the full significance of Christianity is to be realized.

**41** It is difficult to see much meaning in the Pauline conception of Christ's death as a sacrifice of Christ for the sins of mankind, a punishment borne by Him to save men from their own punishment by God, the price paid to God to satisfy a divine sense of justice. Paul's conception is steeped in the Jewish tradition of sacrifice of animals to appease an outraged and avenging Deity. That tradition is the heritage of the Jewish race and other primitive peoples. It cannot be said to have any significance for a spiritual religion. Every man must bear his own punishment; and most honest men are prepared to do so. The significance of Christ's death is found in its end—the resurrection. If that actually occurred, then eternal life in every sense of that term is assured for the human spirit; and that surely is salvation—as indeed Paul himself also preached and believed.

**42** It cannot be to any man's self-interest to make such claims for himself as Christ did: nor could any man succeed in doing so in his own interest even if he tried. The operations of the Divine Power would not merely be too much for him, they would before long overthrow him. To claim to be a Divine Being is to claim not only to be more than human but to be equal to God; and such a claim, if unfounded, is a form of spiritual pride which, as the Greeks saw, will bring about in due course its own nemesis and destruction. The unique peculiarity of Christ's life is that because He felt or knew He was but doing the will of God, the claim did not produce spiritual pride, or bring about divine vengeance or the humiliation and destruction of His personality. His life to the end was true to His claim. This is an important point often overlooked by those who would minimize His divine nature.

**43** The external conditions associated with the death of Christ seem almost trivial and incidental relatively to the bearing of the main figure in the drama and to the issues which He personally felt to be involved in the course of events. The seizure in the garden by a crowd of ruffians led by a traitor seems a melodramatic episode in a common story when compared with the agony through which He was passing at the time: the trial seems less of a mockery than a mock trial got up on the stage of events to set off the spiritual dignity of the victim; the bearing of the cross to the place of crucifixion and the crucifixion itself seem quite ordinary events when compared with the extraordinary spiritual ordeal which was taking place in the soul of the sufferer. This is out of all proportion to the interest or importance of the external acts and transactions, which were of a kind that took place frequently and were familiar to the society of the time. Two malefactors were subjected to the same treatment on the same day.

It is hardly possible for anyone to imagine or to realize clearly, still less to reproduce in words, the state of mind which called forth all the excruciating torture which He felt in undergoing this otherwise familiar ordeal. And it is significant and remarkable that those who recorded the course of these events did not appear or did not attempt to understand His state of mind. It is most unlikely that His agony was due to the sense of ignominy and humiliation to which He was compelled to submit. Many martyrs before and since have gone through as much with indifference and even with the temper of triumph over their enemies. Their beliefs surmounted the sufferings they endured and gave them a quiet confidence.

What He suffered seems to have had its source in an acute realization that His spirit, which had hitherto enjoyed the sense of eternal life steeped in the love of the Divine, had to face and pass through the terrible and unknown adventure of ordinary physical death: that He had to surrender all He held dear in this life to the powers of mortality and physical dissolution, to admit that nature could destroy spirit, or at least have temporary dominion over it; the very opposite of all He had felt and found to be true in His life hitherto. Possibly He may have thought that, as He had a unique relation to God as the specially elect son of God, the love of the Father would have offered some unique way of permitting Him to pass the boundary of mortality, to pass through earthly to immortal life. This, indeed, would have been a consummation of the love of God for Him, and have confirmed the unique and inseparable relation to God which He claimed. The discovery that this was not to be but that He must go through the ordinary portals of natural death may have created the uncertainty and doubt in His mind that drew forth the agonizing cry at the last moment—the very climax of the torture through which He had been passing all the while—"Why hast Thou forsaken me?" That gives the clue to His state of mind, and is its keynote. If He had been merely human, He would not have felt like that: if He had not been human, He would not have expressed His feelings. On the other hand, if He had realized in advance that to pass through the ordeal of natural death was the only way to triumph over nature and establish the supremacy of spirit and thus realize His divine humanity—His incarnation of the divine spirit—He could hardly have felt the sense of desertion to which He gave expression.

It is clear that He had had the prospect of death in mind for some time, even in the manner by which it came about—that of crucifixion. This makes it all the more significant that the actual ordeal involved should have caused such profound spiritual disturbance as He was passing through it. Light is further thrown on the matter by His utterance in the Garden, "Father, if it be possible, let this cup pass from me": as if He thought that there might be given to Him a way out through the portals of death other than that of the dark unknown channel of natural death common to all men and all life on earth. All His life through He had encountered and dominated the powers of nature and the nether world: all through He had met and triumphed over the wickedness and cruelty of His fellow-men. But here at the last He had to submit to the powers of darkness, the powers of mere nature and the evil wills of men. It is intelligible that when brought face to face with such a situation, altogether new in His experience, doubt and uncertainty of His position, of His unique relationship to God and the unique love of God towards Himself, should have entered His mind for the first time in His life. It was the catastrophic test of the validity and the truth of His claim to be the elect son of God, a claim which He alone made on His own behalf and which He alone understood. It is not surprising that the uniqueness He had claimed for Himself and manifested throughout His life should now take the form of an agonizing isolation of spirit. The ordeal of natural death seemed to test, to challenge, and cast doubts upon the very love of God Himself. He did not seem to doubt His own love for God, but God's love for Him—"Why hast *Thou* forsaken *me*?"—as if He implied "I have not forsaken Thee." The interval between this cry and His last words "It is finished," may have brought about a change of mind, for the words "It is finished" may be interpreted in two ways: either He saw clearly what it all meant, and in that case the words may imply quiet and composed resignation in the expectation of future triumph: or the sorrow and doubt remained, in which case the words are a mute acceptance of an uncomprehended mystery in His life, the only mystery which He could not penetrate.

It is remarkable also that the agony took such an entirely personal form, and was not in any way illuminated by the vision of a resurrection to come later, to which He had always referred when speaking of His death. Had He thought He was undergoing His suffering for others (as so many of His followers have maintained) He would surely have risen above His own personal agony in the consciousness that He was enduring it for others, and that it was being imposed on Him for their sakes. Many martyrs have accepted their fate in this way. But it was apparently not so in His case. He felt the bitterness of natural death as a personal agony, harrowing to His own spirit. And apparently He drew no confidence and strength from the anticipation of His resurrection; for surely the assurance that death would not have dominion over Him would have sustained His spirit and alleviated its agony. It did not, probably because the doubt was cast on all He had previously believed by the prospect of natural dissolution.

Yet from the wider point of view it was a greater proof of the love of God that He should go through natural death, to which all men are subject, than that He should escape it in some way special to Himself; for only so could His resurrection after such an ordeal be the complete vindication of His incarnation, and the guarantee that in fact He was the supreme representative of humanity. That the resurrection should be hidden from eyes and vision in this world is itself part of the darkness and bitterness of natural death. It was the concealment of this from the mind of Christ at the last hours which caused His cry of isolation. Had He seen it, He could not have felt such agony. His spirit had demanded more of the Father than that of other men. That is the reason why human beings can and do accept death with equanimity, an equanimity which Christ did not feel. For on His death, as on His life, the whole spiritual welfare and security of mankind depended; and so He felt: and that, too, added to His agony. This distinguishes profoundly the death and suffering of Christ from that of any other human being. He lived for all men in every sense of the term; and since in His resurrection all men overcome death and live again, His death is the death of death, the salvation from death, for all men.

**44** The resurrection cannot be said to have been accomplished merely to demonstrate to men the immortality of the human spirit. Men might believe in that without requiring confirmation of it in that particular way, which at best was an event in the life history of one Divine Person. The purpose of the resurrection was rather to show the necessary connection between the incarnate realization of the Divine Spirit on earth on the one hand, and on the other its continuous existence through all change, even the change of death, and its necessary unity with the Divine Spirit beyond the earthly sphere of life.

## V

**1** Men's doctrines of God fit any channel into which the progress of man will fit them: like a glacier in motion down a valley.

**2** Anthropomorphism is not so much an attributing to the Divine Being of human qualities and qualifications as a direct testimony to the divinity of man; not so much a humanizing of God as a deifying of man.

**3** Why not allow that the conception of God as a Personal God is not necessarily any more true than the conception of Him as not personal? Could we not consider that the demand made on the absolute by a finite spirit will be amply and fully justified by the absolute, no matter what form that demand may take (provided, of course, it has in itself what are necessary elements in religion—reverence, fear, etc.)? Is not the absolute fully equal to all our needs and all our claims on God?

We can, of course, agree that if men make claims on the absolute as a Person and take it to be such, their claims will all be met in a real and true sense, and not be disappointed. If that is the highest conception they can have of the absolute, there is no reason why they should abandon it. Yet, surely, at the same time this does not prevent others from taking the absolute to be impersonal if their nature leads them to believe that a Person cannot fully express all that the absolute is, and must be, to them. And they, too, will find their demands and needs realized in and by the absolute in the form in which it is conceived by them. There seems hardly anything contradictory in such a view; for men at different times have conceived God differently—different nations and peoples have done so—and yet to them all God has been God in deed and in truth, and they have found themselves at one with Him in their lives. It is, however, essential that in each case the demand made shall be in that form which, to those who make it, is felt to be so and cannot be felt otherwise; if not, it would simply be caprice, and this can satisfy no human spirit, nor can a capricious attitude to the absolute ever be maintained in earnest.

**4** It is sometimes maintained that because religion exists in the sphere of "feeling," of representation, of "Vorstellung," it is, therefore, untrustworthy, inadequate, unstable, untrue. One form which this criticism takes is the position that religion is "bad philosophy," that religion contains and exhibits in imagery, in obscure thoughts and ideas, what philosophy clearly and fully presents in its true form. There seems in all this an entire misunderstanding of both religion and philosophy. Religion, just because it lives in imagery, in "feeling," etc., is embedded in the concrete, in the actual full reality of life. By having its being in feeling, it absorbs, controls, is infused with, the whole of life; only if it existed in and through feeling could it do so, and the fact that it makes use only of concrete ideas and expressions shows that it must needs do so. It is not, in the first instance, the function of religion to have "clear and distinct ideas" or, again, absolutely adequate and true thoughts and notions of what it is dealing with. Its ideas must, before all else, be concrete, filled with actual reality. If, in addition to being so, they are also clear and adequate notions, so much the better; but this is not the first necessity. Religion is embedded in concrete life and experience, it is there that it moves and has its being; and the experience of it is, by its very nature, full, rich, concrete. Religion therefore does not require to pass from the concreteness and obscurity of feeling and "Vorstellung" to the abstractness and transparency of thought and notions, and cannot do so without losing its proper nature. To suppose that thinking is a substitute for feeling and a higher form of it is to mistake contemplation for action, truth for experience, abstract thought for fact.

In whatever way, therefore, we are to relate the "feelings" of religion with the thoughts of philosophy—however the latter may be used to influence and mould the former, we must at any rate guard against any attempt to identify the two, or to annihilate the former by establishing the latter. Instances of both these mistakes have occurred in philosophy.

5   The mind, whose life is spent amidst the flux of events and absorbed in the detail of experience, never seems able to rise to a higher conception of God than that of an "over-ruling Providence," i.e. a power controlling and ordering the "accidents" of the world. This is the ordinary bourgeois view of God.

6   Rationalistic criticism of Religion seems to begin when the vitality has gone, or begun to go, out of religion itself. It is symptomatic of the decay of religious belief as well as a cause of it, by hastening the process of decay. This can be seen by the fact that it is only when religious life has become reflective about itself and formulated its process in conceptual, i.e. non-individualistic, terms and, as a second stage, has begun to act from the formulae and taken them for the ground of belief instead of the result of it—it is only then that critical, rationalistic discussion begins. The field has already been prepared for this by the labour of religious analysis itself, of analysis in the interests of religion. Criticism of its doctrines merely carries one stage further the analysis of the living reality into formulae. No doubt this criticism

tends to the decay of the religion; but so do the first steps of analysing it. When the organism has become a shrunken corpse, it is already prepared for the knife of the anatomist.

7   In one way at least agnosticism has a singular resemblance to gnosticism or mysticism. The latter speaks of God or the Absolute as the "ineffable," the "nameless," the "unnameable": the former uses the terms "unknown," "unknowable." The difference between "nameless" and "unknown" is itself merely a difference of expression: both all the while lay the stress of their positions on the inadequacy of knowledge to its object. The result is the same if God transcends knowledge (mysticism) or if we don't know at what point knowledge ceases to carry any meaning (agnosticism).

8   The abstract attributes or conceptions which men apply to God—like being, existence, cause, etc.—are really due to an attempt on man's part to get rid of anthropomorphism when thinking about supreme reality. It seems odd at first that the most that man can say about God is such barren information as that God "is" or "exists" and, odder still, that they seem to be content to say so little. But it is inevitable that, if man strips off the functions and features which to him are all significant, there should be nothing left but qualities or conceptions that have no special significance for him at all. If we try to get objectivity at the expense of the subjective, then clearly we can't expect to find the subjective reinstated or comprehended in the result. Hence it is that the "heart" is constantly revolting against such abstract conceptions in the arguments produced by the "head." And the revolt is justified; for in the Supreme Reality we ought to find the subjective as much as the objective, man's full personality as well as objective ideas. In fact, it is a barren God which cannot produce man, and a worthless conception which cannot sustain the things that give worth to human life.

Nobody was ever edified by proofs for the "being" or "existence" of God who did not have a conception of God of another kind, and drawn from other sources. And it is noteworthy that those who content themselves with "proving" God's "existence" go on afterwards to assume that all that men ordinarily attribute to God, and require of God for ordinary religious purposes (goodness, mercy, holiness, forgiveness, etc.), can now be accepted as certain and asserted of God because He is proved to "exist"!—as if there were not just as much necessity to prove those qualities of God as to prove that He merely exists. The fact is there is no escape, and no necessity to escape, from anthropomorphism in dealing with God's Reality. Man, after all, is not just quite so worthless and bad that God should be ashamed of him and have nothing in common with him, not even spirituality!

**9** Religion is sometimes spoken of as if it were a kind of bad or imperfect philosophy, and as if philosophy should supplant it. The truth seems rather to be that in religion we have as a concrete experience what in philosophy we try to translate into terms of thought. In religion, we have that *experience* of relation with Reality which philosophy tries to interpret in formal terms. Philosophy therefore can no more be a substitute for religion than physiology can be a substitute for organic activity, or the theory of music for musical enjoyment.

Philosophy is to religion as soul to body, form to content, abstract to concrete. And how little philosophy can accomplish even of what it aims at!—a few truisms and pompous platitudes.

**10** If God were merely the conclusion of a philosophical process of reasoning, religion would be impossible.

If God were the premise of all reasoning, no proof would be required from philosophy.

**11** The only atheism of any importance is that which means the failure and ruin of the religious attitude of mind, which deprives the mind of any sense of the power and presence of God in daily life. Intellectual "atheism" is a sport of the imagination and has no real interest or value to anyone.

**12** The great mistake, which has been made by many philosophers and theologians, is to regard God as a "principle of explanation" of the "world." An explanation must always be abstract and in some sense distinct from the object explained. Yet God is not abstract nor distinct from the world He explains; He contains the world. Moreover, the measure of the value of an explanation is the extent of our own confusion, darkness and ignorance: this makes God relative to the quality of mind of the individual. An explanation, again, should make things clearer than they were before: "God" does not: the term only adds another obscure concept to our already obscure knowledge. The world becomes no clearer to us if we say that God "made" it, unless we can say how and why God made it—which is precisely what we cannot say.

The fact is that God is the supreme object of worship and source of all knowledge in our minds; the most concrete, therefore, of Realities, outside which we neither are nor think. God makes all explanations possible and, therefore, is not Himself a particular "explanation" of anything.

**13** There seems an inveterate habit in the human mind to put back the order of things to some remote time in the past and to resist every attempt at concentrating it into the present. Thus even the plan of the world, the course of providence, the train of events of each day, is looked upon as *pre*-ordained, *fore*-seen. Doubtless this is due to man's veneration for the past and his sense that the order of things must be enduring if it is to be respected and acquiesced in. But why should not the scheme of the day's events be arranged by a "mind" or spirit as each event comes into being? Why should not the order be determined *during* the happening of the events instead of before them—as an artist finds the beauty of the work growing under his hands? Why should it be supposed that the plan was once fixed in indefinitely distant ages and then, once decided upon, carried out with undeviating consecutiveness? People do not seem to see that if the plan of events was fixed once for all in some antecedent aeon of time, God Himself becomes no more than a spectator of His own work, helpless and constrained to carry out an "eternal order"; He becomes as much determined by His own plan as the human and other beings whose careers the plan governs. Such a God is not worthy of either respect or attention, for the only matter of any consequence to human beings is the plan ordained, not the power that *once* ordained it but now looks on helplessly at its course.

The absurdity of this view is dimly felt in the belief which so many have in the reality of "miracles" and the miraculous generally. This indicates an obscure admission that God must be allowed to "interfere" with the pre-ordained course of things if and when He thinks fit! There is this much to be said for such a view that it does escape, or try to escape, from the mechanical fatefulness which characterizes a pre-ordained fixed plan of things: it is a confession that the conception of such a brutally determined plan is not the whole truth. Yet this way of escape is equally absurd. For the spontaneous work of God is nothing more than a capricious accident if He only breaks through the plan now and again and merely "when He likes": God, so to say, shows He is not to be constrained by the plan He has formed, shows that He is still alive and still active, but only does so in capricious inroads and interruptions of His own pre-arranged plan. This is like a musician showing that he is master of his own compositions (and not his compositions master over himself) by introducing a jarring discord every now and again: or like a wealthy man proving that he is free in the control of his wealth by throwing some of it away in sheer waste.

What is required is to give up altogether the conception of a fore-ordained plan, and to suppose that God's mind is ordering the world *as* the world goes along, and is manifesting His mind in the life of actual things which live and move and have their being in His activity now as always.

**14** The difference between a primitive and a developed religious consciousness is that between regarding God as exclusively identified with a particular place or nation or tribe or power or virtue, and regarding all qualities, places, powers, etc., as conditions under which the one identical God is manifested, as ways in which God "appears." This is also the difference between intolerance and tolerance in religion. Primitive religious life is necessarily intolerant: it could not maintain its position otherwise, and that is the source of its strength: it must and does exercise force, physical force for the most part, to dominate its own adherents and to beat down external enemies who worship other gods. This intolerance is the main source of the endless wars of primitive peoples: for while the worshippers of different gods might be willing to remain at peace, the gods themselves cannot; they each claim supremacy and there is only one way to test this supremacy and so keep up the faith and heart of their respective worshippers—they must fight it out. Hence the very strength and intensity of primitive religious belief becomes a source of weakness. For the worshippers may be defeated in the conflict; and when that happens the god loses his sway and disappears.

The developed religious consciousness is necessarily tolerant, for the "God of the whole earth" is not the private deity of any nation or individual. This is a source of strength, for God is always on the side of His sincere worshippers, and God is always and without challenge supreme. It is also a source of weakness, for it easily leads to the view that God is indifferent to any one form in which He is worshipped and does not prefer one more than another. God comes simply to be taken for granted: the "spirit" of the worship becomes everything, the form nothing. The only way in which this indifferentism can be avoided is by maintaining that some ways in which God appears, and some forms under which God is worshipped, have more value than the others, more value to the worshipper and more value to God. When this difference of value is accepted, at once there arises ground for controversy and strife. This is the source of the intellectual warfare, leading in many cases to battle and slaughter, which has prevailed in the history of Christianity. Instead of being a warfare between gods, it has been a warfare between doctrines.

**15** Overmuch emphasis on the historical origins of religion leads to a perversion of religious life. People come to consider religion as promising things to come in the future because of what has happened in the past. The future never does fulfil the highest "promises"; it merely creates the promise of more to come. Hence religion becomes a perpetual looking forward, a constant aspiration; and in default of the fullness of realization being found within a given time, because of repeated "hope deferred," the actual realization is put off to another life altogether, a life without the chances and changes of history, a life in "another world." But this is just an admission that the life of religion is not a life confined to historical conditions at all; it is a life which is above historical and temporal conditions, an "eternal life." This should have been accepted from the start as the essence of religious life, and then it would not have been supposed that religion had to do with things that were historically to "come to pass."

It is equally clear that if the security of the religious life is not bound up with what is to happen in the future, it is not bound up with events that may have taken place in the past, however important these may have been at the time. The value of religion does not depend on our ancestors any more than on our successors.

People lay so much stress on historical factors because they are in general unable to deal directly with things unseen and untemporal.

**16** People are prepared to agree about theological dogmas in much the same way as they willingly agree to interchange the conventional compliments of ordinary intercourse. There is no vital truth underlying either; the main point is that people should get on somehow together, and understand or at least use the same language. To such a pass have the strifes of centuries come.

**17** It is generally held that the power of a divine personality is seen in the enactment of "miracles," in "contravening the laws of nature": the performance is said to be a "proof" of "divinity." If this merely means that spirit is not nature but transcends or triumphs over nature, it is a commonplace. If it means that there is something superhuman in contravening the "laws of nature," at least for a good end, it is nonsense. It is a sign of weakness rather than of strength not to be able to accomplish one's ends by utilizing the resources of nature according to the laws and terms of nature. It means that the agent is defeated by the powers of nature and cannot bend nature's order to the ends of spirit. So far from this being superhuman, it is *infra*-human: ordinary men can do better than that.

**18** It is remarkable that, when religion becomes exclusive and esoteric, it adopts the same device for maintaining its doctrines and preserving them from the peril of change, as that employed by abstract science: it employs a dead language to express its doctrines and ideas. This is deliberately done in both cases for the same reasons, to secure uniformity and unchangeableness of meaning in terminology and thought, and to secure unanimity of consent for all time from all those who accept the thoughts conveyed in the language.

Such a procedure may be justified and successful in the case of science, for scientific truth professes to be impersonal, and that means lifeless and indifferent to life: there is no harm in science using a dead language since science is detached from life. But in religion it is perilous and indeed impossible to adopt this device. Religion clothed in a dead language tends inevitably to become dead, a mere formalism, an external garment of the living spirit, incapable and indifferent to development which is the essence of life.

**19** In the greatest spheres of life, in the sphere of man's relation to the Divine Spirit of the world, thought is so incapable of articulating insight, and language still more inadequate to express the whole truth, that there can never be much difference between the learned and the unlearned, the great in intellect and the simple. It is a mere delusion to suppose that those who talk about religion and write about it have more of the real experience than those who cannot reduce the experience to speech. People write about these things, and indeed about many other things, because they do *not* understand them but merely wish to understand them, being often more interested in the experience from this point of view than in the realization of it as a living force. The intellectual interpretation of religion has been in many ways the chief enemy of religious experience. The calm assumption of the learned that those who write most about religion are best able to lead others into the way of truth is but an idol of the schools, a mixture of the love of power and self-glorification. The man who can give reasons for his conduct is not necessarily the best man: the man who can give an explanation of beauty is not necessarily an artist at all. The power assigned to and assumed by the man of articulate intelligence is one of the curious prejudices and illusions of the higher civilization. In the Kingdom of the Spirit all men are at best but children, and to become childlike is in fact one of the essential conditions of belonging to it.

**20** A good deal of so-called philosophy of religion consists in half-conscious patronage of the Almighty, in finding reasons which are little better than excuses for God's actions, in giving explanations which are thinly veiled apologies.

**21**  The question, or the doubt, "whether there is a God" is a superb illustration of human vanity and self-importance. It means almost in so many words "is there a greater mental power than mine?", "is there a higher spirit than myself?"—a question which turns in mocking irony on its proposer.

**22**  Men try to identify God with cause, with truth, with beauty, with goodness. Such reflection has a touch of pathos. It is like an attempt to identify a man by his size or his colour. Except as ways of describing what God means, these terms are of little value: and the attempt to find God solely in any one or more of them is just the old attempt to find a "sign" of God's presence. This is sure to fail, for it implies that the invisible can be found in one visible embodiment. There is no harm in finding God in everything: the mistake is in trying to find Him specially in one thing, one act, one object in the world. When we realize that God is the spirit animating all and in all, we never seek a "sign," we always find Him directly revealed.

It is curious to notice that most people accept the person of Christ in much the same sense as one might take an act or an event to be a "sign" of God's presence. God is supposed to have been "incarnated" in Christ in a unique and exclusive manner: Christ is supposed to be *the* revelation of God, *the* presence of God in humanity. All this is a natural perversion of the half-convinced mind seeking to convince itself of the reality of God's spirit in the world. People want a "sign," and amongst so-called Christians, Christ becomes the personal "sign." Paul understood Christ in this way, and so did most of the other disciples. Fortunately Christ is more than a "sign," and God does not confine His spirit to any one person; nor does anyone who communes with the reality of God need a sign of any sort. We must commune with God in spirit and in truth, as a real abiding presence (and not simply through an attribute like truth, or cause) if we are to appreciate in any vital sense the nature of God's relation to man.

**23** From the religious point of view, knowledge (more especially science) is the discovery of the wisdom of God; work, in all its forms, is the discovery of the power of God; the sense of beauty is the discovery of the love of God. The glory of God is the union of all three supremely realized and inseparably blended.

**24** There is a paganism of the intellect as well as of the imagination. Paganism essentially consists in making God after man's image; spiritual religion in regarding man as made in the image of God. Philosophers do not make use of images, but they generally construct God after man's conceptions and insist that no other God can be accepted. This is paganism of the intellect.

**25** The difference between a philosophy of the Absolute and religion is that for philosophy God can only be an object of thought, the conclusion or the starting-point of a process of reasoning, whereas for religion God is a communicating spirit responding to and corresponding with man, sustaining, inspiring and renewing man's spirit as the needs of his finitude require. Philosophy, being a process of human knowledge, must reduce God to human terms and fit God into the scheme of human thoughts. There must be continuity between all objects of thought; and in fact all objects of thought have the same general character as objects; they are fixed and complete even if the completeness has to be obtained by the artificial process of definition. Knowledge assumes its capacity to grasp what it knows, and if necessary will reduce its object to such terms as can be made intelligible to the human mind. Its process is one-sided; the object does not communicate itself, the mind rather communicates with itself in dealing with the object; and whether the object be dead or alive the process is the same.

In religion, we have an entirely different attitude. In his relation to God, man is conscious of the frailty, the imperfection, the incompleteness of his whole mind, whatever the process of the mind may be: man does not even pretend to "understand"

God, rather he takes it that God understands, and alone understands, him, raises him out of his finitude into a fuller spiritual existence; purifies his mind by a greater vision than of himself he can claim to possess; surpasses all the objects of all his thought; and substitutes the peace of spirit which passes all understanding for the understanding of the world which regulates and stills the restlessness of the human intellect. God gives Himself to man that man may commune directly with Him, and spirit meet spirit in a conscious union and fellowship of unbroken intercourse.

Hence the terms in which religious communion is sustained and completed are entirely different from those in which philosophy or knowledge finds expression. Knowledge finds satisfaction in a connected scheme of ordered thought. Religion finds satisfaction in love of the Divine Spirit, in faith in the Divine Spirit, and in hope in the Divine Life. There is nothing in knowledge or the aim of knowledge comparable with these states of mind. And no knowledge can produce them or reproduce them. The most that knowledge can do is to give us an "idea" of God: it cannot give the spirit of God. The same is true to an analogous extent of our knowledge of other minds: we can by knowledge acquire an idea of another mind, but the only way we can realize another mind is when that mind directly communicates with us, acts with us, sympathizes with us. Our knowledge of it is quite different from its communication with us.

Hence it is that for philosophy the ultimate object of thought can be expressed as "the Absolute," which is at once less and other than God, because merely an object of thought which may even be regarded as lifeless or spiritless. But in religion God is the Soul of our souls, a revealing, consoling and indwelling Spirit giving man life and immortality, joy and fellowship.

**26** It is possible that modern developments of physics may give men a new apprehension of the reality of God, and pave the way for a new movement in religion. The conception of the continuity of matter, the identity of all energy, the functional significance of space (instead of the former idea of space as an indefinitely extended empty "room") give the mind a picture of the continual physical presence of the One Reality such as was hardly possible with the help of the old physico-mechanical conception of the world. It is an easy step for the religious mind to imagine the continuity of a Divine Spirit with a human spirit, once it grasps the sense of a continuity of the physical being of God with the physical existence of the individual.

**27** Philosophy is an undertaking on the part of man only. Religion is God's concern as well as man's: it involves reciprocal communion. That is the great and vital difference between philosophy and religion as forms of experience.

**28** It is entirely a mistake to suppose that the only possible attitude of man to nature is that adopted by science. Nature is not merely an object of knowledge, whether of knowledge for its own sake or of knowledge obtained for the purpose of using nature for man's ends or man's welfare. This view of nature lays too much importance on man in the scheme of the Universe; and in a sense also too little importance, for it implies that man is merely a being who thinks scientifically. Man can never be completely satisfied with the purely scientific outlook on nature; still less can he exhaust the meaning of nature by scientific methods; for scientific methods require him to take nature to pieces, and nature is a whole and not a collection of pieces. He wants to be conscious of his union with nature as a whole, and is not satisfied unless he can realize this. His first instinct as a conscious or self-conscious being is to establish and maintain this relationship to the whole of nature. This is in a manner sounder and healthier than the purely scientific attitude. And it is also his first attitude in point of time. To begin with it takes the form of religion, the religion of nature or nature-religion.

Man loves to feel undisturbed union with nature in its entirety and will go to any length to secure it—by worship of natural objects as centres of communion with all nature, the crudest form of which is fetish worship, the highest form the adoration of the splendour of the Divine in the starry firmament, the worship of the sun and the like. This nature-worship is itself natural to man as a creature of nature: man realizes his dependence as a creature on God (the root of religion) in the first instance through realizing that he is a creature of nature. But it is susceptible of transformation by artistic and poetic insight into a higher spiritual expression: nature becomes a veil of the glory of the Divine, a "garment by which we see God" (Goethe), "a presence which disturbs us with the joy of elevated thought" (Wordsworth), a "thing of beauty which is a joy for ever" (Keats) revealed, it may be, by sculpture or painting, or best of all by music. Art in this way is the developed, spiritualized form of that communion with nature, which the cruder intelligence of man carries on by selecting particular natural objects as objects of worship, of fear or adoration.

Christianity has rarely done justice to the value and importance of natural religion. It has almost invariably taken it to be a degraded form of religion, something to escape from and condemn. It has too much emphasized the value of spirit at the expense of nature, too much emphasized the importance of man in the worship of the Divine. So much so that spiritual religion in Christianity is in many cases indistinguishable from the devotion of man to man himself, the love of God being identified with love of man—the crudest expression of which is the frank "religion and worship of humanity" of Comte.

Properly understood, nature-religion is an inseparable element in a complete religious experience: for nature is a means of communion with God and on that account an object of worship, and a channel through which man can approach and realize the presence of God, and which can convey God's message of love and understanding to the soul, which feels

> In nature and the language of the sense
> The anchor of my purest thought, the nurse,
> The guide and guardian of my heart, and soul
> Of all my moral being.

It is well for Christianity to treat nature and its processes of life and death as symbolic of the relation of the Divine to the human spirit; but it is more than a mere symbol of God's relation to man. Nature is the very Shekinah of the presence of God in man's life, where we can find Him and where He meets us face to face.

**29** An image or mental picture of the relation of the Divine and the human is of far more practical help to the religious life than a dogmatic formula or a theological conception. This accounts for the power of Eastern religious thought compared with Western.

**30** The characteristic feature of Greek religion was that the gods were powers of nature, revealed in nature, embodied in nature, controlling man's life as forces of nature, summed up in the general power of fate: this meant the worship of nature and at once the distinction and the union of man with nature: in that sense the Greeks were higher than the peoples of the East, where man is the slave of nature's forces and little better than a part of nature himself.

But the Greek gods were not revealed in the history of the Greek people. For the social life of Greece was confined to the city-state; and this had no conscious history, for history has a larger sweep than a city can supply.

With the Hebrews, on the other hand, God was not a power *of* nature, but a power *in* it and over it, and was revealed in the history of the Hebrew people, the basis of their existence as a people. There was, therefore, only one God (not many, as inevitably follows from making God a power of nature), and the Hebrew people were God's people, and the people of one God.

From such a conception it naturally followed that the Hebrews thought that the one God of His own "chosen" people would reveal Himself in a unique manner within and to His people at some time, always some time to come, in the future: for thus only could the peculiarly personal relation of God to His people be fully realized: they felt they must see Him face to face, on earth in a personal form—as a Messiah. This was as natural a frame of mind as it was for the Greeks to look for their god or gods in a natural form—it was in fact the same tendency of thought, but directed in a different way. And with the Hebrews it was more likely to occur that a divinely human person should appear to reveal and represent personally to His people what the Divine presence in man's life is.

Thus the Hebrew view of religion is higher than the Greek. Indeed, if the idea it embodies—of a personal manifestation of the Divine in human form—be attained, it is the consummation of religion at its best.

## VI

**1** It is only suffering and struggle, moral and intellectual or spiritual, which give rise to the problem of Immortality; only in reference to these does it seem to have any significance or importance. Abstract these and what is left to suggest it? What is there in the mere existence of a human being to require it, fortuitous as that existence in its origin often is, fragmentary in its activities, momentary so often in its duration, imperfect—painfully so—till its very close, let that come when it may? In sorrow and pain, surely, lie hid the very secrets of our human life.

**2** To a large number of professedly, and perhaps honestly, religious people the belief in immortality seems to operate in a way which is distinctly prejudicial to their religious life. They put off being as truly and completely good as they might be till they get to the next world, lose interest in the struggle towards light and truth and console themselves for their deliberate indifference towards them by their high hopes of what they expect to attain in the after life.

**3** The thought of pre-existence and perhaps, too, that of immortality may be said with truth to have their root just in the very fact that we are so conscious of our continuity with this world. We feel ourselves so much a part of it and are bound up with its whole life in such endless ways that we feel ourselves necessary to it, and it as necessary to us. And we are so familiar with it and it is so familiar to us that we feel we never have been away from it. Hence, since we are bound up with its very being, and its very being with us, we are inseparable from it and therefore think of ourselves as having been with it in some form or other always—as pre-existing: and as continuing with it in some way always—as immortal. We must, of course, even to have these thoughts, think of ourselves in some way as distinct from it—as we can do in virtue of our consciousness of self. But we only think of ourselves as distinct in order at once to think of ourselves as connected in another way—in the past or in the future. And why? Because the self we think of as distinct has been moulded by, and gets its content from, that very reality from which we think it to be distinct. Thus the process is like all other thinking. Our ideas are ours, but they refer to reality, because they arise from it, or are connected with it from the start.

The situation is a little pathetic. The self we think of as immortal is the very self we are acquainted with and no other. And yet this very self is just in time and space all the while.

**4** Is it because we do not remember having been born that we think we can never die?

**5** Any experience which seems to falsify or negate the ordinary idea of time suggests the possibility of immortality. Thus when, in dream or waking experience, we realize in what is in the ordinary sense a mere fraction of time, a long tract of our history, it is thought that we get a glimpse thereby of what an immortal life may be.

But this is really due to a misunderstanding. Our standard of temporal succession is arbitrarily fixed by the motion of a part of the physical system, by the movement of the earth in relation to the sun. This shapes our whole normal idea of temporal succession. We must regard historical sequence as occupying a certain duration measured by this standard; and since the standard is constant and invariable in its rate, events must take a certain time to go past. But the standard refers to a phase of reality, the physical world, which is completely heterogeneous in nature and content with that of conscious or self-conscious experience. Hence the course of conscious life may be realized with a fullness and comprehensiveness of range which may very well defeat or contradict all measurement by a physical standard of time. It does not, therefore, necessarily prove the possibility of immortality; it merely reaffirms or confirms the heterogeneity of the processes of consciousness and of physical nature.

At the same time, if in the case of conscious life we think not of the processes as such but of the quality of the experience, we can see that the point suggested conveys a truth, conveys even the central truth of the conception of immortality. For in the conscious process we have a concept or principle or law which contains within itself an infinity—of detail; and though we cannot go over this piecemeal without a long "historical" sequence, it can be envisaged and gathered together into a single pulse of thought. To realize this endless detail is certainly to realize infinity, the infinity of thought; and to be conscious of it is to be invested with immortality. But this experience is not found in dreams so much as in waking life; and then at the highest levels of consciousness.

We must not confuse the process by which, or in which, this experience is focused, and the principle realized in the process.

That is what is done when we think, for example, of a dream state (which is a purely psychical event or process) as typifying the experience of immortal life.

**6** The great difficulty in the idea of immortality is that it has to take a part for the whole, and tries to satisfy the whole through a part. Man is clearly a whole, a unity, of body, soul and spirit. It is as a whole that he seeks immortality, and only as a whole that he will be satisfied with it. But part of him obviously "dies" —so much is against the immortality of the whole. It is then argued that this part is inferior *because* it dies, and that man is immortal in the other part—spirit. But immortality of spirit is still not immortality of the whole, and so not "personal," "individual" immortality; hence the sense of dissatisfaction felt when it is offered as true immortality. This antithesis is the source of all the objections raised against immortality, and of the only arguments for it that have any claim to acceptance.

**7** It seems odd that people who accept the supremacy of spirit over nature should regard death as an obstacle to the acceptance of immortality. They admit that death is essentially a natural event, an event *in parte naturali*: they also admit that, in many ways (moral, religious, etc.), the whole significance of the experience lies in the fact that spirit uses nature, rises above it and transforms it to spiritual ends. If so, then an event in nature alone cannot possibly be an exhaustive or final expression of the life of spirit. But the question of immortality is one that concerns spirit and spirit only. Death, therefore, leaves the question of man's immortality untouched either one way or the other. It does not prove immortality, it does not make immortality impossible. It seems evident that if in the ordinary life history of man on earth spirit controls nature and employs nature as the material of its realization, the energy of spirit might very well employ the process of organic dissolution as a means to its own further expansion.

**8**  It is a curiosity of history to note that the communication with the dead, which was once banned by religious authority, should be revived again, even in the name of science, by a "Society for psychical research"! How humanity revenges itself on the enemies of its instincts!

**9**  It is often said that man's individual immortality is unnecessary and indefensible because his individuality is partial and, if it has immortality, it is only immortal as part of a corporate life, for example the corporate life of society. But what more reason has a corporate whole to expect or claim immortality than an individual soul? If the one is possible, so is the other: surely the difference of size is not the vital issue.

**10**  People who picture themselves as living "in another world" after this seem to imagine two ways of "living": one consists in doing nothing but "praising God," by "singing" in most cases and musical exercises generally; the other consists in being busily engaged in "serving God," which is supposed to mean "helping others," or helping God Himself.

There is a childish comedy in all this. It reminds one of nothing so much as the play of children who construct a world of make-believe mainly because of their want of experience of the real world in which they are, and of which they are not yet fully aware.

The conception of the "other world" as an everlasting concert or a Royal Academy of Music is a pathetic testimony to the jarring discordance of the present world with the aspirations of man's spirit. And the imagination of an eternal life of "service" shows how deeply ingrained in man is the life of social dependence and interdependence with his fellows, and his sense of the imperfection of the world: God Himself is conceived of as imperfect and needing man's help to carry through and maintain the universe. It never seems to occur to these fanciful children that if God is as weak as that, the universe would be in a very bad way indeed. They forget that the only service God can require is recognition of His will and communion and fellowship with His spirit, and that these are something more important and higher than all acts done either "for others" or "for" anything. Artistic enjoyment is perhaps the nearest analogue we can have of this aspect of eternal life.

**11**  Immortality is exile for the worldly man, exaltation for the saint.

**12**  Is it not possible that death may be a form of finite change which is itself subject like any other change to a further transformation? Why suppose that death is just termination of life? Every change is both a beginning and an end, is in fact part of a process, or a kind of process, which as a process implies an identity running through it in all its variations. On this view both life and death may be but stages in a process whose inner constitution is more fundamental than either of them.

And if it be asked how we are to conceive it, we may suggest that just as life emerged from an arrangement of energies, perhaps physical and chemical, so it may in its turn be the pre-condition of a further realization of the same process, the first step to which may be the event of death. After this there may be a new re-creation or transformation just as real as that which gave rise to life, but to our way of looking so different in kind that we cannot even imagine its character.

The argument that the human individual is resolved at death into physical and chemical elements and therefore vanishes does not seem so strong as it appears at first glance to be. For if the individual is resolved at death into physical and chemical elements, it is because he is composed of such elements in actual life, and yet his being composed of them does not (and is not held to) prevent his being an individual in the full sense of the word. The argument, in fact, that the individual is dissolved into physical and chemical elements at death and therefore disappears, proves too much; for it makes it impossible to explain how he ever was an individual at all. His resolution into elements may well be the preparation for a new arrangement of elements (not necessarily the same) which will constitute him a new individual.

**13** Perhaps one of the strongest reasons for believing in the immortality of the individual is that no spirit, not even the Supreme Spirit, can exist alone and solitary. The Supreme Spirit may require other spirits to communicate with or through whom to communicate its own life even to itself. If the Supreme Spirit needs other spirits to be itself properly spiritual, every spirit may well be immortal; for each is different, and by that very difference contributes something distinctive to the full realization of the Supreme Spirit. Difference of individuality, so far from being an obstacle to immortality, thus becomes a presumption in favour of it. In fact there is as much evidence for immortality in the difference of individuality amongst finite spirits as in the alleged identity of the human spirit with the Divine Spirit.

A human being might well feel sorry for God if there were nothing but God, and God alone were a spirit. For one thing a spirit that was alone would have no other spirit to love and would be incapable of love. It would be less of a spirit than man, who can love another human being.

It is remarkable that in this way the spiritual nature of the Divine Being and the immortality of finite spirits are so intimately connected with each other. It hardly seems worth while being immortal except for the possibility of communion with an eternal spirit; it seems hardly worth while being the Divine Spirit except for communion with other spirits, finite or otherwise.

The Divine Spirit may find itself through communion with finite spirits much as a musician finds his composition expressed through a variety of instruments, or a dramatic poet his plan of life through a variety of characters.

**14** Perhaps to be conscious of God and to commune with God is just the basis of immortality, not only in the sense of immortality *in* time, but immortality for *all* time. If we can commune with God and God with us as a real experience, then God cannot or will not do without us, or be without us.

**15** Nothing but a fact of the natural world, a fact of sense will convince some men, perhaps most men, of immortality. That perhaps may explain or justify the occurrence of the resurrection. Yet even the resurrection could not bring immortality into this world and make immortality a condition of the realm of human life on earth. Being an event, it passed away, and the reappearance of Christ gave way to His disappearance once again. In the long run, therefore, immortality has to be believed in; it cannot be a fact of this world demonstrable to sight. And those who grasp it in this its real significance appreciate its meaning most clearly and are independent of things seen and temporal. Their confidence is greater on that account. "Blessed are they who have not seen and yet have believed."

**16** It is not an impossible speculation that human souls are reincarnated and replaced on this planet after their term of life is over. If this were so, it would provide at least specious answers to a number of questions. For example, a serious obstacle to accepting the individual immortality of each member of the human race has always been that his existence in all cases is so contingent, in many cases is due to mere caprice and impulse, in some cases to brutality; and, again, that human individuals exist in different degrees, few being fully individuals, most being fragments, some being definitely distortions of personality. But if the number of souls in the world is not without limit and if they reappear in slightly varying bodily form, the contingency of their advent on the planet does not seem to matter, nor their very partial fulfilment of individuality. Similarly, their reincarnation would at least appear to explain the ease with which they adjust and adapt themselves to their environment: "not in entire forgetfulness, nor yet in utter nakedness" would they return to earth; they could keep to use again what has been gained; they would suffer for what had been done amiss; they would be in touch with former associates and associations; they should be on familiar ground, though finding it new each time in virtue of a new embodiment; they would have residual and permanent memories, as well as memories acquired by experience; they would not feel utterly lost when they died. What is more, there would be no waste of soul life: spirit would be ever resurrected from the dead: the destiny of the world might have an intelligible as well as a purposeful ending, with nature transformed as the instrument of spiritual life: man and his planet would for ever remain inseparable: Christian eschatology might become an historical as well as an eternal reality. It is a possible speculation.

**17**  So much to know, so little known: so much to do, so little done: so many opportunities missed, so hard the fight with nature and circumstance—what a tragedy is human destiny if earth and time are all. Surely our only hope of recovery, our only chance of success, lies in immortality: nothing less can give us what we really want and make us what we feel we are: with less than this in prospect, our hearts must break with agony, yearning and disappointment.

**18**  Past generations of men on the planet disappear into such complete silence, their very achievements in course of time vanishing from sight and sense as if they had never been, that human beings and human events seem more like notes of a piece of music than the stuff of a substantial world. The performance of a symphony is an event or succession of events: why may not the events or series of events constituting the world's life come into being and pass away like a symphony of sound—real while it lasts and real to the performers, real most of all to the composer, but insubstantial as pain or joy?

**19** People so often regard immortality as a sort of reward of desert. It is small surprise that this view carries little conviction in many quarters. Surely immortality should be rather a demand of desire, the desire to know more, to share more, to live more of the life of God. So very little can be accomplished in this short life, so very partial is our experience of God's riches of love and truth and beauty, that to give us so short an opportunity to appreciate so much is merely to offer us the fate of Tantalus.

**20** If man actually knew he was immortal as an individual, this would undoubtedly exercise a profound effect on his whole life in this world. The difficulty is to understand why a conviction of continuity of this kind should be left open, a matter of hope rather than a matter of knowledge for the everyday life of man. If it is so important, why should we not have knowledge of it and thus be relieved of all doubt about it?

**21** It is sometimes suggested as an argument against immortality that we receive no direct communication from the other world and know literally nothing about the conditions or character of another life. Such an argument seems unsound, at least on the assumption that the Divine Spirit loves the human spirit—which is the essence of spiritual religion.

In the first place, immortality is an experience, the experience of a life in another world: no amount of knowledge, even if obtained, *can* give us or convey to us what an *experience* is: experience has to be lived to be realized, and any knowledge that is to be intelligible to us must be furnished in terms of present experience which, by hypothesis, is totally different from experience in another life.

In the second place, love, and above all a Divine love, does not give beforehand what is in store for the beloved: in fact to withhold beforehand what love has reserved for a later time is of the very nature of love.

**22** There are those who hold that the disappearance of the individual from the earthly scene means his final dissolution, and that as his "body" is resolved into dust and merges with the substance of the earth from which it came, so his "soul" merges with the "general soul" of the world like a wave falling back into the sea.

This is an interesting example of the influence of sensuous imagery on the construction of an abstract theory. Those who think in this way are wholly under the control of what takes place before our eyes—the break-up of the physical constituents of the body and the mingling of these with the earth—and yet they claim to speak of what transcends the sense altogether—the nature and life of the soul. One would have thought that the very difference between soul and body would have necessitated a different fate for each, and that what happened to the body would not happen to the soul—whatever else might happen to it.

**23** It may fairly be asked, why should this world be the only scene of individuality? Why should individuality emerge under the conditions of physical nature and no others? If individuation is necessary to the realization of the Divine in this world, why should not the Divine conserve the individuals it creates? This is particularly relevant in the case of personality, which is the highest form of individuality we know, and is so distinctively real that it is conscious of itself and can relate itself consciously to the Divine, and indeed regard the Divine as distinct from itself. In the simple language of religion, if God needs man so much that He has created man "in His own likeness," why should not God need man always? If man emerges in this world into separate existence, that is justification for supposing that he will *not* merge into some general soul in another world. There would be no other "world" at all without the emergence of individuals, without their separate existence: a world without individuals is not a world, it is not even as good as chaos; it is a mere being and that is as good as nothing at all. So that a world without individuals is without a "general soul" into which individuals can merge; it is a world without God, since God is meaningless without a world in which to manifest Divine Power.

The final disappearance of individuals, therefore, means the disappearance of the Divine! If the Divine ceases to be in another world, it is evident that there is no Divine in this world, and, therefore, no need for any explanation of the dissolution of individuality. In fact, individuality becomes an illusion here as well as hereafter!

**24** It was common long ago to concentrate the religious mind on the prospect of death. There is more value in this attitude than we are apt nowadays to think. After all, it was a way of thinking of man's end and of bringing the end to bear on the present; and this is an important point of view. The mistake lay in identifying the end with the termination: this is a crude conception of the end since the end is, or should be, a purpose, not a full-stop. But even that aspect of the end has to be taken into account in thinking of life on earth; for it certainly does come to a termination. To forget this and live solely in the present, as if it never could cease, is as great a mistake as the other. The process and the termination are inseparable factors for the individual, and must be thought of together.

**25** "God is not the God of the dead but of the living" is one of the most remarkable sayings on record. It is the essence of the meaning of immortality. God is life, and death counts for nothing but a transition from one stage of life to another.

**26** There is much to be said for reincarnation into this world as a solution of the problem of immortality. It may well be that the number of finite spirits inhabiting this earth is itself finite, and that they reappear through successive generations or ages in different places, times and conditions. This seems in some ways easier to believe than that the appearance of every human being at birth is an absolutely new creation brought about by the desires of the parents, who thus become responsible for increasing the number of immortals.

**27** It is said with truth that if God loves man and gives to man the power to love Him, then God cannot dispense with man's life or with man's love. Man, therefore, must be immortal, otherwise God's own life would be impoverished.

But much the same can be said from the point of view of knowledge. Man's knowledge is the realization in man's mind of the rational order of the world: it is, as Aristotle and others indicate, a process of sharing the divine reason up to the limit and level of man's capacity to do so. In a sense, therefore, man in knowing truly is knowing or discovering the "mind" of God, or sharing God's mind, communicating or communing with God. If so, it is unintelligible that God should destroy or extinguish a creature capable of such an achievement. To share the mind of God is to share the life of God, and that is immortality, an immortality based on man's "eternal part," as Aristotle held and, in another sense, Spinoza also.

## VII

**1** May the success of the Romish Church not lie just in this: that it is so near the concrete, and tries to bring the abstract facts, or the purely and highly spiritual facts, of religion into visibility and tangibility? And this does not seem to be to the detriment of the value or worth given to the supreme objects of religion.

The light of the temple is indeed artificial; but what if that is the only light which human eyes can endure, the only light in which it is possible for man to read the mysterious secret of his own existence? After all, it seems very reasonable that a compromise should be made between the glaring sunlight and absolute darkness; and the compromise exactly suits the ordinary mind, and can in itself do no harm to those who can appreciate the sunlight.

**3** There is a fine natural wisdom in the attitude of the unreflective mind towards the views and statements enunciated by authoritative persons on the momentous questions of man's destiny and life here and hereafter. It is difficult to say with how much reservation audiences in church accept what they are told about their relations to God, etc., or with what toleration they listen to the attempts of the preacher to express and illustrate his views on these matters. If they thoroughly, and without qualification, accepted all his ideas, not to say his figures and phrases, then surely the only action possible to them as rational beings would be immediately to carry out to the letter all his conclusions; and this would involve a complete alteration of the facts and forms of their life, both good and bad. But they feel that all that is said is at best not more than half-true, and the true half they already are more or less aware of and are carrying out. All this talk of "separation from God," "perfect freedom from sin," "complete satisfaction of God," "absolute wickedness of man," etc., they feel avoids blasphemy and falsehood only because it is a well-meant exaggeration of a few simple, ultimate facts known so well by everybody that they hardly need to be communicated. This easy indifference regarding public statements concerning man's destiny is the great charm of the "naturally religious" mind; and it is to be found in some degree in all religious men in all religions. No wonder "conversion" is said to be "difficult"!

Preachers should not forget that really God has as much or more interest in keeping men religious than they have in "making" them so!

**4** A clergyman is often regarded as the sort of precipitate for the crystallization of the religious life and sentiment of a given part of the community. He does not often see that, while he may solidify their fluctuating emotions, the solid lump which results holds his own life and activity immovable for ever.

**5** The irony of a universal religion is that, while no religion can exist except where men exist (i.e. in a society of individuals), a universal religion places the individual at a point of view above any specific society, outside it in a sense, so that the religious man can look on his specific society as subordinate, as lower, as even a means to the end of his religion. But, as soon as he does so, he has begun the dissolution of the society, for each individual is then likely to look on himself as part merely of the "Kingdom of God," and as such related solely to the whole. The specific society to which he belongs is not so related because religion is an individual relation and not vicariously procurable through society; to think it can be is to commit the error of ecclesiasticism. Hence, if each individual looks on himself as having this relation only to the whole and, at the same time, looks on the relation to his specific society as subordinate and unimportant *sub specie aeternitatis*, he is bound to be assisting in the dissolution of society. If a vast number do it, the society is bound to go to pieces when the issue is logically worked out. But when this is done, there is no longer a society in which religion can appear, and so religion itself, even universal religion, ceases to play its part in man's life; it cannot control the whole of life, for the life of society has, by hypothesis, ceased. Universal religion thus becomes an abstraction of the worst kind.

This tendency on the part of universal religions may reveal itself in two forms. It may create an *imperium super imperium*—that was the position taken up long ago by the Roman Catholic Church in its attempt to control the State and to dissolve the feelings of nationality which support it. The other way is that of extreme protestantism, e.g. presbyterianism, which seeks to disestablish and disendow the Church and religion altogether, to separate the Church from the State. This tends at once to disrupt the State, for it dissociates members of the Church from the State, as we have just seen; and, because membership in the Church is higher than membership in the State, a person in one nation comes to have, through religion, a closer connection with a member of another nation professing the same faith than to his own compatriot professing a different faith (and faiths must be different because religion is individualistic). But this tends to make religion override State distinctions, i.e. to dissolve nationality. Strange how extreme protestantism and extreme catholicism thus join hands!

These difficulties seem inevitable. But they are practically got over by (1) establishment of a Church, i.e. returning to a tribal form of religion, (2) making religion more and more ceremonial and institutionalistic, i.e. binding it up with the concrete life of the nation.

**6** The proof that the Church is higher than the State, more enduring, is that the Church may break up into fragments indefinitely without provoking revolution in Society, without destroying its cohesion, and may even advance the interests of religion in the process; whereas division in the State is inimical to the safety of the State and in the long run issues in civil war which threatens its very existence. Division in the State is a herald of revolution and ruin; but division in the Church is not merely consistent with the continued vitality of religion, it may actually be a means of maintaining it. Although separation in religion is not usually in the interests of the *institution* of the Church, it may be and often is in the interests of religion. For in the case of a universal religion a distinction can be drawn between spirit and form, *institution* and *ideal*. The ideal is in "another world," a "kingdom of heaven" beyond "the" world; the institution, like the institution of the State, is in the actual world and cannot fully at any time embody the ideal. Hence the conflict and contrast between institution (Church) and ideal (religion itself), a conflict which may go on indefinitely and not affect either religion or State. In the State, however, this distinction cannot be drawn in the same way: the ideal, though equally requiring to be embodied, cannot be conceived apart from its embodiment—i.e. apart from the institution. In fact institution and ideal must *actually* coincide; to attempt to oppose their union means revolution and ruin.

Both Church and State exist inside *Society*, are aspects of its life. For we must distinguish *Society* and *State*: "Religion" is to Church what "Society" is to State.

**7**  Christianity as a system of doctrine has tended to depress, or at any rate to repress, the human spirit in the pursuit of the highest forms of human freedom: and this is clearly seen in the emphatic suppression of the human intellect which was long inculcated as a maxim, and still exists as a sentiment, amongst certain Christians.

The reason for this amazing result of a religion, which ostensibly claims to free the human spirit, is that the doctrines of Christianity when formulated become, not merely *expressions* of the belief of the generation in which they arose and for which they were formulated, but *standards* of belief for all succeeding generations, and more especially for those immediately succeeding. Hence any desired or expressed deviation from them was at once met with reproof, either from the outside authority of the "Church" or from the inside authority of the believer's "conscience." Cravings after wider spiritual freedom were thus strangled at their birth; for only if this was done, it was held, could the individual gain "everlasting salvation."

It may or may not be true that the human spirit cannot be satisfied by Christianity because Christianity does not meet all its wants and fulfil all its demands: but at any rate it certainly is true that any doctrine or belief which is enunciated in the name of Christianity, and which checks the aspirations of the human spirit after freedom, must be set aside and suppressed.

**8** The equalizing of all individuals by the Christian religion has had a powerful influence in the development of Western democracy. The Church, as an institutional system, has always acted on the principle that all human beings are equal in the sight of God, that God is "no respecter of persons"; and for this reason the Church has welcomed into its clerical orders the intellectual talent of individuals in whatever social station these were found, and has given an open career to talent to display itself in the interests of the institution. Thus we have, in all ages of Christianity, the poor man of talent finding scope for the display of his natural ability in the service of the Church, and rising by this means to supreme power and authority, and so installing himself in high position politically and even socially. In the Middle Ages this was the only way by which individuals could overcome the political and social superiority and inferiority stereotyped by the feudal system. The Church conserved the inherent rights and dignities of human individuality by providing an avenue along which the natural ruler, the talented individual, could advance to his proper status in the community, and develop his capacities in the interests of humanity. While in many respects the Church system of the Middle Ages rivalled in worldly splendour and glory the secular splendours of the court and the castle, its power rested in an altogether different basis and conception of human worth. It was not tradition or heredity or wealth, or physical force, or secular advantages of any kind, which gave the individual his position in the hierarchy of clerical dominion, but his inherent talent and the gifts, spiritual and intellectual, which he could contribute to the common life of the institution. Thus the clergy did not marry and so could not hand on their power to their children, and hence could not perpetuate their system by the ordinary secular laws of inheritance and traditional privilege. The clerical hierarchy was being constantly furnished with new talents and new gifts by fresh individuals coming from all classes of the community. This was in itself a source of great power, and was a constant source of danger to the secular orders of the State which rested on, and were carried on by, the ordinary process of family inheritance. The Church thus never depended on *chance* for its rulers and its governors, but always on *choice*, the selection of the best minds and best individuals it could attract to its circle; the secular system depended on chance, the chance of what a given marriage might produce.

Similarly the power the Church wielded was not that of physical but of spiritual force; and in the struggles of humanity intellect and spiritual activity are sure to succeed in the long run against brute force.

Thus the Church has been the conserver of human personality with its dignities and inherent claims to recognition. If the Church of the Middle Ages accomplished no more than this, it has done well and deserves well by humanity.

**9** Superior and inferior, higher and lower, seem distinctions inseparable from human life in any of its forms. Even in the "religion of the poor in spirit" we find them cropping up. What is the origin of ecclesiasticism but the attempt to make a deeper knowledge of the nature of religion the esoteric possession of the privileged few who have seen deeper into the mysteries, and who claim, therefore, higher privileges in consequence? The paradox and the comedy lie in supposing that deeper insight into the nature and conditions of spiritual humility (the attitude of the religion of the poor in spirit) should create any claim to higher privileges, that the deeper knowledge how to be lowly should be used to raise men higher in their own eyes, and in the eyes of their fellows! No wonder that the wiser minds saw the dangers of this insight, and put a curse on the intellect, as Paul did. For, clearly, humility of spirit should affect the intellect too; otherwise the intellect becomes a means of destroying the very spirit which it pretends to assist.

**10** All the trouble with "sects" and "-isms" in the history of religion (especially Western religion) arises from an attempt to realize, through mundane social conditions, a state of life which essentially professes to be non-mundane and *supra*-social. The vessels of the world simply cannot contain the active wine of the spirit.

There are no "sects" in a secular society: if these arise, they are at once treated as enemies and removed as criminals. This process cannot be adopted in religion, which seeks to conserve personality at its highest; hence the trouble of sects. Rome tried the secular method in the inquisition, and the self-contradiction brought the Church down.

On the other hand, where a religion is hostile to individuality and suppresses all finite selfhood, the difficulty of "sects" does not arise so prominently.

**11** The reason for ceremonial and cult in religion is that man, in his daily life, is accustomed to depend on, and use, his senses for the guidance of his thought and action. Since this is required for mundane existence, it is required for *supra*-mundane existence: since it is the way of man's communion with nature, it is required for man's communion with God: since it is the condition of self-maintenance in the natural world, it is the condition of self-maintenance in the spiritual. And it is as valuable in the one case as in the other.

**12** Extraordinary the vagaries of extremists: the Reformers of the sixteenth century revolted from the oppression of the ecclesiastical system of Rome, in the name of individual liberty of conscience in religious matters; and then evolved the doctrine of predestination which sapped the root of the religious liberty of the soul! They gave up the tyranny of an institution and substituted for it the more terrible tyranny of fate and foreknowledge!

It is also a singular paradox that protestantism should have made its appeal in the interests of spiritual freedom, and then have declared that all the individual could "do," all his "works," were of no avail for his salvation at all, that all the "doing" had been done for him already, that his salvation was purely a matter of "faith." Yet surely liberty which is liberty to *do* nothing, or liberty which issues in deeds without spiritual value, is not liberty worth having.

13   The attempt of the Church to dominate Europe in the Middle Ages was the inevitable result of the Asiatic origin of the Christian religion. And the outburst of the Renaissance and of the scientific spirit was the reaction of the free spirit of the West against the oppressive influence of an Asiatic religion. It is not, therefore, because Christianity encourages the spirit of science that the two have co-existed in the West; the two have constantly quarrelled and still constantly quarrel, and are at war in their heart of hearts. It is because Christianity does not satisfy all the demands of the free spirit of the West—a spirit which has given rise to free institutions as well as freedom of intellect—that the break with the initial attempt of the Church to control Europe was inevitable.

14   The relation of Christianity to human society has oscillated between two extreme positions. It has been treated, especially by reformers, as a levelling principle, reducing all men to a common denominator, which has alone been considered important: it has also been used, by the institutionalists, as a principle to justify the grading of society into levels of prestige and power, as is seen in the introduction of hierarchy even into the organization of the Church. These two extremes are quite contradictory, and the conflicts between the "world" and Christianity have been the inevitable result, a conflict which has seriously affected the institution of the Church itself. The fact seems to be that Christianity is useless in the secular affairs of man: it can give no clear light or guidance, and never has done so. Claiming to have its source in a non-secular realm of things, it has brought little else than confusion into a world built after another pattern altogether.

**15** The relation of the Church to its doctrines has now come to the rather comical pass that pastors and people try to keep up each other's belief in the doctrines for the sake of one another. The one side holds them because it is assumed that the other side wants them or believes that it believes them! The doctrines are accepted in much the same way that a motion is passed "unanimously" at a public meeting, by "universal consent"; when nobody in particular really wants the motion or knows exactly what it means.

**16** When law and the State take charge of religion, the spirit of religion is doomed. It is a matter of time when it will become a mere instrument for governmental uses, a kind of reserve police force, or a round of conventional forms and ceremonies of the same value as the ritual associated with the dignities of the State.

It is impossible for religion to accept the protection and direction of the State without the State requiring a *quid pro quo*. The *quid pro quo* is always a surrender of the claims of religion to its predominant influence in man's life.

**17** Laymen sometimes criticize the clergy on the ground that they seek to make the best of both worlds. This is hardly a fair objection: it is rather a merit if they succeed in doing so, and in any case it is their duty to try. Besides both worlds are necessary to their scheme, and the least they can do is make a virtue of the necessity.

**18** The clergy so often complain of the indifference of people to religious ministrations and even to religion. The indifference exists and perhaps always will be found to exist as long as the clergy speak and act as if they had a monopoly or even a privileged intimacy with God; as if they were a kind of trust for the distribution of divine ideas and ideas of the Divine; as if, like the priests of primitive peoples, they manufactured idols and images of God for the benefit of the worshippers. This attitude is perhaps natural among a professional class, but the reaction from it and against it is equally inevitable; it is the reaction against professionalism. What belongs to a profession does not greatly concern another profession or class except for professional purposes; and this is what the so-called indifference comes to.

**19** All sects are apt to be intolerant, no matter how they may protest the contrary. They so often refuse to meet on common ground, and in any case do not desire to meet as often as they might. There is an implied fear that frequency of intercourse would blunt the finer perception of their own peculiar differences, and might even make these appear ridiculous in their own eyes by being known to be ridiculous in the eyes of others.

When a sect refuses to meet with another on common ground—a common occasion, to express a common belief, etc.—the implication is that such a sect regards itself as a repository of the whole truth. Thereby it contradicts itself and destroys its whole value. The great use of sects lies in emphasis, not in language or substance: they are the italics of religious doctrine. Nothing is so objectionable as to speak always in italics: nothing so harmful as the domination of Society by a particular sect. Sects have their utility in the fact that they correct and check each other like the colours on a counterpane.

**20** Nonconformity in some of its forms is Christianity without manners: conformity in some forms is manners without Christianity.

**21** An English cleric is expected to have just enough piety to be a good parson, and not too much to prevent him from being a good fellow.

**22** The Church has been far too intent on being large, comprehensive and powerful. This has confused proselytizing with conversion by conviction; and has produced conventionality in religious observance instead of change of heart and spirit. We cannot expect to have "large congregations" and sincerity of spiritual life.

**23** The Church has been too much on the defensive on behalf of religion. Religion needs no defence but experience of the Divine. More harm has been done by using authoritative organized force (spiritual and physical) in the interests of religion than by leaving the religious life alone to justify itself. Let the tares and wheat grow together till the harvest is reaped.

**24** The great advantage of the definition of belief by the Church is that it diminishes uncertainty concerning the objects of devotion and loyalty. Most men have a very limited experience of the Divine life.

**25** What protestantism demands is not so much the right to think for yourself as the right to decide who shall think for you and in whom you will trust.

On great questions it may not matter what the individual thinks: he may be unfit or incapable of thinking to any effect, his thoughts may be worth nothing, and he is not necessarily bound to make up his mind. The question for most men is, what have great men thought on the subject? To know that is enough for most people. The only difficulty is, who are the great men? Men who are better than ourselves?

**26** Christianity has been a real danger to political life. Dogmatic beliefs produce fanaticism; and when Christian sects have different dogmatic beliefs on fundamental issues, strife of the most violent nature can arise. Witness England in the seventeenth century. The stability of the State is imperilled by fanaticism.

## VIII

**1** It is possible, and indeed seems actually to be the case, that the religious experience of men who have attained to a high degree of religious insight and lived a high religious life, becomes for others a *standard* of religious attainment by which they judge their conduct. In these circumstances what they desire to be becomes transformed into what they ought to be, becomes an ideal of religious life; and hence, as a direct consequence, when they do not possess the grounds for their standards in their own experience, when the experience of others is forced to be their own experience—they seek and must seek to force *their* experience to conform to that of the others (or vice versa), to find in their experience some basis of fact corresponding to that represented by others. Hence at once the artificiality and the dissimilarity of the lives of many Christians.

But we must ask whether such a method of procedure is really correct. Is it not transforming religious life into a form (possibly a higher form) of the moral life? Is it not simply making a religious experience into a moral ideal of living? Entirely subsuming religion under or making it identical with morality? Nothing seems more evident than that one man's religious experience, for example that of Bunyan or Carlyle, can never become in very deed an ideal of righteous living. Its results may be expressed in the form of principles, which may guide or test other men; but the experience itself it is impossible (fortunately) for everyone to undergo. Religious experience is a growth, and its expression in literature is the direct *outcome* (not the *basis*) of actual endeavour, actual attainment or desire of attainment. Religious emotions, etc., are the outcome of a practical moral life carried to its ultimate issue. Their expressions are therefore actual experiences. Perceptiveness cannot be given to any man *ab extra*. Hence the dangers of dogmatism and formalism of all sorts. Hence, also, in religion more perhaps than anywhere, the supreme importance of direct contact with real fact, and of accurate expression and belief in that fact. Nothing, surely, can be of higher authority than what appeals to a man as, in very truth, the truth of God, the clear revelations of his own spirit. To resist these, or disbelieve them—that is unutterable!

**2** The doctrine of "relative morality" pushed to its extreme makes "practical" religion non-existent. For religion can only be practised on the assumption that the laws of morality are absolute, are the decrees of God; and if it is a matter of indifference what laws of morality exist among men, then clearly their fulfilment cannot be recognized as a religious duty, the essence of which lies in the recognition of the unchangeable character of its nature and of the objective/law regarding which the duty is felt to exist. The religious mind could only avoid this conclusion by supposing that each stage of moral development is ordained by God as the best for the corresponding stage of human affairs. In this case, the only view of God would be a Deistic one, and the laws of morality (even the highest known to us) would not be eternal decrees of God's nature. God, in fact, would from our point of view be non-moral, though the appointing of what is best for men seems to indicate that he would in some sense be moral.

**3** To cut morality off from religion, to induce men to strive to work out the great ideas of goodness single-handed and alone, is like trying to encourage a brave army to venture on a campaign without a general. It may be possible, but it can have only a melancholy hope of success.

**4** There seems little doubt that the alienation of the spirit from the flesh which is characteristic of certain forms of the Christian religion has its roots in the moral or aesthetic repugnance or dislike shown towards the filth and decay with which bodily processes are associated. This comes to light in a curious way in the attitude of Paul and others to marriage; his whole view is governed by his attitude towards its physical basis; and this, again, is controlled by the fact that the principle of reproduction is associated with the principle of organic waste, the largely aesthetic sense of "shame" attaching to the organs of organic waste being, by a singular perversity, attached also to the organic function of reproduction.

5   The danger of regarding religion as above morality (whether as the crown or as the security of moral ideas) is that religion and religious people will make morality subservient to religion, and religion the justification for immorality.

6   Religion arises to a large extent out of the incompleteness of the moral life, and its aim is largely the completion of the sense of personality acquired under social conditions. Paul's interpretation of religion is a curious example of this. The antithesis between good and evil self-hood, which is involved in and arises from the moral life, is carried over bodily into religion and re-appears as an antithesis between the whole moral personality and the ideal fulfilment of that personality in the Divine Life of God. In contrast to the fulfilment of the spirit in God, all our moral effort and attainment is still a long way short of perfection, no matter how good or evil it may be. Hence, relatively to the divine life, there is as great an opposition between our best moral attainments and God's perfection as there is between evil and good *inside* the moral life itself. Paul *identifies* straight away the terms of these opposites in the sphere of religion and morality respectively: hence the phrases "all our righteousness is as filthy rags," when we have done our best we are still unprofitable servants. Our very righteousness becomes in religion equivalent to what is evil: it *is* evil, and has to be put aside in order that the "new man" may appear.

7   In religion, the tendency is to insist on the relative unimportance of differences of individuality. What is important is the unity of all individuals in God, and in relation to Him all differences are insignificant. In morality and the social order, the

differences of individuals are and must be accentuated and emphasized as strongly as is consistent with the maintenance of social order: without this, actions have no value or significance for the individual life, and Society becomes a dead level without growth, without interest, without progress: hence the contrast and the constant opposition of the point of view of religion and that of morality. In religion there are no "distinctions of persons," and no grounds of distinction are permitted, e.g. differences of property, race, family, etc. In morality, races, nations, classes, powers, etc., are all-important.

**8** The operation of religion on human nature is very closely allied to the operation of morality. In both, the emotions are subdued to a law. In religion, the emotions are overawed by the supreme power, overawed into submissive acquiescence and, it may be, peace. In morality, the emotions are checked and guided by an ideal of social order. It is because of the control exerted in both cases—the negative operation—that there is the close affinity between the two in actual life.

**9** People speak of religion supporting morality: but the real difficulty is to say whether morality supports religion, or religion morality.

**10** The old idea which catholicism at its best stood out to defend—that in this finite life the most important purpose of a finite spirit's existence is the salvation of the soul—is just the idea that has been overlooked in the planning of life in more recent years. The individual is to be "equipped," "educated," made "efficient," but when we ask for what, the answer generally given is for "his work in the world," or for "membership in the society in which he is born." This is a poor return for all his efforts, even if he can attain his end; and who can ever be sure that he does attain it? Men's jealousies and bitterness towards each other make it hardly possible for any man to feel that he has accomplished anything for "his society," "his world": gratitude is the rarest of virtues, want of generosity the commonest of vices. And what a poor return to dismiss as vague and irrelevant to the individual mind all but the limited sphere of social interests! Why should a man be deprived of his birthright share in the fullness of the universe? What shall it profit if a man be honoured by all his society, and have no place in the plan of the universe? Shall the world's applause be reckoned more worth having than the "joy of the Lord"? Shall a public funeral make up for the "life in God"?

**11** In morality, man is under the control of finite ends; hence their constraint of him, amounting often to oppression. In religion, he is liberated from the constraint of all finite ends whatsoever: he can afford to "be himself" and be his whole self, "bad and good" together, knowing that both are completely "understood": he is himself and nothing else, whatever that be, knowing that his self is rooted and nourished by the one Reality in which he lives and moves and has his being. The very notion of "end" seems to disappear in this experience. In fact man has no "end" in religion; to be his "own end" is equivalent to having none, and to have an "infinite end" is the same as having no end at all. The life of religion is an "endless" life in every sense of the term; and from that comes the sense of freedom and expansion which its votaries enjoy. So keenly is this felt that religion can *oppose* morality, as well as rise above it.

**12** There are in general two ways in which religion is connected with morality in "popular" life and thought: (*a*) it is a means by which men cancel their mistakes, rise above their weakness, a city of refuge for the doers of evil; (*b*) it is an inspiration for good deeds, a support for the morally heroic.

The first is a negative influence, the second a positive; the first is the more common and the easier of the two to effectuate. Rarely does anyone unite both.

**13**  It is pathetic to observe in the history of the early Christians how often sensual love was treated as the great barrier and obstacle to the higher life of the spirit. Renunciation of sensual love was looked on as the first condition and necessity for the emancipation of the spirit. How the early saints gloried over the suppression of the desires of the flesh! This became almost the chief triumph of their lives, and the main end of their earthly struggle. Abstention from marriage was the first and chief step to spiritual holiness: it was the beginning of the "purification" of the soul.

All this strikes us as extravagant and astonishing; but it is easy to see how it arose. There is no more difficult form of religion to sustain than a religion which consists in spiritual love—the religion inaugurated by Christianity. Spiritual love leads the soul to love all things and all persons in all ways. It, therefore, does not abrogate but tends to refine and give a new value to the desires which have their source in sexual impulse. Yet these very desires are in themselves so clamant that the added refinement of them not only makes them more attractive and interesting than normally they can be if left to themselves, it also by contrast gives them greater prominence. To strengthen their power is of all things the most perilous to the life of the spirit; for the spirit seeks to transcend the cravings of the flesh, and regards the flesh and its mere natural cravings as the enemy of the spirit.

Hence the dilemma of the early Christian. If spiritual love animated his soul, inevitably all the powers of his soul were awakened into new significance: part of these powers have their source in the life of the senses, in the energy of the "sensuous soul," the aspect of his soul whose energy is that of the senses. But if these lower energies of his soul were aroused into greater activity, if their own innate force were increased by the added energy of spiritual exaltation, the spirit, so far from getting rid of the desires of the flesh, was merely giving new life to its enemy and fostering its enemy within its own household: it was feeding its enemy on its own heart's blood. The dilemma was inevitable;

for the human individual is in reality one and indivisible, and the life of love accentuates this unity more than anything else, for love is the consummation of life, love is supremely healthy life. We need not, therefore, be surprised to find that the discovery of this result of the adoption of the principle of spiritual love should have alarmed and dismayed the early Christians, or that their way of escape should have been that of sheer emancipation from the desires of the body altogether. The complete suppression of these desires seemed indeed to be the only way of avoiding the dilemma in which the principle of spiritual love placed the individual. But this form of heroism was in reality a form of cowardice and afforded no real solution for the dilemma. For the elimination of natural desires from the region of spiritual experience is tantamount to an admission that the spirit cannot control the flesh at all but must escape from the flesh; cannot rule the flesh but must run away from it; cannot subject the flesh to its ends but must destroy the flesh altogether. But if this is so, there is either no meaning in the life of the spirit or else the spirit has no place in the world of time and nature; for there is nothing for the spirit to do or to attain if the body is utterly destroyed, and no possibility of its being realized in the world if it ignores the conditions of time and natural existence.

**14** An anti-orthodox and anti-clerical philosopher has recently made much of the phrase of Keats that the "world is the vale of soul-making," the place where people make and shape their souls, and that this is the meaning of the world. It is amusing and interesting to see extremes meet in this way. Evangelicalism has held the same doctrine for generations. "Making your soul" and "saving your soul" are two ways of saying the same thing.

**15** It is certainly very remarkable that the greatest control over Nature has been exercised by nations who have professedly imbibed a religion of renunciation of Nature: and that the greatest riches have been in the possession of those nations who have professed on religious grounds to despise riches. Perhaps it is that the strenuousness of individuality which tends to be created by a religion of renunciation can take the form of dominating Nature and subduing it to the level of a mere means to human ends. It is as if man sought to recover by the forceful enslavement of nature the imperious self-importance which he has to surrender at the demand of his religion. He, so to say, shows himself the lord of Nature to compensate himself for being the servant of the Lord. In a manner it is even logical; for if Nature is to be brought into subjection, in what better way can this be done than by making it an absolute slave to man's will?

Yet how this process restores man's self-sufficiency and self-importance in his own eyes, and thus tends to counteract the operation of the very principle of self-renunciation! Thus it is that riches "lead astray," and power feeds the passion of self-assertion. Hence it is indeed hard for those who "love riches" to "enter the Kingdom."

What an ironical process this development turns out to be! *Si naturam expellas furca, tamen usque recurret.*

**16**  The reason why saints have felt so keenly the vividness of temptations is that the very excess of concentration on spiritual interests intensifies the contrast and opposition between the spirit and natural conditions, between "the spirit and the flesh." It thus gives a greater independence, reality and power to Nature than Nature would otherwise have if it were harmonized with spirit. Having this independence, Nature is felt to intrude itself on the presence of spirit at every turn, because the cultivation of the inward life of the spirit is only carried on by incessant opposition on the part of spirit to Nature's demands.

**17**  It is impossible to accept and apply literally some of the injunctions in the "Sermon on the Mount." Some pacifists base their objection to war, for example, on the command "resist not evil" literally interpreted. But literally interpreted this would countenance and encourage sheer immorality. We should have to say that when a man has an inclination to do evil he should not resist this evil inclination in himself. Or again, when a human brute seeks to ravage a woman she should not resist him but let him have his way. Such an interpretation may be literal, but it means nothing less than a permission, a command rather, to give free scope to evil passion whatever the form it assumes. It is incredible that Christ could countenance such a flagrant perversion of the moral life and of moral principles.

The statement must be interpreted in such a way as to be consistent with supreme moral ends; otherwise it undermines social well-being and would have to be condemned not as impracticable but as immoral.

Similarly "love your enemies" must be interpreted in the light of supreme moral ends.

**18** It is often said that men must hold fast by righteousness and truth because they are the will of God. Whether they are the will of God or not, men must hold to them with all their heart and strength, for without them it is quite impossible for human society to be carried on.

**19** God must have other ends and conditions of human life in His plan besides righteousness and truth; otherwise why should He allow evil to prevail against them even temporarily?

## IX

**1** It is those who can command the resources of the next world who have the greatest power in this; and that is the difference between the value of religion and the value of science.

**2**  Religion can very readily be used as a justification of human indolence, a sort of consecrated *laissez aller* on a grand scale, doing nothing *in majorem dei gloriam*. So many people fall back on religion simply to save themselves trouble.

**3**  The relation of religion to daily life (e.g. to morality) is closely similar to the relation of living activity in general to the manifold acts in which life is expressed. Life is not simply a series of acts, but a principle manifested in all living actions. The living agent is not interested in the first place in living activity as such, but in the acts of his daily life: still, the living activity is operative in, and is implied in, all these detailed acts. So in religion: religion is a consciousness of the presence, in all details of life, of the one Supreme Reality, but this consciousness does not relieve us from the necessity of finding out how in particular we are to act when face to face with definite problems of conduct.

**4**  Even a slight realization of the religious attitude, provided it is sincere and deeply grounded, will make life tolerable and even cheerful for any man.

**5**  In religion a man acquires or possesses the secret of living on the best of terms with his whole self, more especially with that part which contains the unfathomed reserves of his nature. There is a part of each man which is a kind of well of surprises: if he distrusts or fears this, his life can become a fine torture or a gnawing misery: if he is assured that this, too, is guided and inspired by the same spirit which holds the plan of his everyday life in its keeping, his undivided heart is full of confidence and strength. To become and remain in peaceful unison with this vast background of his life in the actual present is one of the supreme achievements of the religious attitude, as the confidence of having so attained is a perfect test of the vitality of the religious mind. This does not make a great difference to man's life; it makes *all* the difference.

**6** Religious people tend to lay too much stress on the "consolations of religion" and even to regard these as its main significance, as if religion only came into play when men get into real difficulties, out of which they cannot of themselves escape. This ignores altogether the equally important influence which religion has for the healthy and the happy-minded, those afflicted with no great sorrow and not affected by any great obstacles: this influence consists in the renewal of the spirit of the individual, the restoration of jaded and jarring energies, the revivifying of the gladness and joy in life.

This second influence is quite as real to many people as the first; and it is evident that it is as true to the essence of religion. God is not the God of the dying and the dead only, but of the lively and the living.

**7** Any religion which so emphasizes self-condemnation as to imprison the soul instead of giving it liberty is itself condemned by its own procedure. No sane religion can lead to spiritual suicide.

**8** "Salvation," which the old religions laid so much stress on, means simply the consciousness of being "safe" and "secure" in the Power and Presence of the Divine. In this sense, therefore, it is true to say that "Salvation" is the essence of religion.

**9** People constantly speak of religion as being mainly concerned with "ideals." It is not with ideals that most men are concerned: and certainly religion is not so much, and not at all exclusively, concerned with the ideals of life as with its foundations, not with life's aspirations but with its elementary emotions, not with its flowers and fruits (so few have either or both) but with its very roots and stem.

If a man has a sense of security in regard to the simple basis of his life—his elementary hopes and fears, the confidence and despair which make up so much of everyday emotion—he has achieved most of what he requires of religion.

**10**   The maintenance of the religious attitude in the life of every day should resemble the consciousness of a strain of music in the changing scene of sense-experience, the consciousness of love of friends when in contact with a crowd, the consciousness of light when looking at a varied world of visible objects.

**11**   It is everything to a man's life if he has some immovable basis of reliable trust, some supreme reality which he knows is with him at all times to secure his life and give meaning to his purposes and make the stages of his life intelligible. Without this centre of confidence, this fortress of strength, life is just chaos and disquiet. When this is shaken, there is a spiritual earthquake and he knows not where to place his feet.

Yet surely physical earthquakes help to settle the world more steadily to its centre of gravity: in the same way spiritual earthquakes may help to establish one's spiritual existence more securely in the long run.

**12**   If God has any use for us we shall be given the opportunity and the means to be of use.

**13**   For the security of the primary conditions of moral individuality—courage, confidence and self-possession—a religious basis is in the long run indispensable. Habit is not enough, and that is the only possible alternative.

**14**   It is essential for the sanity of religion that the religious life should be kept in the closest contact with the smallest details of the everyday world. This frustrates all tendency to vagueness and artificiality, and obviates the dangers of hypocrisy and insincerity which hamper the mind when it tries to inhabit two separate worlds at the same time.

Religions have been shattered by dualism in the religious life: religions are vitalized when "this" world and the "next" are inseparably interfused through act and thought and feeling.

Religion is "holy living" as well as "holy dying."

**15**  The gifts or "fruits" of the spirit—joy, peace, love, faith—are not man's by nature, and cannot be obtained by unaided human nature, or by discipline or by education. The natural man neither needs nor wants them. They come through communion with a divine life and are of grace, for they are graces.

**16**  Men always come back to God in their troubles: if they would commune with God with greater constancy, they would have fewer troubles.

**17**  We have not realized the religious life until we are constantly aware of a Divine Presence in the life of every day.

**18**  "Seek first the Kingdom of God and all things will be added to you." Yes, for the search is so all-absorbing that the good it brings is all-sufficing, and other "goods" seem relatively of little importance; they are just "added" on to it.

**19**  Everything which produces quietness of mind has the blessing of God, since quietness of mind is a portion of God's peace.

**20**  People speak of the hardships, the severity of discipline and sacrifice required by a spiritual religion at its best. They seem to forget that the demands of a natural religion, i.e. a religion of Nature, can be and have been much more severe and more exacting, with fear as the dominating motive throughout. Roman religion as illustrated in the *Aeneid* is a pathetic frame of mind for a human being to sustain.

**21**  By far the best way to live in the present is to live in the Divine Presence.

**22**  What we want above all is to engage our minds in something inexhaustible in its interest. Very few finite things have this quality.

**23**   If you seek to do the will of God, you will not even try to do your own: you will have so much to do that you will forget you have a will of your own at all.

**24**   To trust anyone is to double your own strength. To trust the divine is to increase your strength to the power of infinity.

**25**   The Jews have made the great mistake of believing that their religious vision and interpretation of their own history constitutes them the specially chosen people of God. There is no connection between these ideas. As well might the Greeks maintain that, because objective philosophical pursuit of the truth started with them in Europe, the truth was their proprietary possession. To interpret national history by the light of religion is a gift, an accomplishment, of the human spirit, which is of value to all men: it does not imply that the race in which it is exercised by some of its remarkable men has a privileged position in humanity. The Jews showed merely how religion may inspire national life—that is all: and it is a point of view from which any nation may and should regard its life and its history. It is a universally applicable view of human experience. And in that sense the Jewish religious view has been taken over by other nations and has been applied by them to their own case and their own experience, with necessary changes to suit their own circumstances: though too often these other nations have taken the Jews at their own valuation and regarded them as the "chosen people."

# X

**1**   Note that the consciousness of sin dawns with the period of complete, or completing, development of the full powers of personality in man and in woman, and is thus contemporaneous with the attainment of moral and intellectual responsibility in the eyes of the community. It is noteworthy, too, that this is the period of greatest intensity of moral "feeling," greatest acuteness of moral "sensibility," and, consequently, because of the emphasis on the individual life, of the keenest sense of sin, of weakness, of instability. Sin has not yet come to be recognized as part of the destiny of the individual; perpetual contact with it has not yet hardened the spirit or produced the intrepidity which makes us careless of it or of temptation to it. The habits which form the character have not yet been secured; sin, shame, failure, wrong are new experiences which, because new and personal, seem exaggeratedly strange and terrible and, in the light of the good, awful. Hence it is that, at this period, character is more susceptible of good influences, and that personality can be most easily moulded just for the reason that its chaotic situation and its indefiniteness call out for guidance. It is, therefore, with a beautiful and natural appropriateness that the Church chooses above all this period for the admission of men and women to its ranks; indeed, this is the period when individuals most readily and naturally seek its aid and feel the need of it. This period also seems remarkable for the moral and spiritual regeneration of all kinds exhibited amongst men and women.

**2** The great defect in men's ordinary attitude towards sin is in not laying sufficient emphasis on what is essentially implied in it— namely, the absolute union of man and God. Sin is regarded as something positively in ourselves as individuals, against which men do and must fight, but which, when it is taken as their own, they never get rid of. By no amount of struggle with oneself will one abolish sin. To struggle with it, in fact, is to accentuate it and, partly because of this and partly because sin implies a relation to God, sin becomes magnified into an absolute reality, and is regarded as something "overpowering" us, "stronger" than us, etc. All this is fundamentally erroneous. To deal with sin we must necessarily lay stress on what essentially constitutes it—man's relation to God. Till this is grasped, the whole question will lie in confusion. But when we see this, we can understand that sin is abolished by acquiescence in a relationship which actually exists, and which can be continually restored by consciously adopting as our own the conditions or laws by which it is constituted. Sin is overcome, not by struggling with ourselves, but by abandoning ourselves, by asserting our union with God, without which there would be no sin. It is overcome by resignation not by warfare, by re-adopting as our own what is there all the while.

3  The treatment of original sin by the Hebrews, viz. their tracing sin to an historical origin in man's life, is an attempt to combine two distinct ideas—the idea of the universality and apparent inevitableness of sin, and the idea that it is something that should be dispensed with, that is not necessary but capricious, that has to be removed and is thus not essential to man's life, but inherently "contingent." Both these aspects are characteristic of sin, and both must be recognized in any explanation of it. The Hebrews' explanation does in a way recognize both. For something historical, a mere human event, has the element of contingency and caprice required; and at the same time, its having taken place in the life of the first mother, shows why it might well be expected to affect everybody.

4  It is in virtue of the idea of the "divine transcendence," i.e. the *supra*-human nature of God, that religions have insisted on forgiveness of sins and removal of evil of all sorts as an essential function of the Divine Life: it is in virtue of the idea of the "divine immanence," i.e. the indwelling presence of God in the life of man, that religions have laid stress on atonement, the oneness and communion of divine and human life. We often find these conceptions (forgiveness and atonement) identified or confused, atonement being equal to penalty or payment of penalty, and forgiveness equal to the restoration of union or the condition of such restoration. But, strictly, forgiveness is the negative side,

and atonement the positive side of the same experience (viz. the concrete unity of divine and human as a conscious experience). Forgiveness follows necessarily from the negative relation of man to God as transcendent; for it is in the transcendence of God that man is contrasted or opposed to God, and because of that transcendence that God is so altogether supreme that in order to sustain and assert his own supremacy over all man's life, even in its weakness, He can and must "forgive." Atonement, or harmonious union, again follows necessarily from the indwelling presence of God in man's life: the two are spiritually continuous and God is all in all as a conscious experience.

5   It is often asked what comfort sufferers have who suffer innocently, or suffer because others have sinned. The comfort lies in the knowledge that such sufferers take upon themselves the burden of others' sorrow, and save these from suffering; and in the healing sense of intimate union with the lives of others which that knowledge brings. It is the thought that we bear our own sorrows and sufferings alone that tortures and kills the spirit craving to share and be united with other spirits. If we see that, even in and by our sufferings, we are bound up with others and they with us, the suffering passes into reconciling atonement, and its sting is removed. If others share our suffering, even by their pity, and still more by their eagerness to help and soften its pain, the agony is tolerable: and if we see our suffering as endured for others' sake, it becomes atoning sorrow, not meaningless torture. There is satisfaction, too, in the thought that wrong does bring punishment and pain; for that is the way the unity of spiritual life is realized, and its completeness maintained. There is a reasonableness in pain following wrong and sin: it would be unreasonable if wrong had no such consequence. The restoration of the disturbed harmony of spiritual life is essential if spiritual life is to exist at all; and such restoration of disturbance can only involve further disturbance—the disturbance of suffering. Spirit must be reconciled to itself and restore its own life at all costs.

Only so is it controlled by law. We do not object to this truth if the sinner himself suffers in an obvious manner: why should we object if one man sins and another man suffers, since both are bound up together in a single spiritual whole? If we praise and appreciate the value of all men being members, one of another, in the same spiritual body, we must accept the consequence of this in the case of suffering as well as in the case of happiness. If happiness is shared and if love is realized in common, suffering must be shared one with another, and one for another.

6 When suffering is looked upon as part of the order of things, it is perhaps inevitable that man should come to look upon it as sacred, and come to cultivate it as part of the divine plan. That is, at any rate, one way of meeting its problems.

7 There is always a great obstacle in the way of self-reform, at least of the moral kind. The resolve to turn over a new leaf seems constantly hampered by the thought of the leaves that have been turned down. These, too, are known to be part of the Book of Life and they catch the eye and chill the enthusiasm to proceed with the new page. The remembrance that wrong was done humiliates the individual who desires to do the right. His shame for the past makes him ashamed in thinking of the good he seeks to fulfil in the present. His previous unworthiness makes him seem unworthy of the good he wishes to win. The better he would attain condemns him for the bad he has done, and the higher he goes the more this is felt.

There is no doubt a great deal of morbidity in this attitude towards moral progress. Taken literally and without qualification, it leads to the paralysis of all moral effort whatsoever; for all advance must involve a condemnation of the past, whether the advance be from good to better or from bad to good: and this advance is of the essence of morality. To make it ineffective is thus to oppose the life of morality.

It is this mood of mind which is emphasized in the so-called consciousness of sin or guilt as understood by religion. It is said that as long as the sense of evil remains the individual cannot lay hold of the good; and that the only way to advance is to get rid of the sense of the evil he has done. But since he cannot accomplish this of himself, for the evil is in himself, he must be assisted externally to get rid of the sense of evil altogether.

St. Paul has this feeling very acutely developed, and complains bitterly of the haunting sense of evil in his progress towards good: "the good that I would I do not," etc.

Over against this experience must be placed the healthy courage of Shakespeare's saying:

> Our doubts are traitors,
> And make us lose the good we oft might win,
> By fearing to attempt.

In point of fact there should be no more obstacle in the way of moral improvement in spite of past failure than there is in intellectual improvement in spite of previous errors of judgment. The only honest course is to recognize the wrong done as wrong, confess we were mistaken and insist on our claim to the good that we now find making its call upon us.

**8** The so-called "forgiveness of sins" has the great drawback that it tends to stereotype the disposition to evil; by constantly "passing over" the mere acts which spring from that disposition, and leaving the disposition itself untouched, the acts come to seem of no importance, while the disposition, being left unaltered, comes to be treated as part of a man's "nature" which he cannot "help" and which calls for pity and toleration.

What is of vital importance, however, is precisely the disposition to do the evil, or think the evil. If the disposition is not or cannot be changed, forgiveness seems either useless or an endless process; the individual will require forgiveness till "seventy-times-seven." In either case the sinner has the best of it; for he both gets his own way and is forgiven and in addition has the privilege of keeping his tendencies of mind unaltered!

It is the disposition that has to be removed as well as the act. Strictly speaking, we cannot alter the act but only the disposition. And apparently we cannot forgive the disposition but only the act. The only way the disposition can be changed is for the sinner to "forgive himself," to do "penance," to react with his whole mind against the disposition to evil, and so change his "natural tendency." "Forgiveness," in short, must be a double-sided experience; it must be both an act done by the injured to the offender, and an act (or reaction) of the offender towards the injured; it involves at once pardon and penitence. If it is either alone or exclusively the essentially spiritual character of the process is unrealized: for it always implies a relation of a person to another person, a relation in which both are interested and co-operate. Pardon without penitence is futile; it may be a mere encouragement to the repetition of the act, or a ludicrous assumption of superiority, or again a moral insult. Penitence without pardon is equally futile; it may be self-torture for no purpose, or it may issue in the complacency which makes a merit of its own agonies, or again it may be the expression of a heightened sense of superiority to the duller sensibility of others.

What holds for the relation of human persons to one another, holds with the necessary changes of the relation of man to God. In the latter case, forgiveness involves perpetual pardon on one side, and recurrent penitence on the other.

9   Christian teachers have perhaps made too much of the importance of "forgiveness of sins," and have not laid sufficient stress on other aspects of the religious life which need to be considered in connection with it. Men, no doubt, require to be redeemed and forgiven for sin; but they also need to have their strength of mind daily restored, their confidence and courage daily renewed. In short, men require to be renewed in the "spirit of their mind" as a whole. They need the assurance of God's strength to over-

come their weakness, and so to cancel and remove their imperfection of thought and will. They require to feel that God is reconciled to them and they to God in spite of defects and imperfections of every kind, and not only in spite of "sin." Unless God restores and renews the whole man, the joy of the divine life is unattainable.

**10** Men may repent and regret, but they cannot forgive themselves. No amount of penance will produce the state of forgiveness; penance is rather a token of having been forgiven. Forgiveness must lie beyond the individual who does the wrong. It marks the completed stage of the cancelling of the wrong done. And in the long run no individual can forgive another to the extent of cancelling the wrong entirely, for the wrong concerns the individual wrong-doer, who as we have just seen cannot forgive himself. The suggestion seems clear that forgiveness is only to be accomplished by a divine act, an act of the divine life in man; and then it is accomplished in the interest of the divine life as much as for the well-being of the finite individual. It is the process of restoring the complete communion between the divine life and the individual which has been broken by the wrong (the "sin"). Hence forgiveness is the Divine prerogative and also the Divine nature. God must necessarily forgive, for God is spirit at one with Itself in and through all finitude.

**11** It is often said that the evolution theory changed the old conception of the "fall" of man into a "rise." The difficulty, however, for the evolution theory is to explain how man comes to fall so often now that he has "risen"; and still more to explain why he should regret so keenly the successive falls when they do take place. The "fall" as an "explanation" is in some ways easier to believe than that man has risen; for in trying to do His will man is always falling away from God.

**12** It is necessary that God should forgive, because the permanent alienation of finite spirits from Him is inconsistent with the harmonious unity of a divine life. Hence it is said God is always "plenteous in mercy" and "ready to forgive." The difficulty is for finite spirits to believe this and forget themselves in God's forgiveness. Their pride makes them unwilling to accept forgiveness unless they can forgive themselves—as if this were anything more than another form of pride and, therefore, another sin requiring forgiveness. It is because the sinner finds it so difficult to realize this aspect of the divine life that priests and confessors have been found to be a means of guidance to the perplexed. It is in this, as in other matters, hardly possible to be judge in one's own cause.

**13** Religious people usually look on the "forgiveness of sins" as some special favour of the Divine done to the sinner to relieve him of his sense of guilt and give him a new start. It is difficult to see much wisdom or value in this. It may even be a bad thing for the sinner to be relieved of his sense of guilt; he may become a worse man in consequence.

The point of forgiveness is rather that the fulfilment of the Divine will by man demands that man's failures should not be allowed to arrest his innate desire for goodness, block his progress towards it, or undermine his belief in its ultimate triumph under the power of God. If the sin were not removed—"forgiven"—the very sense of failure, which the consciousness of sin implies, would create, or deepen into, a sense of incapacity to succeed at all in the moral life, and this again would lead to further failure and, perhaps worse, to the feeling that failures are inevitable. Failure in that case would produce more failure, and the individual would come to submit to failure and thus "lose heart" or lose interest in the moral life. Brooding on inevitable defeat prepares the way for new failure or paralyses effort altogether. "To mourn a mischief that is past and gone is the best way to draw new mischief on." What man needs, and what God requires if His will is to be done by man, is to get rid of the sense of guilt which arises from consciousness of wrong-doing (or wrong thinking). He may forget it, but it is not easy to get rid of it in that way in normal experience; we cannot deliberately forget, anyhow; there is no certainty that we will forget; and we may remember just at a time which will impede our next effort or an effort in a situation similar to that in which the wrong was done! Hence the only way in which finite moral experience can be saved from its inferiorities is by recognizing that the Divine Spirit itself cancels our failures and our "sins" in its all-embracing love for the finite spirit which shares its purpose and its life. Forgiveness of sins, in other words, is a necessity of the Divine nature quite as much, and in the same way, as it is a necessity of human nature. In neither case is it an incident or accident.

14   There is a great difference between saying "be merciful to my sin" and "be merciful to me a sinner." It is not everyone who willingly and truly says the second. Most people are willing enough to say the first.

15   Self-will is said to be the source of all sin. Possibly it is; for self-will is finitude claiming to be omnipotent in its own right, acting solely because it desires to act, seeking ends of its own designing and its own desire regardless of all else. This, in the sphere of finitude, is will claiming to be supreme. But such a claim for supremacy can be made and sustained by God alone. Self-will claims the privileges and powers of the Divine Will for itself as finite will, and for the immediate ends of finite will, to satisfy the will as finite. Self-will is thus necessarily sheer hostility to the Divine Will, for it admits of nothing higher than itself. And that is certainly the root and essence of sin.

At the same time, it is the implicit divinity of the finite spirit which makes such a procedure possible. Self-will can only claim supremacy because it has the capacity for infinitude. It has been endowed with that capacity by the Divine Spirit; so that the possibility of sin lies in the very creation of finite spirit and finite will. Such creation is the Divine act and the Divine purpose.

In that sense the Divine Will is the source from which this manifestation (like all other manifestations) of finite will springs and proceeds.

**16** The suffering, the sin, the evil in the world have been too often regarded as a cosmic misfortune, and in that sense contingent in the scheme of things. They are, however, inevitable in finite experience, and in that sense are necessary to the realization of the whole. And, indeed, they seem worth while, for in no other way, it would appear, could Infinite Power and Love in the Divine have been brought home so vividly and convincingly to man as through overcoming and reconciling to Itself the evil, the sin and the suffering in finite experience. Evil is God's opportunity to manifest and realize eternal Love.

**17** One of the profoundest truths of Christianity is that all a man can do "of himself," unaided by a divine power, is to do wrong.

# II

# HUMAN NATURE AND CONDUCT

### I

**1**   There is a vein of pessimism in all men's view of life. How easily, for example, we see that evil has been done, misfortune has happened, grief has overtaken men, loss has been sustained, the desired good has not been attained! How hesitatingly we allow that good has been done, how doubtfully we admit that what appears good fortune actually is so or will remain so, how tremblingly we accept life's joys and happiness!

**2**   It seems certain that real security and confidence of spirit, of "mind and heart," in the world, assured supremacy over it, are attained, not by intellectual comprehension of it, not by "understanding" it simply, but by moral rectitude of will, by consistent unswerving obedience and devotion to the purposes and ends which are highest. It is possible to understand the whole plan of the world and yet live in terror of it, or it may be even hate it. But ready obedience to what we know to be the highest and continuous service of it give a strength, a resource, an immovable fixity, a *raison d'être*, a consistency and unity to life, and are even necessary for the acquisition of intellectual comprehension of the world and for the love of truth which that requires.

It is in morality that we seem to touch the meaning of our own lives, the purposes of our being; it is there that reality seems to meet us face to face. And this view seems borne out by ordinary judgments.

**3** It is a mistake for those who consider Freedom to be liberty to do what you please to suppose that this Freedom can, or need, consist in the number of objects or ends which you may choose, and that the more numerous your ends or aims the greater or truer your freedom. As a matter of fact, most men find themselves to be free, and to be most truly free when their aims are few and limited both in number and nature. A plurality of purposes and objects tends rather to create distraction and to make men the prey of their circumstances instead of master of them; and this is not freedom in any sense.

**4** A man's past is like his children: it is born in the present; but it is no sooner born than it begins to assert itself and finally establishes an independence of its author which will confront him with a reality equal to his own, and from which he cannot cut himself loose precisely because it originally shared his life.

It is thus that the past becomes a kind of objective destiny where a man reads his fate, knows what he was and learns what he is. Out of this arises the endless agony and pathos of regret; for it is there that the individual discovers the deeper currents that carry him onward all unbeknown to the goal of his life, and is compelled to acknowledge his past as continuous with his present, and to claim as his own the deeds of vanished years. In that continuity lies the source of his regret; for in the gathering years he has garnered a wisdom which enables him to judge the past and yet obliges him to recognize that the past which he judges is as much a part of the truth about his life as his power to judge it. This union of increased knowledge with an unalterable past is the essential quality of his life, and at the same time the pathos of its meaning. To escape it is impossible, for it is himself; to approve it is to wrong himself; to acquiesce is to be unworthy of himself. Yet own it he must; hence the wild yearning and misery of regret.

5   What determines a man's happiness or misery, his security or instability, is not so much the thought or the object he has immediately before him as the undercurrent of thought and feeling or interest which accompanies it. If, in this sphere of his conscious life, he is at peace with himself, little else can really disturb him. The reason is that here he has his immediate experience; here the past has modified his structure, making him what he is. And in the same way what determines whether a man gives his whole mind to an idea is the undercurrent of reflection which accompanies it. If this undercurrent of reflection is active, the new idea enters into his mental structure with more completeness, with the only completeness of which he is capable. Hence in many cases the distinction between a great man and a feeble man just lies in the fact that the one brings with him a vastly greater accompaniment of reflection to bear on an idea brought before him. But of course the new idea does modify and determine this undercurrent of mental activity.

6   No one can be really efficient in his work unless his activity is exercised with that joy and complete self-possession which are characteristic of the artistic life. Genuinely good work, a man's genuine best, must be produced with that free spontaneity which is both the accompaniment and condition of joyous exertion. Joy is not inconsistent with labour; it can only be taken to be so when joy is looked at as equivalent to frivolity and labour is regarded as a sort of penalty. Labour is serious, but human perfection is still more so; and the realization of perfection is only to be found in the joyous life.

Hence it is that we find the best work and the happiest lives amongst those who are doing the work for which they feel themselves "fitted," and who at the same time, when they put forth energy, never overreach themselves but always do something completely in their power. It is doubtful if work has its true moral value under any conditions if a man is doing what he is not fitted for, or what is not fitted for him, or if he is doing more than he is fitted for—he will produce bad work, and be a bad workman. Nothing is more painful than to do (or see another do) a piece of work with the straining exertion of a man in a catastrophe. Such work will never be regarded as satisfactory; it will even at its best have the incompleteness and roughness which necessarily belong to an attempt to master what we know to be, to some degree, not completely under our control. We ought, for the best work, to have more power than the work really requires; for only thus have we self-possession, and self-possession is essential to the best work.

**7** A good test of our capacity for happiness and of our possession of it is to see whether we prefer sleeping to waking.

**8** The way to secure lasting content and a basis for happiness is to learn to regard the necessities of life as luxuries.

**9** It is a mistake to regard the feeling of pleasure as merely of subordinate value in the conduct of life. In a great many cases, it is of primary importance, and is the only guide we possess. Acts of momentary significance, novel situations requiring immediate attention, courses of action where the balance of reason seems equal for and against, intimacies of social adjustment where considerations of feeling alone enter into the substance of the situation—in all such cases, feeling of pleasure and pain is the only test of what to do and avoid.

**10** There is this to be said for the seeker of enjoyment, that if he gets it, even to a limited extent, at any rate he really has got something out of life of which he is perfectly certain, and of which he can say that for the moment it *is* worth having. This much cannot be said of the truth-seeker, the self-denier, the ambitious and, in general, those who fly after higher things.

**11**   The conduct of life would be more than half assured if, when men were really happy, they knew and could lay hold of the principle constituting their happiness. As it is, happiness comes upon most men and then leaves them like a beam of light on a cloudy day.

**12**   It is easy to reckon our pleasures and enjoyments as part of our spiritual wealth. But we have not attained to our best nor made use of the full resources of our spiritual activity, until we can utilize our sufferings and our pains so as to enrich our spiritual life. We run away from these, or we avoid them, or we shrink from them. So long as we do this, they are not only waste material, they are alien material, like poison to the body, and yet they are ours as really as our pleasures. There is only one way of meeting them and dealing with them consistently with maintaining spiritual supremacy, and that is that we must cheerfully accept them as they come, dominate and control them for our own ends and establish the power of our spirit over them, however recalcitrant they may be. This enriches because it strengthens the life of the spirit.

**13**   Joy requires restraint and direction quite as much as sorrow: but joy comes so seldom to individuals that there is little opportunity to learn the art of controlling it.

**14**   There is a joy in things which is as much above laughter as the power of a calm sea is greater than that of a waterfall.

**15**   Happiness reveals a man in all his weaknesses and crudities of instinct much more than is possible when he is under the restraining influence of convention or self-discipline.

**16**   The great value of the senses to the human spirit is that their free and full exercise gives man the feeling of companionship with the world and prevents him feeling solitary or lonely. That is why the life of pleasure is so satisfying—while it lasts: and that is why people will always be drawn to the life of pleasure, in spite of all that so-called philosophers and others say to the contrary. Those who cut themselves off from the activity of the senses and the satisfaction such activity can assuredly bring are sure to find, some time or other, that they are isolated from the world about them, as "strangers and pilgrims"; they will feel themselves estranged from the world in some form or other. Their refuge and safety in such cases is to try to make the mental life by itself sufficient. They become "saints," or they pursue science or philosophy; or they try to keep up their union with the world outside them by "struggling" with it, by fighting its temptations, by curbing the flesh and so on—an indirect and painful testimony to the mistake they have made in cutting themselves off from the exercise and satisfaction of their senses. For the satisfaction of the mind through the exercise of sense is essential to the possession of the feeling of security and continuity with the world.

The most natural way in which this union with the outer world is maintained is through the life of art. It is the best and fullest realization of the activity of the senses; and thus brings the sense of joy in life in a way that nothing else can. And that, perhaps, is the spiritual purpose of the artistic experience.

**17** Happiness is so rare with some people that it can be as disturbing as pain: they hardly know what to do with it; and often the first impulse is to distrust it, and to get rid of it by doing something that destroys it.

**18** It is often suggested against the theory of pleasure as the end of life that to get pleasure we have so often to forget it in the pursuit of the means to it. But this is true of any conception of a supreme end. It seems a mistake to seek *the* end of human life, as if it were something by itself, and something to be had in detachment from everything else. The end is not to be possessed by itself, and, therefore, cannot be sought as a thing apart. In a sense it may be said that the end is to be found by not seeking it; as we walk by the aid of light, but do not look for light as we walk.

**19** One of the greatest sources of strength as well as happiness in a man's life is the recollection of his past as an orderly development and continuity of thought, action and desire. Nothing helps a man so much as the constant presence of happy memories in his life. Nothing so imperils a man's happiness as the importunate recollection of defeat, weakness, failure, mistake, or nameless dread, or broken will. If a man can link up present and past in an unbroken unity of purpose it is much, indeed very much: if he can link up the present life with the stuff and substance of the past—its ideals, its beliefs, its interests, its friends—he has most of what the heart of man can require for real happiness and security of mind and spirit.

A mind not at ease with its past is necessarily restless and unhappy: just as a people that recalls constantly the misdeeds of a bygone generation of its nation is in a constant state of insecurity and incipient rebellion.

No soul can be so unhappy as that which is torn asunder by its recollections.

**20** The ingredients of happiness for most people would probably be a little love, a little wealth, and some peace of mind.

**21** There is perhaps no better way of finding out a man's real nature than by ascertaining what makes him unreservedly happy.

**22** One of the great secrets of life is how to make a choice which, when worked out with all its results, can be cheerfully accepted as a destiny. Those who know this secret are successful and happy in life: those who do not know it are neither successful nor happy.

**23**  It is easy to control pains and fears, compared with the difficulty of controlling pleasures and happiness.

**24**  We hear much of vicarious suffering, of one for the many, of some for others; but in truth there seems to be vicarious enjoyment as well as vicarious suffering, vicarious labour, vicarious reward, vicarious achievement. All the greatest goods in human life have been accomplished by a few, one or two, and when accomplished they are passed on to, and shared by, the many. The great builders of civilization, even of its material prosperity, and the great poets, artists, thinkers, have all been few in number: they have laboured, and others enter into their labours, they have struggled, often without seeing fruit or external reward, and others reap the results of their efforts.

There is nothing so remarkable in vicarious suffering that it should be singled out for special recognition or wonder. It is a glory to suffer for others as much as it is a glory to interpret the divine vision to others. And the accomplishment of something universal, for all, must always be a joy in itself.

**25**  Sincerity in the pursuit and possession of pleasure seems far more difficult than sincerity in the consciousness of pain. We are seldom mistaken about the latter. Few seem to know what pleasure they really want or whether they are really pleased: hence the smirk, the pretence, the effort to please or be pleased, which often deceive others in the attempt to avoid deceiving oneself.

**26**  It is not possible for anyone to be wholly happy unless he can look back on the past with gratitude and revive it with delight. Without this, happiness can never be more than partial and fragmentary.

For most people, there is so much in the past which they would gladly forget or wish had never been. A man whose happiness lies in the future and feeds on hope is merely escaping from disappointment: his life has been spent in a prison-house.

**27** "Heaven lies about us in our infancy." Yes, and is only recoverable by those of later years who acquire and preserve the childlike spirit. The heaven of maturity is, however, so much fuller, in that the acquired childlikeness of those who attain it is enriched by the stabilized judgments of experience and the tried standards of life: it has the serenity which contemplates the present in the light of everlasting values, and supplements the confidingness of trust by the confidence of a steadfast hope. Being vaster by the width of the horizon of the maturer mind, it both contains and surpasses the heaven of childhood. Hence we find those who possess it seem to return to the beliefs of earlier days and bring them to life again.

> After the last returns the first,
> Though a wide compass round be fetched.

**28** One of the main problems of practical life is to balance the powers and claims of the environment with the conditions of mental stability, with quietness of mind. In youth it is possible to allow environment relatively greater power: the mind can still keep a certain equilibrium even when the individual "lets himself go." But in later years it is more necessary to subordinate environment relatively to the mind, if peace and stability are to be maintained. Hence it always seems pathetic and sad when we find a man of advanced years carried away by the appeal of the senses, running after new pleasures, carried away by new sensations stimulated by his environment. It seems more fitting that these things and states should be special to youth. It becomes the older mind to preserve a certain detachment of spirit, to dwell in quiet with eternal things and to take the "world" for granted.

**29** We wonder at the security and stability of our bodily life, which depends on such a delicate balance of complex parts and functions. On the other hand, while a slight maladjustment may disturb the equilibrium of the organism, its stability is such that it can be maintained by little effort of any one part, and by slight adjustment or by delicate direction of function. It is only when the organism is seriously disturbed that strong or violent effort is needed to maintain its integrity.

Much the same is true of the spiritual equilibrium of man's life. How little is required to keep it steady, provided that little is of the right kind and is constantly supplied: how much is needed to restore its stability once this is deeply shaken, and how easily its balance is disturbed by a wrong purpose or a wandering desire!

This is a truth with which many old people are instinctively familiar. "Si la jeunesse savait ce que la vieillesse reconnait touchant les choses qui conviennent à la paix de Dieu!"

**30** At our best we should live like actors in the drama of life, conscious that we are actors and conscious only of our part. To be conscious of ourselves as well as of our part spoils the play: it means we are either bad actors or have not yet learned our part properly.

We have to make up our mind whether the play of life is a "Divina Commedia" or a "Comédie humaine." This will make all the difference to our acting. The best acting in the drama of life is done by those who feel sure their part is set for them by the author. For he does not merely give us our part but the power and ability to play it, and prompts us when we pause. If only youth knew this secret early, what misery of self-consciousness it would be spared, and from what failure it would be saved!

## II

**1** Would the Theistic assumption really be a sufficient guarantee for the identity of Duty and self-interest which is regarded as a logically necessary postulate of ethics? Suppose every breach (voluntary) of clear duty were to be punished and every performance (or performance on the whole) of duty were to be rewarded, would it even then be to my interest always to do my duty? And if it was, would not my sole motive be self-interest, and *not* duty? Again, if the duty were painful and my interest pleasant, would it not really be to my interest to take the present pleasure, even though punished for it afterwards? In any case, it would just be a matter of shifting the time for suffering pain (not the amount); for both the person who does the painful duty and gets his pleasure afterwards and he who suffers afterwards for taking present pleasure (from self-interested motives) get both pain and pleasure, differing only in the times when they get them. The one gets his pain now and pleasure afterwards, the other his pleasure now and pain afterwards; and how does this help with the problem of the identity of self-interest and duty? Nor can it be said that eternal pleasure is a better and greater reward than present experienced pleasure which is fleeting; for eternal pleasure is not what is known to us as pleasure and can't be so described, and if the pleasure *in infinitum* be what we call pleasure it will *ipso facto* not be eternal.

**2** Exercise of will depends on the presentation and more or less continued presence before the mind of an idea whose realization is prefigured and thought of. Hence the tension in the absence of the realization of that idea. Hence, to destroy the misery of such tension and the remorse of conscience, etc., we must remove the idea alone, and should not think of the tension. But how can we remove *Desire* itself?

**3** There is a strong divergence between the limits, applicability, etc., of a *rule* and a *law*. You may break the former with impunity at times but not the latter.

**4** It seems quite a mistake (though a natural one) to suppose that, in order to feel or thoroughly appreciate the sinfulness of sin, the beauty of goodness, the excellence of virtue, yes, even the comforts or worth of riches or of poverty, it is essential to have a living actual experience of the states in which these are or are to be found. This of itself will never give the required appreciation of their full significance. For in being in these states, in living through them, we are in a sense living them, and the mere existing in a certain state does not of itself involve a judgment on the nature or meaning of that state, since conscious judgment is by its very nature *re*flective whereas life and living are *pro*gressive, forward-looking. Now all appreciation of the meaning and worth of a thing must be expressed in a judgment and so must be reflective. Hence, fully to understand the value and significance of, say, *sin*, what is required is a complete and clear comprehension of the nature and meaning of the laws or principles which it is the nature of sin to contradict. But obviously this can be attained without any real experiencing of sin, that is to say without committing a sin, and indeed is not likely to be attained as a result of committing one. And the same could be said, *mutatis mutandis*, of our understanding of the worth of goodness.

Incidentally, this shows that any other basis for ethics (or any judgment of value?) than reason in itself, and for itself, will prove quite inefficient when dealing with the facts of our moral experience. For if we depended entirely and uniquely on *feeling* as such, on pleasure or pain, then we could, by no possibility make any judgment on the nature and meaning of any particular experience—or rather on the value, the *moral* worth, of the experience. All that could be said would be that such and such an experience is so and so, is pleasant or otherwise. If we say when it is painful it ought to be pleasant—keeping to pleasure and pain as our sole criteria of worth—this can mean either that, if things had been otherwise, we should now have pleasure instead of pain; or, if the life we have is to be quite efficient, we should have pleasurable feeling, not painful, since pleasure is the expression of the efficiency of life, of the proper state of living. The former alternative is a mere absurdity and contradicts the admitted significance of the law of causation; and in any case to say that the constitution of things ought to give us pleasure, and not pain, is to cease to talk seriously. The latter alternative does at least furnish a standard for judgment, and in so doing abandons the criterion of mere feeling; for it implies that we can judge feeling itself, and we could only do this by appeals to reasons founded otherwhere than on feeling as such, founded in fact on the constitution of things. But it would involve the hardly less absurd position that the man with a bad liver or aching pains is less *moral* than the man whose body is working accurately and faithfully. And this completely contradicts our moral judgments and our conception of moral ideas as revealed in our expressions of moral worth or in our ordinary practice. In other words, it explains morality and our moral ideas by explaining them away, or by denying the facts which themselves condition the existence of the problem. Feeling, after all, is a mere state of being in the present; and we cannot merely, in and by the present, judge the value of the present. To do this we require to transcend the present state, to have a standard which is other than the present state and wider than it. On this feeling theory, too, any anticipation of the worth of the future or of the universe as a whole, and any judgment of value on them, is rendered quite impossible because (1) we can never precisely anticipate the future state of our feeling (which is *always* present), (2) the laws of ourselves and of the world might alter and with them all our experience, and (3) feeling is peculiar to us as *self-conscious* beings and is not found elsewhere in the universe—the so-called feelings of the animals being little more than a sense of being alive. Indeed, what chiefly makes the feeling theory plausible is the stress which is laid on the *body* as an animated organism, the physical basis of mental life. The other extreme theory lays stress merely on the soul, spirit, e.g. mystical morality, etc. But both body and soul are abstractions if treated apart from one another. We must start with some conception of the nature and significance of spirit.

**5**  It is wiser and better to take a determinate decision and resolutely act upon it, even though it may afterwards require to be modified, or even though, through weakness, one's resolution to act on it may falter or fail, rather than to maintain or submit to a halting indecision and impotent irresolution. The latter implies, in general, weakness of the will, a moral or spiritual weakness; the former is weak only in so far as the object or idea which is carried out is erroneous or in some way wrong, i.e. the error here—if error there be—is only due to misunderstanding or misconception.

**6**  From the doctrine that morality is relative it is possible to draw two conclusions, (1) that just because morality is relative each man or each age should act completely and fully up to the conditions laid upon him, the laws known by him, should do the right earnestly just because he knows it to be right, (2) that because it is relative we are exonerated from any ultimate necessity to fulfil its conditions as they appear in the present state or age, that in fact because it is relative, and therefore presumably advancing, we should seek not to do its commands as given in the present, but "live and act for eternity," i.e. either do "better" than present morality enjoins or do as we please and have little or no respect for present morality.

That two contradictory positions can be taken up regarding the same doctrine augurs ill for the truth of it!

**7**  It is doubtful if many men ever get beyond the purely negative view of goodness as avoiding something which we must not be—the main Hebrew conception of it. Yet this is quite disastrous to the highest moral life. No man can rejoice in a negation. Indeed, there is something of the nature of the devil in such morality; destruction, negation, is the character both of the devil's work and of the conduct of the man whose sole view of virtue consists in refusing to do wrong. There is hatred in both; and it is surely significant that negative morality is the morality which we find in pugnacious people and in people with morose, sour tempers.

**8** In drawing, particularly in a medium where the conditions are the simplest, like line work or pencilling, the great secret is to know what to draw in order to suggest the most or, negatively, to know what to omit. That is true of all artistic work. There is an artistic aspect of life and conduct, too. This is expressed in the idea that a man must know his limits and act within them. To do this properly is "to know what to omit"; and that is one of the great secrets of conduct. If one's personality is to be anything like a complete whole, one must give up something; for a whole must be balanced and have the proportion which gives at once strength and grace. This art of omission, limitation or, rather, of keeping within due bounds, appears as what is called "refinement" in the moral life, and a "cultivated mind" in intellectual pursuits.

**9** The attempt to claim high or higher value for the "primitive" state of man on the ground of its innocence is due to a confusion between moral innocence and innocence of morality: the latter is the condition of the brutes and of "primitive man," the former is the highest achievement of the moral life.

**10** So many of the "text-books on morals" have been written by bourgeois men for the bourgeoisie that people have come to identify the study of morals with the study of duties and virtues of the most elementary description and ideals of the poorest substance. Such discussions of the elementary virtues and duties merely testify to the primitive level of the morality of the writers. Better people never think of such elements of good living: they are more concerned with the graces of life and take the rudiments for granted: they know it is not enough to be an honest man if one is to be a gentleman. Those who make a great to-do about strenuous honesty and find it requires a struggle to execute duty and practise the cardinal virtues are not far removed from the primitive man, and their conduct is not typical, still less is it the standard of excellent living.

Kant's ethics deal with the morality of the half-civilized peasant, and would seem ridiculous at the Court of King Louis.

**11** Philosophers and others write and discuss much about a supreme moral ideal as a governing principle of conduct. In practical moral experience there is no single supreme ideal in operation: the supposition that there is one is not based on experience, but is due to the projection into the field of experience of the mere concept of unity which the philosophers and others must work with in order to bring to a focus the manifold ends which actual human beings pursue. They (the philosophers) suppose that what they seek is what is actually exercising a dynamic agency on individual wills, and they therefore proceed to identify this central unity with some moving factor in moral experience—like pleasure or law or reason, etc.—and thence try to resolve all other aims into this one. The very perplexity into which such an attempt leads ought to have made them pause and question their starting-point: the result of not doing so is seen in the abstractness of their theories or, what is almost worse, their bending and twisting facts to make them fit the theories.

What we have in actual moral experience is not a single controlling end, the same for all men, but *types* of moral life under which individuals range themselves. The number and variety of these depend on the kind of society or community in which an individual finds himself; and the individual's selection of the particular type to which he shall belong is primarily a matter of the kind of interest in the moral life which he feels. For myself I find no "supreme" ideal in my own life or in that of others, but a number of ends related to a type of moral life, and changing from day to day. Such types are those of a man of business, an official, a scholar, a workman, a controller of a household and the like. Within or round these types, some of greater range and some of less, the various ends, the fulfilment of which connects a man with his circle or the community, are gathered: thence proceed his several duties; and each has its corresponding virtues as well as its rights. This limited sphere of interest in the moral life is all that, in actual fact, a man has to guide him as a "moral ideal."

**12** Gratitude is not a lively sense of favours to come; if it were, more people would show gratitude. Gratitude is, however, the rarest of virtues, is indeed a grace rather than a virtue. It is a sense of thankful dependence on another; and few can bring themselves to feel and recognize this dependence.

**13** It is curious and significant that science, art and religion all take up a detached attitude towards the moral life in different ways. To the student of nature the good and the bad man are of equal interest; they present problems for solution and nothing more; and the natural sciences regard them with equal favour and concern. Those practical sciences which apply the knowledge of nature to man's needs never allow the moral character of individuals to prejudice or interfere with their work: e.g. medical science must treat with equal care the erring mother and the lawful mother: their children are produced according to the same natural laws.

So in art: the moral lives of individuals are but material which enter into the domain of art and are welcome equally as material, supplying the material of tragedy and comedy, sorrow and joy, beauty and pathos of physical expression to the painter or sculptor.

In religion again, we find that the religious point of view transcends moral distinctions, wipes out or forgives the sin, treating righteousness even as "filthy rags," encouraging the moral agent to look beyond the present struggle of good and evil to a state in which moral effort passes into joy and temptations disappear.

**14** Objection has often been taken to the expression of moral laws in a negative form, e.g. in the Jewish code, on the ground that such laws do not tell us what to do, but merely what not to do. The assumption underlying this criticism is that such moral laws are useless as guides to practical conduct and leave the individual to find the positive direction for his moral life either in customary convention or in the prescription of his private conscience.

The criticism seems superficial. Negative moral precepts pull the individual up and compel him to keep his mind on the beaten track of the moral experience of his society. They imply that he is by instinct or by nature anxious to do the right thing, to do what is good; that he is first and foremost good and on the side of goodness and therefore does not need to be told what good he should do, but rather what he should avoid doing. They assume, too, that man as social is anxious to live well with his fellows, and that this is the strongest tendency of his moral nature and will keep him right: not that he is naturally evil and requires to be restrained from dominating evil tendencies within him. In a word, they imply that man is inherently a healthy-minded moral agent, and only occasionally, when under the sway of passion, is inclined to depart from goodness. If therefore he has goodwill towards his fellows from the start, fellowship with them will lead him aright, give his conscience play and induce him to accept the guidance of the established moral order of his society.

From this point of view, it is better that moral laws should be expressed negatively than positively. Their negative form induces respect for the positive moral order, gives the impression of authority and points to the dangers of disobedience; and at the same time throws the individual back on himself and emphasizes his individual responsibility for his conduct.

**15** There is a strange worldliness of outlook in the Hebraic conception of righteousness. Not only does the Hebrew mind expect prosperity as the reward of righteousness, and feel grieved and disappointed if prosperity does not attend the righteous. It attributes to the righteous man an attitude of sanctified moral conceit which is worldly in a hardly less obvious sense. Righteousness makes him vain, self-confident, and proud. On this view righteousness is a kind of possession which he claims as his own by right, and of which he must not be deprived, and the deprivation of which is a ground of complaint against the nature of things. It is not a quality or condition of personal life to which or for which the individual should be asked to sacrifice himself. The Hebrew mind does not believe in suffering for righteousness, either temporarily or permanently: suffering is an unjustifiable hardship and should not be imposed on the righteous man in this life, otherwise he will rebel and is entitled to rebel. No nation has *used* righteousness for its own glory and self-glorification as the Hebrews have done. On the other hand, this selfish interest in righteousness, paradoxical as it is, has been the source of the strength of Hebraic religion.

**16** Mercy is the generous overflow of goodness without passing judgment. And the good need it as much as the bad.

**17** There are virtues of impotence as well as virtues of ignorance and of innocence. They are a great advantage for the maintenance of social order, though they do not add to the merit of the individual.

### III

**1** Is warring with evil the best way to destroy it? It seems rather to increase its hold on the mind, just as we find that touching, handling, scratching, or even thinking about a wound on one's own body has the effect simply of irritating it and preventing its cure. The simplest way seems to be to ignore it persistently.

**2** An "evil conscience" is the peculiar possession, the uniquely private experience of the individual who "has" it! We could not if we would, and we would not if we could (except in rare circumstances), communicate it to another; it is not really communicable; and it is questionable if it ought to be communicable. But a "good conscience" is common property, or can be made so and, in fact, is made so; for the world and its business are only possible on the basis of frankness and openness of life and conduct. This is, perhaps, the reason why sin and all it implies is made in religion an affair between the individual and God, and why it is an exclusively religious concept.

**3** Is not the greatest of evils to believe in evil?

**4** There is, perhaps, that which is worse than a consciousness of sin, and that is a consciousness of none. . . . But to make a virtue of the consciousness of sin is itself sin.

**5** It is possible for men, by persistent wrong-doing, to render themselves positively incapable of choosing and doing the good. Yet even when they readily and persistently adopt the evil, they always do so in the knowledge that it is evil: the distinction between good and evil never seems to get confused. Consequently, the whole conscious state of the individual, who pursues evil more readily than good, reveals continually, even to the agent himself, the contradiction, the misery, the disappointment, attendant on the adoption of evil. In no case does evil become good. That men should choose evil when they know good even only a little, or that when they have seen the good more fully they should not seize on it as if the whole world depended on the choice—that seems the endless enigma of human action. Explain good and evil how we may, the absolute and irrevocable difference between them can never be too much insisted on, and can never be removed.

**6**  The argument in favour of "sowing wild oats" seems specious, and is really nothing more than specious. For if a man would employ, even in mistaken efforts to do good, the energy, opportunity and activity which he uses in deliberate attempts to do evil—he will know more of good and less of evil, and be as much wiser and better a man as the longer, and closer, acquaintance with truth and good cannot fail to make him. To suppose that a man, by knowing more of evil, will thereby know more of good, seems nonsense even on the face of it. All that acquaintance with evil can do is to intensify our opposition to it, and the repugnance which it incites in us; it cannot increase our knowledge of good. This can only come by direct experience of good. We may say that a man who knows evil and the ways and rewards of it will be better equipped to avoid it, and defend himself against it. But, clearly, if a man does not do evil and knows nothing of it (or as little as he can help), he will not need to defend himself against it or to know how to do so. The knowledge would therefore be useless and the energy of acquiring it would be entirely misdirected. And to acquire such knowledge for the sake of others is quite palpable nonsense; no man in his senses ever would become a beast in order to teach others how not to be beasts!

The truth is that the reason why "best men are moulded by their faults" is because they are to start with best men, not because they have faults; they are best in spite of, and not because of, their faults. To convert the statement, "we learn the truth by making mistakes" into the form "we should deliberately make mistakes when we have learned the truth" (and this is what "sowing wild oats" means) is the most obvious stultification.

**7**  There is perhaps no end pursued by men which can so thoroughly corrupt the inner motives of action as the acquisition of wealth. Nothing can so readily foster hypocrisy and insincerity of purpose, and distort the native goodness of human instincts. And there are many reasons why it should have these effects:

that it ought only to be a means and not an end; that it cannot be, and is not, by anyone really considered to be an end; that it is a personal possession; that it is bound up with the very nature of subsistence and self-preservation in society, and requires, or obtains, possession of all the forces necessary to self-preservation; that its attainment in a complete state of society depends so much, and so often, on the presence or absence of mere trifles and trivial circumstances or deeds; that as a rule, and for the generality, it can only be obtained in small doses, and that the possession even of these requires continuous application, with the result that our conduct in seeking it is as petty as it is itself.

8  The only proper attitude of a human being towards sin is repentance and sorrow at the very thought of it. Morbidly or remorsefully to dwell on it is to substantiate, establish it, give it a reality which it essentially cannot, and will not, have. This attitude towards it is only a stage removed from vice and wickedness which assert and believe in, and seek to establish, evil as a positive reality. Hence the close affinity between morbid and wicked people, often noticed by observers. On the other hand, to ignore and be indifferent to sin and evil is to treat it as non-existent, and that is certainly false also.

9.  It is when evil deeds become sinful habits, and evil desires become sinful dispositions, that we first realize that our moral life is threatened from within its own citadel. We will admit that we consented to the evil act or evil thought, and will blame ourselves and repent; but when, after repetition, these come of themselves and assert their presence in our best and highest moments—it is then that we refuse to feel ourselves responsible, and rebel against a destiny which seems to seek our moral ruin and to compel us to sin "in spite of ourselves." Yet our weak moments would not be a prey to evil thoughts and deeds were it not that repeated consent in times of deliberate choice has made the invasion of our lives at those weak moments possible.

Nothing, therefore, can be gained by seeking to throw off connexion with the inevitable consequences of our own acts; we must accept, even against our will, the consequence of many repeated acts as much as that of a single action which we admit as ours. Everything is lost by refusing to recognize as our own what could only come from ourselves; for, by refusing, we split our moral life into isolated and conflicting tendencies; we destroy the organic unity of our own purposes; we admit an inimical destiny to a share in the direction of our fate; we paralyse utterly the spontaneity of our will and produce the painful and awful spectacle of a mind unable to act without first of all discovering if it is not compelled to act by a force it cannot control, a mind in helpless conflict with itself, in fear of its own inner destiny, which has lost control of the ends of its own being.

On the other hand, by honestly and freely confessing those products of evil habit and disposition to be our own—though they come "of themselves"—we establish the very condition which is essential if we are to regenerate our lives and uproot the evil within us; we assert without equivocation the unity of our individual life, and admit the evil to be an organized element in its constitution; we claim it as ours, as the product of our will, of our freedom. Moreover, by doing so, we can at once determine whether we shall further acquiesce in the habit which produces it; we judge our past and present conduct in the light of our highest purposes, and decide whether such acts as produced such habits, or such habits as created such acts, shall form part of our individual life. Our will is thereby made a single will; our purposes are in harmony; our acts, even our evil acts, are our own; no inwardly conflicting self-determining tendencies control our lives; we decide and consent to what shall be ours and what shall shape our destiny.

Better be in harmony with oneself and one's iniquity as a part of oneself, accepting the misery of self-condemnation and self-abasement, than divide oneself from one's inner destiny and suffer the agony of acquiescence in an uncontrollable defeat.

Reconciliation with oneself is the first condition of self-restoration and moral renewal. To divide ourselves from ourselves is to attempt the impossible feat of maintaining, as distinct from our own lives, the destiny which all the while we assert to be their inmost reality.

**10** It so often happens that the only reality which we seem able to lay hands on, or which seems most attractive to us, is that of evil. I believe that men will at times do wrong because they have ceased for the moment to believe in the right and yet must believe in something to keep themselves from sheer mental vacuity or self-desperation. For if action is where we, for the most part, make ourselves real, it is clearly inevitable that a man will act wrongly rather than not act at all, if thereby he can make his life a substantial fact to himself and not an insubstantial illusion. Nothing is so paralysing, so heart-breaking, as the feeling of hopeless desertion by the wider life of "sense and outer things" which forms the medium where we can carry out our purposes. Action of any kind which has a conscious purpose in it—even an outburst of temper or a childish romp—is preferable to no action at all and gives a man that comfortable feeling of being at home in the world (at least in the world of sense) which carries him beyond his private existence and makes a substance of him and not an ineffectual shadow. Of course, doing evil to make oneself real is the illusion of the faithless and unbelieving, for evil in its very nature is unreal, and its unreality and worthlessness are proved by the deception and remorse which it brings in its train. It is probably when this is discovered that the individual is brought to the real test of his moral life; for if that which seemed to be real turns out a failure or disappointment, only two courses are open to him—he must either repent and return to his belief in goodness and truth or else proceed immediately or by slow stages to his own destruction. In the latter case, he either destroys himself right away—and this seems the cause of so many suicides—or continues to believe in evil, and acts upon it till disease, ruin and death carry him off in spite of himself. Destruction in one or other form cannot but await him; for the man who believes in a deception and a negation has nothing more to hold on to. While he is holding on to an unreality and a lie he becomes himself an unreality and an untruth—a diseased body and a diseased soul. And this can have only one end: the negation of the individual himself.

**11** Men are apt to overlook the homogeneity and organic unity of all evil. If evil is repudiated completely in one quarter, it is thereby rejected in another; for our attitude towards it is in all cases the same, and our grounds for rejecting it likewise the same. On the other hand, to acquiesce in or tamper with evil of one form (which means to tempt oneself with it) is at once to lay oneself open to evil of other forms, for if we seek it in one direction, why not in another, or even in every direction? Hence it is that the man who deliberately chooses or plays with evil of one sort soon finds himself surrounded by all sorts of temptations, and goes "from bad to worse."

Hence it is that most men have a general distrust of a man who is weak "in one direction," no matter what that direction is. And, similarly, the man who is conscious of a habit of evil choice soon comes to distrust his general moral nature, and finds himself, in extreme forms of this experience, inhabiting a "world of demons."

**12** The great mistake in dealing with the devil is to put him outside you. If once evil is externalized, it can only be fought as an enemy with an independent reality of its own: this makes the contest both meaningless and comical, instead of being, as it should be, serious and tragical. For if evil *is* outside you, what have you to fight with? Why pick a quarrel with what does not concern you? To pick a quarrel with the devil is to turn yourself into a sinner. If evil is outside you, then let it remain there! No fight will then be possible for you. But if it is inside, as it is, do not put it outside you, for then you cannot end the quarrel; at any rate the quarrel becomes insincere if you fight treating as an outsider what you *know* to be inside. So all the saints have done.

**13** Societies of men differ fundamentally in their practical attitude towards human weakness and evil. One class of societies acts on the principle "how much can we tolerate?" the other class acts on the principle "how much can we suppress?" These two attitudes indicate totally different conceptions of human life and totally different ideals of civilization.

**14** Forgiveness of sins is a great puzzle to our ordinary ways of thinking, but not so difficult if we keep in view one or two fundamental ideas. The first is that forgiveness has nothing to do with forgetfulness: it is a definite act or attitude towards what has taken place. Forgetfulness is a mental effect due to the peculiar mental endowments or processes of the individual mind. Forgiveness represents a universal judgment; forgetfulness a particular incident or event. Forgiveness implies the presence of the past deed in consciousness; forgetfulness implies its absence.

The second point is that forgiveness does not involve the blotting out of the past, its disappearance, but its recognition. Forgiveness does not make a wrench with the past or a breach in the continuity of events. The supposition that it does so is the great obstacle to seeing how forgiveness is possible; for it is said, if the past is still there, how is it forgiven? Unless the past is recognized as real, though past, forgiveness is quite unnecessary: there is nothing to forgive; something must have happened, that is, must be recognized as in some way real, to give forgiveness a meaning. Forgiveness is an attitude to the past event; and so we must recognize the past event as real.

**15** It is often thought that worldliness means solely a love of the world, of passing things and shows, for their own sake and for the pleasure they bring. That is only one sense of worldliness. It is equally worldly to be afraid of the world, to be fearful of anything the world contains, whether small or great, transitory or permanent, imaginary or actual, past, present or future. And this latter form of worldliness is perhaps more common than the other, or at least as common; and is more deadly to the complete freedom of the mind. This fear of the world may take many forms, from anxiety to positive terror. It is the worldliness of the coward, the sycophant, the timid and the vast crowd who are wanting in self-reliance in the face of events.

Both the love of the world and the fear of it are forms of worldliness for the same reason: they spring from the same source—pure self-seeking, consideration solely for one's particular self regardless of all else. For such self-seeking really reduces the self to the level of things of the world, neither more nor less: hence there are possible for the self-seeker only two courses of action, two attitudes of mind: he must either use other things (and even other persons) solely for his advantage—this produces love of the world; or he must be used by other things (or persons) for *their* advantage—this produces fear of the world.

There is only one remedy for, or protection from such a frame of mind—that is to love the spiritual whole of which one is a part and in which one lives and moves and has one's being. This will inevitably replace the "love of self" by enjoyment of the larger and completer Life, and the "fearfulness for self" by awe and wonder.

And how to do it? Admiration and adoration form the main conditions: much depends on these, and they are in our power; the rest follows after.

**16** One reason why people repeatedly delight in evil seems to be that somehow they feel that they would like to have every kind of experience. They think of complete satisfaction as being satisfaction in the largest number and greatest variety of ways regardless of the kind of object or source of the satisfaction. To be active in any way at all seems better than not to be alive.

**17** There is a form of worldliness which loves the world and the things of the world.

There is another form equally prevalent which dreads the world and the things of the world.

It is difficult to say which is worse or better. But in respect of worldliness there is not much to choose between them.

**18** There is a great danger in too close an association of the consciousness of sin in the religious sense with the consciousness of moral evil in the strict sense (i.e. in man's relation to man). There is apt to be calamity if the two are completely identified, as has sometimes happened in human history.

If moral evil is inseparably connected with the consciousness of sin, the sense of evil in the individual's life becomes so deep, constant and ineradicable as to overshadow his whole moral life, and make it unendurable. For the moral life is at every point subject to defects, defeats, failures and imperfections. Many of these are not moral evils at all. They merely arise from variety of duties and conflicts of duties, and from the general limitations of individuality; and they are the very conditions of moral experience. But the consciousness of sin makes the individual so alive to defects and limitations relatively to the supreme perfection of God that the very limitations under which morality works become identified with sinfulness. Moreover, consciousness of sin gives a permanence to moral evil which it would not normally possess in the moral life. This deepens the memory of moral evil so that the individual becomes almost incapable or afraid of pursuing good lest more evil arise. Consciousness of sin also tends to attach an importance to moral evil which is far beyond what moral evil in many cases calls for; and even tends to attach equal and "infinite" importance to every moral evil, which is in flagrant contradiction to the procedure of the moral life, where we distinguish between evils of different kinds and different degrees much as we distinguish between kind and degree in goodness. Some evil acts and thoughts and desires are transitory and trivial; some are more enduring and far-reaching: just as some forms of goodness are trivial, others of lasting significance.

**19** It is not only evil acts or evil thoughts that disturb the happiness of the individual. These will pass or may be forgotten. A more potent source of unhappiness is the disposition to do or encourage evil which they leave behind them.

**20** The reluctance to admit having done a wrong usually rests on a deeper evil than the wrong done. It generally proceeds from the vanity of self-righteousness or the moral conceit of thinking ourselves better than we really are.

Very few have the moral dignity to confess a wrong willingly, and with unabashed regret. People who are mean about their faults cannot be expected to be lofty in their virtues.

## IV

**1** Probably temptation is most keenly felt as temptation by those whose whole nature is essentially on the side of the Good, whose dominant purposes are really identified with it. And this is not merely in virtue of the fact that an intense consciousness of good must heighten the contrast between the desires which it stimulates and the evil which provides the temptation, it is also because, in the very acquisition of good, in the assurance of the identity of the will with the supreme good, there is a consciousness of mastery over the good, a consciousness of its being the personal possession of him whose will is one with it. And the consciousness of these things seems at moments to become self-conscious (in the worst sense of the term), and to induce a mood of self-assertion in which we feel able to defy the good or set up another, create another in its place, purely for the sake of manifesting the strength of will in which we feel ourselves supreme. That is a subtle, and might be a terrible, temptation; but it seems only possible to those of a high moral nature. It seems almost certainly to have been one to which Christ's nature was open, and if He overcame what is perhaps the worst temptation a moral nature is capable of (just because it lies so near to the heart of the moral life and is purely internal to it), surely any temptation may be surmounted.

2   One of the subtlest dangers in the moral life is that the calls of the highest are passed by, or shrunk from, owing to the feeling of helpless unworthiness arising out of the consciousness of having chosen evil, or failed to choose good, in the past. The presence of this feeling may easily paralyse all hope. And, again, being aware that we have failed and have deliberately adopted evil makes us hesitate to believe in our own constancy of purpose, and thus takes the marrow out of our moral courage. Experiences like these, however, lose sight of the fact that such restraining feelings are themselves evil and wrong, and ought not to be acquiesced in or admitted to influence us.

3   It is possible to have such hatred of evil in every shape, and fear of doing it, that good action is rendered difficult or impossible; there is a paralysis of moral will.

4   The man who "can't forgive himself" or accept the forgiveness of Heaven is distorting his moral nature by making a virtue of his misfortune, and is playing hangman to the devil in his own cause.

5   How singularly subtle evil shows itself! The sheer delight with which some virtuous men and women talk of evil and of the evil ways of others is mistaken by them for superior virtue; but it is in reality one way at least in which they show the mark of the beast upon themselves.

**6** One of the most serious and gravest difficulties in the way of moral improvement is just the sense that such improvement has been achieved. And this is not simply because the feeling that he is better than he was is apt to make the individual self-conscious and thereby to prepare him for another fall, through the pride that comes before it. In addition the improvement deepens and widens the gulf between us and our old self, our old evil ways. This accentuates our disgust with the past and makes our remorse more profound. Rather than endure these feelings, we would in some way keep in touch with our past; we would not, at least, go so far beyond it as to destroy our sense of continuity with it, which we must do if we set it up and condemn it, and so ourselves, out and out. To create such a gulf is to produce torture of the worst kind, and since the torture must be attributed to the heightened knowledge and attainment of the good which has caused the gulf, we shrink from further moral effort, and either fall into a routine of moderate attainment coupled with the toleration of the past which a lower ideal can make possible, or, by isolated acts of evil, connect ourselves with the old life and begin the struggle over again with the same issue and result—hence the ebb and flow, the rising and falling in moral development. Very few can resolutely defy this power of the past over the present, condemn it utterly, endure the pain, if necessary, and break with it altogether. Hence it is often supposed that only a "supernatural" power can do this for a man; he needs and gets "forgiveness" (which is reconciliation with his ideal in spite of his past); he has to be "born again" to keep the new life. This is the sphere of religion not morality.

**7** One of the greatest and commonest mistakes of the moral life is to confuse negative vices with blameless conduct.

**8** Most people take a keen interest, many have a great satisfaction, in the wrongdoing of others. People find in the deeds of the wrongdoer an expression of their own evil nature and their own evil desires; by observing and following the course of the evil in the mind and life of another, they can in a certain manner enjoy or appreciate the inhibited desires towards evil that stir in themselves, without themselves suffering the penalty that follows the evil deed. By reading and hearing of the crimes of others, they can satisfy their natural interest in wickedness and keep a whole skin and a safe reputation. This is the source of the strange phenomenon of "Schadenfreude."

Since all men have this interest in wrongdoing, it is only because some men have actually committed the crime and endured the punishment that everyone is not tempted to do the wrong himself, and take the path of evil to find out what it is like. Eve took the apple first and thereby anticipated, and partly saved, Adam's fall. Doubtless he would have done the deed himself had she not done it before him; his ready consent to taste the enjoyment when mediated through her invitation to share it proves how close he was to the path of evil all the while.

Thus it seems that the evildoers are the safety-valve for the general evil desires that prevail in all mankind. Some do the evil; and others are thereby prevented from actually doing it, because doing it is unnecessary when they see it done.

Vicarious sinning seems as real a fact of human experience as vicarious suffering.

**9** If the greater forces at work in the world and man's history employ or require the spur of evil to urge forward the achievement of vaster and more substantial good, how much more must the individual need the constant prick of pain and evil to keep awake his sense of the future and brace his efforts for new and finer ends. If God needs the Devil, man can hardly expect to do without him.

**10** The attempt to deduce or derive an action in everyday life from too high a principle is apt to lead the agent to act from mere caprice. The connection between principle and action is neither obvious nor direct; and in the effort to link up the two, the agent has often, in haste or despair, to fall back on the impulse or instinct of the moment. Thus action derived from the principle of "love" to others tends to reflect the natural impulses or private inclinations of the individual rather than a universal law observable by all in all circumstances.

**11** The great enemy of the moral life is the minor virtues.

**12** The reason why many good men suddenly have a dip into sensuality is that their goodness is abstract, aerified, exaggerated; and the unreality of their moral will fails to give satisfaction, or rather their moral will craves for satisfaction in a tangible real form and fails to find satisfaction in the abstract moralities which they pursue. Sense experience is the most vivid form in which reality is presented to most minds, and hence the recoil from morality to reality is a recoil into or upon sense—a plunge into sensuality.

It is for the same reason that mysticism in its extreme form is so often associated with bouts of sensuality. The mind turns from the aerified visionariness of the imagination and, to save its sanity, grasps at reality in its most sensuous and unmistakable form—sensuality.

**13** It seems useless to attempt to reduce human behaviour to detailed calculation. It is man's business and delight to break through calculated order; no sooner is such an order set up than man will at once devise some means of escaping it, or throwing it over outright. Rather than give up this capacity, man will do wrong and think wrong in order to claim it as his "right"!

**14** Those in the right are too apt to forget that, in face of evil and wrong, the right can largely take care of itself, either by establishing itself in time or as a result of the evil defeating itself by its own course of action. Those who defend the right with passion and intensity tend to make the right a private possession of their own, and thereby to fight for it with a bitterness which leads them into evil in their turn. Thus they come to do evil for a good end and put themselves partly in the same category as the thing they oppose.

Evil should be met with the calm majesty of the right which, because right, is above all passionate feeling. People are in too great a hurry to have things their own way even in the interests of right; and to have things their own way is not necessarily to have things in the right way.

15  A man may be so sensitively scrupulous for the truth that he cannot clearly and decisively mark it off from the domain of error lest in doing so some truth escape his notice; a man may be so very good in his goodwill that he will rather find excuses for the devil than condemn the devil outright.

16  A great many vices are little more than moral hobbies in which individuals seek relief from a virtuous routine by doing something all their own and for their own enjoyment!

17  The self-remorse, self-depreciation and self-contempt indulged in by the individual when he recollects the mistakes, the *faux pas*, the misdeeds and wrong deeds, and even evil imaginings, of his past life, are in reality a form of inverted vanity: for such an attitude implies the assumption that he is too good a fellow to have done these deeds or thought these thoughts, implies that he thinks himself a much better fellow than these acts prove him to have been. His sense of shame is like that of a prosperous man towards the poverty of his early upbringing, or a social success towards a poor relation. The man whose regret for his past haunts him in this way is as much under the influence of personal vanity as the man who, looking back on the good he has done in his past, thinks himself a very fine fellow, and prides himself on his goodness. Both states of mind are equally

bad; the one is merely negative vanity and the other positive vanity. And when the haunting shame for the past prevents a man from cheerfully doing his best in the present, his vanity passes into pride. Instead of merely being pleased with himself for being better than he was, he is so conscious of his merits that he refuses to do any good actions at all. He would turn his hatred of himself for wronging the good into hatred of the good which he has wronged, sooner than bend his will before the majesty of the good which he is called upon to perform.

The error of this frame of mind arises from confounding the specific acts of wrong committed with the disposition or tendency to do wrong. With the latter, a finite individual will always have to contend, and his struggle with it is part of his moral and spiritual life from first to last: with the former, he has no more to do, indeed he has less to do, than with the good he has done in the past; being past, it is done, and done with; his real life lies in the present and in the future. With his past deeds he must reconcile himself by acquiescence in the fact that he has done them and by the reconciliation which comes from the knowledge that the good is still with him calling upon him, drawing him on, a good which is all the more precious in that it has not deserted him in spite of the particular wrongs which he has committed, and is known to him all the better and all the more clearly because of his experience of the evil. With the disposition or tendency to evil he must continue to wage war: with this he cannot reconcile himself except by the suppression of his inclinations to evil as they successively recur.

18  The charity of sinners towards one another is much greater and more sincere than the charity of the saints towards one another or towards sinners. And it has the merit of being based on a common experience.

19  It is the vulgarity of mere goodness which makes it so unattractive and ineffective.

**20**  It is often difficult to say what really are vices in mankind Even vanity is in many cases of the greatest use to man; and nothing that has a use can be said to be wholly vicious.

**21**  Good people are not really satisfied by goodness: not till goodness is felt as beauty, as a "beauty of holiness," does goodness seem supremely worth while. Goodness has to be lifted into the atmosphere of religion or of art before it gives man joy; and only in joy can man feel that he is all that he has it in him to be.

**22**  People like the security of virtue with the risks of vice. This gives a fillip to life. Men do not care to be "righteous overmuch" lest life be too dull.

**23**  People who have done a great wrong sometimes go voluntarily into a penitentiary afterwards in order to expiate it. There is a good deal of vanity in adopting this course. It is in a measure an attempt to make up for an excess of wrong by an excess of virtue. It is an exaggeration of their own self-importance to suppose that the whole universe is tainted by their evil disposition or evil action, and that by some unusual course of discipline they can restore the moral health of the world. Seclusion in a penitentiary with its consequent daily concentration on the evil that has been done is necessarily a way of agonizing the soul instead of leading it to expand; a way of perpetuating in the region of memory the sense of an evil that probably lasted a little time, and thus of making evil more important than it should be in the life of the individual; a way of creating a new evil in the heart because of the self-satisfaction induced in the penitent at the suffering he is enduring on behalf of goodness.

**24**  So many people nowadays want to find good reasons for being bad.

**25**  The Victorians seemed to think they had satisfied the claims of morality when they made the major virtues respectable; that the best one man could do for another was to show him the way to prosperity and success, and that the claims of religion were met if the Church was a respected institution with properly accredited representatives in the House of Lords. The inward was sacrificed to the outward and merit was claimed for the sacrifice.

**26**  One of the subtlest forms of evil is found where men find a good motive for doing wrong.

**27**  Some people have scruples about being good lest they be too good.

**28**  We speak of men having the defects of their qualities. But defects often give a spice to special qualities.

**29**  Righteous indignation is a rare state of mind. It implies a completely disinterested attitude towards moral situations; it implies such concern for moral rectitude as to arouse hatred against wrong itself apart from its effect on ourselves; and it implies the capacity to direct and control our personal feelings so that they are ennobled by the cause we have at heart and are not degraded by bitterness, private hostility, selfish malice, self-will or moral self-conceit. Very few can rise to these moral heights. It is not surprising, therefore, that those who show moral indignation or righteous anger so often damage the cause they have at heart, and are generally regarded as having some private end to serve or advantage to secure. This is particularly the case where it is evident that the individual is taken off his guard and flares up in a sudden outburst of anger. Passion is so personal that it is most often actuated by self-will in some form or other, and is more a form of self-assertion than self-subordination to a higher end.

There is nothing nobler than a great passion devoted to and controlled by a great end; and lofty moral indignation can be most impressive and even overwhelming. But, like all fine things, it is difficult to achieve; and the failure to attain it does more harm to the cause of righteousness than cool indifference to wrongdoing coupled with quiet resolution to defeat it.

**30**  If there be an outer sphere of contingency, which has reality like any other sphere of reality, and corresponds to the inner fact of freedom of choice, it seems possible to explain why good may replace and cancel evil, or evil replace and cancel good. It seems difficult to explain such a thing in any other way. If the outer realm of events consists wholly of necessary connections, a good or evil once done could never be altered: it would remain to all eternity. It seems unimaginable that the fortuitous choice of a finite will can possibly create an event or produce an effect that will last for all time in the unchangeable nexus of the outer world.

Again, given that there is a real field of contingency within which the will can effectively operate as a free will, then we can attach meaning to the religious or spiritual concept of forgiveness of evil, as well as to the moral concept of pardon of guilt and the cancelling of wrong. A sin can be wiped out by a spiritual process, if the act of sin does in fact take place in a realm of contingency, where events can *be* as well as *not* be. Forgiveness cannot take effect on any genuine terms if an act once done cannot be undone: the forgiveness could then only be inward; the outer would remain and, if it remained, would mock and contradict the claim to forgiveness.

**31**  Few people are less welcome than moral reformers; for they break up custom and convention, which have given stability to social life; and the insistence on a deeper sincerity in moral relationships disturbs the souls of men and puts them at odds with their own moral purposes, thereby forcing them to condemn themselves. No man lives happily in a state of self-condemnation.

## V

**1** Men do not seem to be knit together by things as such, or institutions as such, or even deeds considered as external facts, but by unseen unmarketable emotions, feelings, spirit-threads. This is so in every case—a truly *sympathetic* look is really of more value to anyone in distress than a purse of gold; and this is proved by the fact that, if you present the gold with a grudge or a scowl, in the majority of cases it will be refused. Hence men are more united and more separated than we know or think.

**2** If all the emotion spent in regret for our misfortunes, and in bitterness at our wounded vanity, were converted into enthusiasm for the truth and the love of righteousness, our life would be infinitely strengthened, our very emotions would become richer.

**3** There is only one justifiable attitude which an honest man can take up towards passion of all and any sort—the attitude of a ruler to his subject. And though a wise ruler will always consider the good of his subjects, he will never parley with them. The game of a good life is half lost simply by treating as reasonable and self-sufficient what, in themselves, are the very reverse, by a man matching his true self as against an equal which never is or can be his equal. And, whenever a man does put himself on a level with his impulses and regard his reason as no better than his emotions, any moment may bring his defeat and disaster; for impulses are precisely what are supreme at moments, what are most effective on the instant or on isolated occasions. Their success lies in guerrilla warfare, rarely in a pitched battle.

**4** The mechanism of life should always be left to the regions of unconsciousness—whether the mechanism be that of acquired habit, physiological process or the external machinery through which ends are pursued and realized. This leaves consciousness to deal effectively with the needs and interests of the present.

The commitment of so large a region of our activity to the region of unconsciousness requires a large measure of that faith in the working of the world which is involved in religion.

It is when the mechanism of life becomes itself an object of attention that the mind is disturbed and necessarily harassed— necessarily because it is divided within itself. And when the mechanism of life becomes the exclusive object of attention, the soul is sick, it becomes confused, it becomes "nerves" and not mind; the mechanism of life, the body in some part or other, is out of order with it.

5   That reason and intellect do not necessarily unite men but rather separate them is evident from the experience of religion in the history of the Church. It is equally evident from the case of morality. Sentiment, on the other hand, does unite men in a more living way than reason. It is a mistake to say without qualification that men are isolated in their emotional life, and united by their rational life.

6   It is difficult to say whether it is worse to have no desires or to have all our desires fulfilled. But it certainly is bad to have desires and to know that they cannot be fulfilled, for that is a sure indication that there is something wrong. Either we should not have the desires in question or else they should not remain unfulfilled: if the first, we are to blame, if the second, the "world" is to blame. Here is one dividing line between philosophies.

7   Habit is no doubt the security of the moral life; but it is a weakness in religion, as it is in art and science. There is no room for habit in the highest forms of experience; for these are man's highest life, and life at its best is as fresh as each new day.

8   There is, especially in the Western mind, a root dislike almost amounting to horror of the powers that lie hidden in the life of passion and emotion. This prevents the individual from

committing himself to the tendencies that prevail in the domain of sense. He cannot trust the lead of sense or any of its suggestions. He prefers to have his mind free to choose, to manipulate its ideas and imaginations, to control by higher ideas the desires that occur and so forth. He does not care to surrender himself to the currents of organic instinct, lest he lose his consciousness of mental freedom. His individuality is his whole reality, body and soul, but his self is only half his individuality, viz. his consciously directed activity of soul. His body he hardly cares to think of as his self at all. It is either "assumed" or "ignored": he is afraid to commit his individuality to that aspect of his nature. He hardly cares even to know about it, still less to think of it as part of his self.

This is very remarkable and accounts for much that is characteristic of Western thought and practice.

**9** The mistake we all tend to commit is to underestimate the emotional value of the world. The only emotions which most people cultivate are those which are awakened by the activity of the organism at its lowest levels. The higher interests of man in his world—the world of nature and of human nature—are capable of giving a return of emotional experience which as far transcends the lower organic levels of emotion as a sonata transcends a doggerel ballad, or a Shakespearean drama transcends village gossip.

**10** Habits are not simply, perhaps not at all, the consequence of laziness or of taking the line of least resistance: these are results of habit, not causes or reasons for its formation. Habits of mind satisfy two needs of mental life; they regularize mental activity in such a way that our ends determine the spontaneous direction of our wills ("habits become second nature"); and they establish the sense of our continuity from day to day and from year to year. So important are these needs that we find people often more prone to keep up "old habits" than to choose new ends so as to form new habits. Our consciousness of identity is as much sustained by the strength of our habits as by the constancy of our "ideals." The development of many people takes place along the lines of established habits, rather than by the selection of new and "higher" ends of life.

**11** The moral life is partly constituted by purely natural conditions; though how far it is so constituted is very difficult in any particular case to say. Natural conditions—health, physique, energy of mind—are involved in goodness and badness alike. Many an individual owes his good disposition to good ancestry and a sound heart; many a one his bad disposition to a malformation of the brain or a diseased internal organ of his body. Only a complete view of a man's life can apportion the due estimate of praise or blame. Man must punish wrong and encourage right, whatever happens and whatever be the natural constitution of the individual. But from the completest point of comprehension probably all evil will be traceable to a defective natural endowment, or a defective adjustment of mental and bodily powers. If so, there is good ground for suggesting that to understand all is to forgive all; and that in the long run God forgives the worst of crimes and the worst of sinners, and wipes away all tears from all eyes.

**12** A man's power consists in the extent of his reserves; his effectiveness lies in the use he can make of them. It is always a sign of weakness if a man is "at the end of his tether," if he has no reserves left; and it shows want of judgment and of balance if a man calls constantly upon his reserves, if he puts all he has and all he is into every occasion, if he "gives himself away" every time. Those who bring their reserves quickly into the field soon become aware that they have nothing left to draw upon; and before long this breeds want of confidence and, what is worse, want of self-confidence, which neither bluff nor bluster can hide from themselves or from others. The positive side of courage and confidence is derived entirely from the consciousness of having reserves in hand, having still something to fall back on, and on which we can safely rely.

The English have the sense of all this perhaps better than any other people, except possibly the Chinese. It is doubtless an instinct or spontaneous attitude of mind; and the English are the last to think about the matter. In their case, it often takes a superficial form—the "reserve" of the Englishman, as he is seen by the outsider: there is often nothing behind this "reserve"; it is an appearance, though not necessarily a pose; it suggests reserved resources which turn out not to be there when the individual is put to the test. But even as an appearance, there is something in it; for it does mean that the individual is at least not carried away by the passing moment and is detached from the immediate incidents or actions at hand. And the cultivation of reserve, even in this superficial sense, is a testimony to the belief in the reality, and to the desire to possess the reserve in which real strength lies.

The reserve resources may come from different quarters of experience. The consciousness of a social background to the individual's life; the consciousness of family tradition or heritage; social status and position; the consciousness of wealth, of firm achievement which commands respect, of difficulties overcome in the past, of an ideal of life or duty for which he stands—all these supply reserves on which the individual falls back with confidence and which usually prevent him from being at the mercy of the doings of the moment or the events of the passing hour. Most of them are of a mundane character, and give the kind of self-possession found in the man or woman "of the world."

The greatest reserve power in experience is undoubtedly that which belongs to the man who feels sure of the Divine Life within him and around him. But few people really feel this except in emergencies. The only self-possession which will stand the test of all circumstances is the self-possession of a man who is confident that he possesses Divine power in himself and that the Divine power possesses him and who rejoices in possessing it and being possessed by it.

**13** The background of consciousness is the main source of the happiness or unhappiness of the individual. If this is harmonious, the serenity of the mind is assured: if it is vacant or perturbed, the mind cannot be at ease no matter what occupies the foreground of consciousness. The unspoken memories, the unexpressed imaginings, the unrealized desires, the hopes and fears of life—all these belong to the background of the hourly experience.

**14** It is a degradation of the dignity of age when an old man seeks to bask in the sunlight of youth in order to enjoy an Indian summer of desire. For that reason most healthy-minded people dislike such a spectacle. The smouldering ashes of the affections should be allowed to die down.

**15** Good habits are better than good resolutions. A bad habit will undermine the best resolution.

## VI

**1** The problem of life seems to be whether a man *wills* or *needs* to develop all his powers, all his instincts, faculties, parts, functions, etc. (call them how we please). For example, is a man less guilty for neglecting the opportunity to cultivate any one side of his nature—say, the love of music or of the beautiful—than he is if he does not give play to his religious instincts or emotions? (If he can do so, for some men can't.) Or can we say he is *more guilty* for neglecting the latter than the former, and will therefore be punished? It does not seem so. Surely *all* our nature is important; and can *we* estimate the degrees of importance of each part of it? Can we, in fact, absolutely fix the value of each part in such a way as to determine the results of cultivating or not cultivating it? It seems not; yet this claim is at the basis of all dogmatic religions. Not that a man would not or might not be *less* of a man if he did not cultivate his religious instincts; doubtless he would be less of a full man because less developed; and just because he can't determine the value of each instinct, he can't be in any way entitled to suppose he can neglect any instinct with impunity. But there are compensations on every side. And in the greater whole and larger life of the future surely there will be fuller life, wiser minds—*Wir heissen euch hoffen.*

2  What if Freedom mean not freedom to act, but freedom *after* action, i.e. greater and fuller development of the self?

3  It is well indeed to insist on the significance of personality as such. It seems very easy to say that the worth of personality consists simply in the ends to which it strives and for which it lives, and that those ends are ideas and that men are therefore symbols or concretions of concepts or principles. Yet might we not with equal truth (or at any rate with great truth) declare that the value of these ends just consists in the fact that it is persons who realize them, that in themselves they do not determine the value of persons, but persons the value of them; in fact that persons, being the most real and concrete of objects, are the only objects capable of providing satisfaction as well as the only beings capable of enjoying it? What, for example, is the significance of Love if it has nothing but ideas before it when it goes out to its object, and if these ideas are merely the highest ideas of the object and not the object as it is? Would not Love repudiate such an explanation of its object, and claim that the object in and for itself—the object with all its sorrows, imperfections and aspirations—is the end of its desire, the centre of its infinite tenderness and sympathy? From another side, does

not the whole significance of the Atonement in ordinary theological opinion just lie in the fact that the Person as a person suffered, not for his ideas in the sense that he sacrificed himself to his opinions as other men do, but in the fact that the supreme worth of a personality was annihilated for persons? And would not the whole doctrine fall if it were merely a species of martyrdom, high though that be?

4   In the last resort it must depend on each individual personally to determine whether he shall serve and aim at the highest and at the realization of this in his daily life, and how far he shall go in the pursuit of it. As a matter of fact, it is no one else's concern to what degree of goodness a man shall attain. That he shall be normally good is everyone's interest; but that he shall rise higher than external goodness, that he shall deepen his appreciation and realization of the good is his affair only. And this arises simply from the general truth that the moral life must have its source in the personal will alone. No one can be moral for another. No one can in reality make it possible for another to be moral. He may make it easier, but the primary initiative is presupposed.

5   There is no need to strain after peculiarity or eccentricity in order to give expression to our special individual outlook, to do justice to our "unique individuality." No doubt, much of the artificiality and exaggeration of modern life has this, in itself justifiable, desire at its root—to be an individual self and no one's duplicate. But strained effort in action or expression is not "originality" at all. To be truly ourselves, to express and do what appeals to us with uncontrollable and easy conviction and certainty, is to be original. And this we cannot help being if we are true to ourselves, for each individual has a distinctive nature and no other, and cannot help having it. The more truly we are ourselves, therefore, the more original we shall be in the only big intimate sense of original. But, in point of fact, few

people have the courage to command their own insight; they feel safer in falling in line with established convention. And their so-called "originality" is merely a superficial veneer over a fundamentally conventional and commonplace constitution of mind.

6   There is a difficulty in idealistic ethics (e.g. Plato's or Aristotle's type) analogous to that found in hedonism of the crudest form. The latter, it is said, endeavours to get the "ought" out of the "is"; implying that duty is to follow as a command what is there, in any case, as a fact—the desire for pleasure. That is certainly naturalism. But in idealism, especially when the content of the moral life is found in society, we are also told to start from the "natural" elements of our constitution, its instincts and tendencies, etc.—and that morality consists in developing what is implicit in those. This is surely, in a sense, getting the "ought" out of the "is." The word "development" covers, but does not hide, the transition, which is *continuous* all the while. This comes out more clearly still when it is said that "good" is the object of "desire," and that all desire is for a good, and all is "desired *sub specie boni*." The distinction between "goods" does not get over the difficulty, for *everything* that is in man's experience thus falls inside the content of desire. The difference between "higher" and "lower" goods must, in such a view, be determined by stages of development. But if we take this view, we must either regard the difference as one of degree only or else introduce an end which lies outside development, and decides what is higher and lower in it. In the first case, we have naturalistic ethics in another form; in the second we must abandon the simple notion that morality consists in becoming explicitly what one is implicitly.

In short, this idealistic view tends to confuse the two senses of development, that in time and that in thought. In the second sense, the end is not found *in* the process at all, it lies outside it, it is that at which we consciously aim. We stand outside the process of our lives and determine that process by reference to the end; and so the end can*not* (either necessarily or in fact) be a mere evolving of what is there already. If it were, we could not state it, since, by hypothesis, it is not attained. If the end is purely and simply the evolution of what is now implicit in us, then we do not *need* a consciousness of the end—that will be attained anyhow. If the end is outside and determining the process *ab extra*, it is not now implicitly there. Or, in other words, if we are evolving the end of our natural constitution by being moral, we are *in* the process and *of it* and, hence what we say of the end of it is relative to the stage we are at, is liable, therefore, to further and indefinite change. There can be no "ought"; we cannot in the long run help ourselves. If we really determine the process for the sake of an end outside the process —which we are clearly aware of and which does not alter, because not contained in the process—then the process is more than a mere evolution of our "natural constitution." In these circumstances all we can do is to take self-consciousness frankly as the end, logically presupposed in action, and the ground of connection of its parts. The moral end is thus not in time but realized through it.

7 There are two very opposite kinds of self-consciousness: there is the self-consciousness of the man who glories and rejoices in the distinctiveness of his individuality from that of others, who even flaunts it in their faces, and despises or ignores them if they cannot share his enjoyment or minister to his satisfaction; there is the self-consciousness of the man who is half afraid, half ashamed, of being distinct from others, whose delight and desire is to find others so much in sympathy with himself that they will absolve him even of the necessity of seeming to be different from them, who no sooner discovers or feels himself distinctive than he at once becomes unhappy, helpless, timid and confused, because he secretly despises and wants to ignore this element in himself that marks him off from others. The first is

the self-consciousness of Beaconsfield, the second that of Amiel. The one makes a man glory in himself and despise the world: the other makes a man glory in the world and despise himself. If there is to be a choice made between these two, there is no doubt that the first is much the healthier, and makes for strength and efficiency of manhood: the second is nothing but weakness and helpless inefficiency.

Both types of character are, however, exaggerations; and a perfectly balanced mind would avoid them both. People of the first type exaggerate the value of their peculiarities to such an extent as to neglect, though not to obliterate, their more lasting and important qualities; in fact they treat their peculiarities as if they were important qualities. People of the other type exaggerate their insignificance as individuals to such an extent as to make even their lasting and important qualities insignificant and useless.

**8** Wherever we find anyone taking his doctrines or his occupation or his ends "too seriously," we may be sure he is out to establish an abstraction, a one-sided, and to that extent, an erroneous theory or principle. He is trying to concentrate his whole personality upon one purpose, plan or idea: and his taking it "too seriously" is really due to the attempt to concentrate the whole aim of his life into one direction. The attempt carries with it the grim dissatisfaction so characteristic of the "over-serious"; for his whole effort lies in trying to hold at bay all sources of satisfaction but this one, and to deny that anything has value except the one particular line which he has chosen.

**9** Have the courage to be yourself, and a self worthy of your courage.

**10** It is perhaps inevitable that people should try to identify the current estimate of their social importance with the final judgment upon their lives, that they should suppose the significance attached to their lives by their contemporaries is reproduced in exactly the same terms in the doomsday book of judgment. People so easily confound the prominent with the important. But it needs no great insight to see that, in the economy of the earth, valleys are just as important as hills, springs as seas, dust as diamonds.

**11**   The "chief end of man" may perhaps best be described as being yourself and doing as many things as possible merely for the sake of doing them and for no other reason.

**12**   The secret of self-discipline consists in applying the same measure of judgment to one's own thoughts and feelings and actions as we apply to those of other people, without self-indulgence or self-excusing and without self-satisfaction or the brooding morbidity of self-analysis. When we judge another person, we expect the rebuke to be taken and we expect a change of procedure: otherwise we consider him radically dishonest or bad. When we judge ourselves, we should accept the judgment in the same way: otherwise we fall into mere self-sophistication and insincerity of mind.

Much, if not most, self-consciousness is due to misdirected or misapplied self-judgment. Those who are self-conscious are aware of themselves without a clear recognition of the standards to which they mean to conform and by which they mean to judge both themselves and others in daily thought and action. We should be as severe towards ourselves as towards others, no more and no less.

**13**   There is a great difference between saying "live each day as if it were your last" and "live each day as part of eternity." Only in the second case do we avoid the insistent anxiety about to-morrow which is the bane of life.

**14**   People talk much nonsense about the importance of "personality" and "great personalities." What they seem to mean by personality is a combination of resolution, or obstinacy, and forcefulness of character. This may be nothing more than a dominating or domineering self-will. A great personality is one who helps others to believe in themselves, not one who asks or expects others to believe in him; and one who does so, not by imposing or impressing his personality on others, but by believing in himself and his purposes.

A true and reliable leader is not one who desires to lead but one whom others desire to follow.

**15** Personality, on which so much stress is laid nowadays, is a category characteristic of Western civilization. It seems to have little significance in the East: there persons are messengers and agents of a purpose larger than themselves.

**16** The English conception of the gentleman goes no farther than respect for personality. Personality is a social status, and hence involves recognition of differences of social standing. It does not imply social equality in spite of being a common social condition: only persons of the same social status are recognized as socially equal. The attitude of the gentleman in the English sense is that of one who seeks primarily to maintain his own self-respect and his respect for others at the same time. If he can, in so doing, secure the respect of others for himself so much the better; but this is secondary. He does not lose his self-respect if the respect of others is not shown: on the contrary, he regards the other who is wanting in respect to him as "not a gentleman." Since respect is a matter of degree, complete respect from others can only be obtained between persons of the same social standing; there only can respect be mutual and equal, for there only can each understand and appreciate fully the person of the other. Under that condition, self-respect can be supported by the respect of others, and the withholding of respect from others may impair the respect for self.

Where respect for personality goes deeper than social status, where in respecting himself the individual respects human personality as such in himself, and in respecting others is respecting human personality in others, the conception of "gentleman" does not apply. It is transcended. A higher, or at any rate a different, ethical conception comes in. It is replaced by "brotherhood" or the love of human beings. Here equality of personality is fundamental, and the emphasis is not on the first person but on the second. The individual seeks to secure the love of others in manifesting love towards them and to find his love for himself in the love he has for others: the loss of their love for him is a definite loss to himself, and a diminution of his love for himself. Moreover, whereas a "gentleman" manifests his characteristic quality primarily in the sphere of action, the love for others takes place primarily in the sphere of feeling. A "gentleman" does not normally display his feelings at all; he conceals them behind his actions. That is why the "gentleman" is one person to the "world" and another person to his intimates. In the sphere of love this division breaks down; for all whom we love are our intimates.

The attitude of the "gentleman" and the attitude of love to others are, however, not incompatible in the same person; respect for self in respecting others is, or can be, a preliminary stage in establishing the completer relationship of feeling involved in love towards others.

**17** It is because human personality is of higher value than the moral law, that forgiveness of sin (or wrong), which is a breach of the moral law, is justified and indeed both possible and necessary. The claims of the moral law cannot be allowed to be an intolerable burden on the human spirit. Not only was the Sabbath made for man, but every moral law as well.

**18** A good test of the quality and character of a man's personality is to consider what sort of drama he would appropriately find a place in and how he would play his part in it. This affords perhaps the best way of passing judgment on him.

## VII

1   The weakness of the morality of self-sacrifice as ordinarily understood is that it presumes that there are no selves in the world but the selves of others. The truth in the idea of self-sacrifice is devotion to whatsoever duty demands no matter what this duty is and, thereby, the annihilation of the selfish, particular, individual will. Duty to other people, surrender of our selfish impulses for their good, is only a part of it.

2   The limits set to self-sacrifice and self-abnegation are indicated in the two "great commandments": "Thou shalt love God with thy *whole* heart," etc., and "Thou shalt love thy neighbour as thyself." No one is commanded to love mankind or individuals with his *whole soul*; only that which is in and for itself wholly perfect and complete requires that consummate devotion. Hence the impotence of a "Religion of Humanity"; hence also the infinite claims of the imperative of Perfection.

3   How lame and foolish men look when separated from that sphere of activity in which their lives are spent, and to which their attention is primarily devoted! They seem just about as helpless as a musician who has entertained the company and laid aside his instrument and can do nothing more for them. Whence this lack of resource to meet the world at all points? Why cannot men be at home at all times, and for all purposes? Is there to be no activity from within, but only activity as it is exercised on the world about us—no satisfaction with moments of rest and detachment? Is there only one field of activity—space? Are men to be only reservoirs, not at all *springs*?

4   Love demands not only that we should love but that we should eagerly welcome love on the part of others.

**5** It seems doubtful if Love, in its highest and best form, has in itself that stability and security which will preserve it from extravagance and even vagary, and without which the moral and spiritual safety of its votaries may be threatened. It would seem to require experience of habit or wisdom or the skill of life to render it an unquestionable director of conduct. Love of itself is no guarantee for the wisdom of the act to which it gives rise. It would seem to require the gentle guidance and the mellowing strength which come from sorrow.

**6** Altruism is the attempt to work the principle of love from the wrong end, to work it from its consequences instead of from its source, to take its result as a principle instead of recognizing that there is no distinction between its result and its cause. Altruism is only justified because it is a virtue; and a mere instance of virtue is obviously less important than the love of virtue itself. To seek the good of others simply without seeking to realize good as such, good as it really is apart from others because embracing both them and us, good as it is supreme over all and in itself demanding reverence, is entirely to misunderstand the purpose of altruism itself. Moreover, it is forgotten that in its religious reference the love of God stands first, and the love of man second; these do not exclude each other, but one is prior to, and superior to, the other; and for obvious reasons. We do not love God because we love man; this seems simply impossible. We love man because we love God. This seems to have been the old meaning. And the statement "what ye would that men should do to you," etc., does not support altruism; all it means is that in these relations which you actually do, and must, have with men, when you actually have to act towards them in any case, act in such a way as you would have them act towards you were they in your place. But this does not mean that *all* our acts are simply to be acts done to others or for others; nor does it mean that we must only act for the sake of others. It applies solely to a limited sphere of actions.

**7** For the accidental temporary purposes of occasional, fragmentary, trivial intercourse with men, it is necessary—and, in any case, valuable—to be able to deal with and communicate trivial matters. It is this that makes small talk of advantage, and gives it such a place in life. And yet it must be manipulated either with skill and ingenuity or with some seriousness. Lack of interest or attention to it, either in giving or taking, is fatal to its effectiveness. To treat it with indifference—and, still more, to ignore it—is to reduce oneself, or one's neighbours, to silence at once, that "awkward silence" which is so embarrassing and discomposing to any intelligent mind. It is the incompatibility of the minds of men of solitary habits, or men of vaster, deeper interests, with the atmosphere of such "small talk" that makes them such unsociable beings, uncomfortable to themselves and to others in occasional intercourse. The capacity to be trivial with dignity and self-respect is what no man can learn unless by frequent intercourse with people of all classes and opinions. The solitary man feels he either is a fool, or is easily made a fool of by being nonplussed; the serious man is a bore and is bored. Sympathy hardly overcomes the difficulty; for sympathy presupposes an identity of interest which, by the nature of the case, does not exist. And nothing works such fearful havoc with a man's self-possession as an insincere pretence of interest. Sober men are the most useless beings for trivial banter and flippant remarks. An experience or two of his incompetence and futility will either make such a man sheepishly ashamed of himself, or cause him to take to sarcasm in self-defence.

**8** In ordinary conversation, silence is only acceptable, and indeed only possible, between friends. It is the natural instinct of all others to shrink from the "painful pause." Are people naturally afraid of each other? Or is it rather that they are afraid to suggest that each is unnecessary to the other?

**9** The best talks are those where at the end both parties feel that the subject is yet unexhausted, that much remains to be talked about. Hence the sound rule of conversation: never give a subject completely away, keep part of it in reserve. A corollary from this is: change the subject before it gets exhausted. It is because of this essential element in conversation that dogmatic talkers, and pragmatic talkers, make impossible conversationalists —the former because they would say the last word in the most final way on the subject; the latter because they deal only in facts which are to be accepted without further comment.

It is imperative, too, that a man should not give himself away, should not throw himself completely into the talk. Very few talks are worth such exhaustion, and very few people are worth the trouble of attempting it.

**10** All men are brothers on a holiday; it is the serious businesses of life which create distinctions and divisions among men.

**11** Social intercourse is a strange mixture of interest and mutual distrust, frankness and suspicion, self-abandonment and shrinking reserve. Let people be as intimate as they may, there is still the same look of questioning in their eyes, the same unrealized sympathy, the same lack of complete ease, self-effacement and happy confidence in themselves and in one another which is the essential condition of social union and harmony. Experience does not seem to assist people in the matter. None seem able at once and emphatically to estimate the newcomer or the old friend at his general value and then treat him accordingly with perfect confidence. We will instruct, we will enquire, we will advise, we will, in fact, do everything to maintain the breach and the division which it is the sole aim of communication to overcome and destroy. Moreover, the necessity of keeping up somehow the externals of intercourse (which to be true should always be unreserved, i.e. from within) is no doubt the root of all the insincerities, the disappointments, the fatuousness of social inter-communication. For it becomes unspeakably difficult for those who seek the genuine result to carry it out in opposition to the transparent reserve and superficiality of those who persist in maintaining falsehood of attitude; and the latter amongst themselves can do nothing else, and will do nothing else. The result is that the feeble, the mediocre and the bad at heart set the style of social intercourse, while the genuine souls escape altogether from it, or make the compromise of amiability between their own self-respect and their duty to society. The talk of the former continues to be heartbreaking to all concerned; that of the latter takes the form of genial humour and anecdotage. But in either case, not a vestige of direct unreserved communion, not a stroke of immediate penetration of the one into the other.

What a strange farce this makes of the "opportunities of life"! Men who will only appear once on this earth, with this single chance of love or mutual self-revelation, and mutual assistance in the education and development of the spirit, pass from stage to stage and from day to day before one another, like men of business in the markets of the world. It is a painful spectacle to find society a perpetual struggle to maintain an equilibrium of fellowship, simply to avoid the shame of discovering, or of producing, the naked isolation of its members.

**12** Love is not a matter of a day but for ever; for it is our very life, and that is endless.

**13** Nothing enfeebles a man in social life so much as the fostering of what he knows to be a private vice or personal weakness. A secret of this sort destroys that complete confidence and interest in the public good and his share in it, which go to make the devoted and trusted citizen of the world.

**14** The easiest form of demonstrating affection is not the safest, i.e. not the best for ensuring that it will be returned, simply because affection and the deeper emotions touch human beings at the finest and most intimate parts of their spiritual nature; hence the failure, which one sees and feels so often, of the "warm embrace" and of the ordinary physical demonstrations of feeling.

You feel you are being invaded before you are prepared for it, or more completely than you care to be at the time; hence the reluctance, and even repugnance, so often felt in such circumstances, even by friends.

**15** The obvious cure for self-consciousness is consciousness of something else!

**16** The secret, in large measure, of strength in social and public life is to stand unreservedly for some principle or principles which are absolutely necessary to human life, and which endure unshaken in spite of all change. This gives one a hold on others and a hold on oneself; it is a claim we must fulfil, and get fulfilled. When the strong belief in such principles has become an instinctive attitude of mind, and we follow them quite unconsciously, then once for all have we got rid of the uneasy self-consciousness which is due largely to timidity of conviction or to connection with principles which are out of relation with life at its best.

**17** The meaning of society as a realization of self-consciousness in the individual life is brought out in a remarkable way by the kind of appearance a man makes before his fellows in a large or small grouping of them. Some men seem princes in self-confidence and self-sufficiency when you take them or find them alone, or when they are "alone with themselves." But set them up before a group of their fellows, large or small, and suddenly by their stumbling, their shyness, their confusion and irresolution of thought and action, you find them craven cowards and slaves, with no more self-possession than a frightened child or a cringing criminal. The larger social mind with which they are implicitly at one, and seek to be in unison, has suddenly revealed them to themselves, and so to their fellows, as fragmentary and immature and pitiably small in soul and spirit.

It is not great ideas or great intentions or great schemes that give the sense of innocent security in the presence of others, in the larger social life, which such people obviously lack; it is a fully developed sympathy with others, an explicit realization, in feeling and will and thought, of unity with the general life, the full-bodied expansion of oneself in and by the social whole. Without this, great ideas, true ideas—whether of artist, saint or "thinker"—may be a hindrance and a confusion in the presence of others just because they are "great"; they are apt to dominate the mind, or stand in the way of close personal union with other minds. For what the individual who has them is aware of is just that he is not in touch with others but abstracted, separated from them by those abstract general schemes and ideas that he possesses: and from this arises his self-consciousness, his sense of being a distinct self-entity, not at one with what his own fuller nature as a social individuality claims and requires. And till he attains some measure of expansion in the lives and purposes of others, for their sake as well as his own, his weakness and immaturity of spirit will be displayed. That his unity with his fellows is what he needs and seeks is evident in the very fact of the sense of strain and discord, in which his "self-consciousness" and "shyness" consist; for that means that his unity with them is implicit and not brought out; hence the pain and the contradiction he feels—a pain and contradiction he would not have but for the implied constraint of the larger whole upon him.

Of course, there is the other type of mind as well, which is one with its fellows completely and rejoices in the security of this presence with its "larger self," and yet when "alone with itself" or with another, it may be "awkward" and "shy." This is not so common—perhaps indeed rather rare. When it takes the form of being ill at ease with the person or persons with whom one is temporarily or permanently associated, it is explicable by the same principles as above, with the necessary changes.

**18** "Unconventional people" are those who have no conventions of their own and are awkward in handling those accepted by other people: they are people who imitate no one and whom no one cares to imitate: they are so careful of their own peculiarities as to be unintentionally careless of the feelings of others: they act in such a way that independence of others comes to mean a lack of regard for anybody: they think that careless manners are the same as easy manners, and gracelessness the same as superiority.

**19** The man who can sustain a condition of constant self-love is not to be despised, he is to be envied. Most people despise this condition because they cannot sustain it. But the man who cannot sustain self-love should cultivate love towards others: this will lead to the same completeness of life as self-love, and will equally keep him in harmony with himself, just as it keeps a man in harmony with others. Most people are so incomplete in themselves that they must seek union with others to fill up their own incompleteness.

**20** Why should not another person exercise physical influence on the subtle energies of the brain just as much as external matter influences or affects our physical body as a whole, for example in the "force" of gravitation? If the latter is not inconsistent with our "freedom," why should the former be? If we can summon the energies of our body to "resist" gravitation or external bodies generally, why may we not also summon the forces of our subtler nervous energy to resist influence of a subtler kind from other beings without us?

**21** The usual process of overcoming the "self-consciousness" shown by individuals in social intercourse is that of "thinking about something outside themselves," "going out of themselves." This is secured largely by social discipline (ridicule, condemnation, increased social experience, etc.) and is perfectly sound in principle, for it does break down the sense of isolation by linking the mind with other things. But the best, perhaps the only real and permanent, security against the occurrence of such a state of mind at all is an abiding sense on the part of the individual that his whole life, in its distinctiveness from other things as well as in its union with them, rests upon and is supported by an abiding and all pervading Reality from which no separation is really possible at all, for in this Reality the very being that feels isolated has its source and retains its inseparable place in the whole. That such a sense does prevent all "self-consciousness" is seen in the fact that the essentially religious mind never suffers from this disconcerting sense of isolation at all, or suffers from it less than any other and recovers more easily when it does feel it. Social discipline has doubtless immense influence, and social experience still more, in arresting or preventing the development of such feelings. But these influences by themselves are never completely sufficient, for we often find the most experienced men and women of the world showing unmistakable signs of their conscious isolation, especially when in a social *milieu* to which they are unaccustomed and which does not yield to their pressure for recognition.

This kind of self-consciousness is really inseparable from social existence; it is indeed often created by it, and is as familiar as social sympathy. It varies in degrees of intensity, as well as in the length of time during which it is felt: it appears also in many forms and reveals itself in many ways, from the mere want of *rapport* and the discomfort and annoyance this brings, to the disconcerting mental confusion which shows itself in weakness of thought or word or feature or gesture. Very few people escape wholly from it, and probably none have ever failed to experience it at all.

**22**   Not merely is it impossible to give out all our individuality to others with whom we are in social communion—we generally maintain that we ought not to do so even if we can. Thus, much of the best of ourselves we shrink from profaning by letting other people, or even only one other person, share it or see it: we feel we ought to keep a secret that is too precious to divulge: we will not "wear our heart on our sleeve," etc. Again, we cannot allow ourselves to tell our neighbours the whole truth, for example about themselves, as we suppose it to be, for this would in many cases destroy what all morality exists to establish—our unity with our fellow-men: it would thus frustrate the communication of truth itself. It is also familiar that we cannot tell other people the truth about our own evil tendencies. To do this puts us in their power; for evil is inherently weakness, and when they know about our weakness they can very easily take advantage of it.

It follows from all this that social life—and, therefore, morality—does not absorb or exhaust or fulfil the whole nature of individuality. We must keep ourselves detached from, as well as attached to, the society with which we are identified.

**23** When people think of love they tend to suppose that there is only one kind of love, of which all others are but copies or illustrations, and they generally take as their type the love of the human sexes. But there are surely many kinds of love: and the love of the sexes is but one and in itself not necessarily the highest kind of love. The love of a mother for her child is as genuinely love, but is awakened by an entirely different occasion. So of other kinds of love.

**24** The grandeur of free beings lies in their capacity for love, for love is the essential act of true liberty, its highest expression. No higher act of freedom is possible than the renunciation of self, the immolation of self, in which love consists.

**25** Discordance, *gêne*, uneasiness in social intercourse or on social and public occasions is ultimately due to unconscious discrepancy of interests and standards of judgment. People are together and have not enough in common and no sufficient community of standard to carry on together, to go below the surface with confidence in each other. And when any individual is aware that he has no standard of judgment in common with another, he is likely to feel "uncomfortable" in the other's presence and perhaps also the other in his. When one feels not only that he has no common standard of judgment with another but has no confidence in his own standard or has no standard at all to guide him, he is almost sure to be "painfully self-conscious."

**26** I object to anyone calling me "Brother" whom I do not know well.

I object to anyone presuming to know me so well as to call me "Brother."

**27** People look for "sympathy." But there are two kinds of sympathy—that of the appreciative critic which is stimulating and draws the best out of a man, and that of genial good nature which enjoys the feeling of being sympathetic and neither disturbs nor exhilarates the object of its sympathy.

**28** Too much wit and too much knowledge are apt to be a source of envy or jealousy in conversation, and arrest its flow when minds are not equally endowed.

**29** In the religious life, as in the life of the scholar, the artist, the scientist, and even the man of business, it is hardly possible to overestimate the importance of social experience or communal fellowship. This is the only human means of at once checking eccentricity, fostering the interests of the individual in the best to which he aspires, substantiating his purposes, and strengthening his will to achieve. A vision increases in value with the number of individuals who share it; it tends to become dim if dependent on the moods and tenses of the individual spirit. Even great wealth may turn to foolishness and contempt, if regarded as merely private fortune to be spent according to the caprice of the individual. Those artists are the sanest who express the common thought on man and Nature. It is not a matter of either using society or being used by it, but of receiving and giving the best that human life has to offer.

**30**  Intimacy has its risks. It is easier and in most cases better to be acquaintances than friends.

**31**  The art of living together consists in letting others feel that even their mistakes are a source of pleasure.

**32**  It is the fashion nowadays—and is said to be the "message" of some prominent novelists—to think that the incorporation of the sexes is the same as the incarnation of the spirit of love in the world. What a travesty of human nature such a conception is! It makes the life of human love an inevitable tragedy, hopeless and unrelieved. It marks the difference between paganism and Christianity.

**33**  Some people proffer you more affection than they have it in their power to give and sometimes more than you are willing to accept.

**34**  Frankness is the true test of friendship. When friendship breaks under that test, the bonds, we may be sure, were fragile from the first.

**35**  Only a man with a sense of his own destiny can confront with confidence and serenity the scorn, the animosity and still more the open hostility of his fellow-men. Most men's confidence in themselves stands or falls by the good will of others and the unexpressed approval and trust of others; so inseparably are men bound together by social bonds.

## VIII

**1**  The complexity and diversity of trades and businesses in our modern life gives rise to the question how we are to determine which trade, which kind of work, is better or worthier than another? This question arises naturally in the minds of most men, and is found latent in the judgments and opinions of ordinary life. Some come to the conclusion that all trades—and all work—are alike indifferent, as work; the main fact for each man is the spirit he works in; the kind of the work is of no import, the *quality* of the work done by the worker is *the* main determining ground of judgment of the work. Hence, since this quality is a moral quality (namely whether the work in any given case be well or ill done), the conclusion is arrived at that all men as workmen are equal; for the same formal moral standard of judgment is of course used in all cases, namely whether the work be done well or not. This is essentially a levelling principle and is at the root of many or most (perhaps all) democratic movements. All workmen on this view are equal; none is higher than another; the kind of work is of no account. And this principle is often advocated as a consolation to the defeated and to the downtrodden, and as a support to "the dignity of labour" of any kind (labour being on this view simply the means for realizing the moral life of man); it is even at times used to encourage the pride of people engaged in kinds of work which are popularly supposed to be of a specially low order.

It seems, however, to be quite erroneous if it is taken, as it often is, to be a means of determining how one business or work differs from another; for, clearly, it does not in reality differentiate one kind of work from another at all; it determines not the *kinds* of work, it determines only the *quality* of the work, and confounds these two elements by asserting that differences of work are in reality not differences so far as work goes, they are entirely *indifferent*, they are accidents in the problem. In short, it does not differentiate kinds of labour by any principle, it declares that there are no kinds of labour at all—it differentiates only moral qualities of labourers, qualities of labour. It does not determine the social question, it determines only the ethical question. It does not furnish the principle by which society separates itself into economic classes, it determines the principle by which men separate themselves into *moral* classes. Its principle is thus far too wide, and its judgment correspondingly abstract. As a consequence it neglects altogether the essentially organic connection between a workman and his work, and fails to consider the effect of work on the workman. In the end it cannot even be consistent, for a villain who did his work well would be as good as a good citizen who did his duty.

Another principle of division is that work differs by the amount of thought required, the amount of exercise of intellect necessary to carry it through. This seems no less erroneous; for it also neglects the effect of work on workman, and the organic connection between the two. A man may be a genius and at the same time a fool morally or a disgrace socially; one whom men refuse to recognize as high and noble either in himself or in his work.

The truth seems to be this: men differentiate (consciously or unconsciously) one kind of work from another by the extent to which it can absorb and express the whole complex personality of the workman. That work is higher which will allow the fullest play to, and give most room for, the development of the personality of the workman as a whole; that work is lowest which does not do so to any appreciable extent. This is seen to be at the basis of ordinary judgments of the kinds of work men engage in. It is no doubt responsible for the widespread recognition of the fact that men are constitutionally and naturally different from one another and suited for different kinds of work, and probably also for the view, familiar since Aristotle, that the highest work in Society is that of the statesman. Incidentally, it is equally relevant to our more purely moral judgments about work.

**2** It is impossible to justify the existence of a custom or doctrine by regarding the continuation of it simply as a tribute to tradition. It must find its justification in a present necessity; otherwise it is either trivial (i.e. useless, or merely ornamental), or actively pernicious. For obviously a custom must be adequate to the need which it exists to meet. No doubt men inevitably tend to take the form in which an idea is clothed for the legitimate, or even the best, expression of it; but they must and should change any expression which the growth of ideas has shown to be a bad one. Man's life is lived in the present, not in the past; and the dead may well keep their own.

There is a perpetual conflict between the value of a custom and its history, especially at the present time where the historic sense is so keenly developed. Men try to reconcile the two by a compromise, holding that, because a custom has had a value, it must still have one, at any rate because it has been, therefore it should continue to be. Both of those inferences are false. We must be able to justify our beliefs by the present and in the present; for life is actual only in the present.

3   The danger of democracy is the vice of vulgarity. Vulgarity is the frank and confessed denial of the sacredness of personal life, and takes the form of touching and handling familiarly (i.e. as one's own, and so as public property) the inner life of other individuals. To the vulgar man, everything is public and therefore common, including the recesses of private life; and democracy undoubtedly tends to encourage this attitude by its over-emphasis on "equality." Equality taken in an abstract way means simply having nothing and being nothing apart from other minds, and so apart from the common mind. When this is taken, as it usually is, as referring to individuals as persons, as members of a community, then the claim to inspect and expose the workings of the inner life of other people is almost a natural consequence. Nothing is hidden, or admitted to be hidden, or private, because this would be a permanent threat against the accepted equality which is supposed to be the safeguard of unity.

It is remarkable that democracy, which starts from the conception of the rights of the individual, should wind up by denying in its actions that the individual has any specific rights at all. It is also notable that democracy, which rests on the idea of the worth and dignity of the individual man, should contain within itself a mode of acting which denies the existence of anything in the individual of any special worth or dignity at all.

**4** To democracy, individuals are living separate units; to aristocracy, instances of general classes; to despotism, vanishing ciphers.

**5** The distinction between human activity exercised for an end beyond itself, and exercised for itself alone, for its own sake, permeates very large tracts of social life and does so in different ways. Amongst other things, it is the basis of the difference between payment for activity and payment apart from it. Thus, if the end of doing anything lies beyond itself, it logically follows that nobody will do it except for some consideration *of value to himself*; this value does not lie in the work itself, *therefore* it falls outside the work; it does not lie in him, therefore it lies between the two, in the form of *payment*. Payment is thus the medium or mediating link connecting a man who is an end in himself with a work whose end lies not in itself but outside itself. (Hence slaves are not *paid* because, though their work has an end outside itself, they themselves are not ends in themselves; they are *kept*, like horses or cattle; they cannot be paid, for that implies property and property implies freedom.) When, however, the work is done "for its own sake," when its end lies in itself, the individual does not need to be connected with it *externally* by a medium, its "reward" "lies in itself," and so far from money-payment being asked or required, it is looked on as in a way irrelevant, with contempt or indifference, as having nothing to do with the work at all. At the same time, the worker must be maintained; and hence he either does something which has a commercial interest and value only, leaving the other side of his nature *free* to do what is of worth in itself, or else payment is given to him from some fund or source apart from his work (a "fixed" salary), or else he puts what price he likes on his work to keep himself alive (e.g. the "fancy prices" of works of art). From this distinction comes the profound difference between a *business* and a *profession*. These two cannot be compared; in the one we work for external ends and are paid, and indeed must be paid; in the other we work for what is an end in itself and cannot be paid for *the work as such*.

Work for ends beyond the work is the simplest, most rudimentary form of activity because it implies no initiative, no individual choice or genius. Hence *everybody* is *expected* to do such work, in other words, to work for a living. Indeed, anybody can be compelled to work in this way, by circumstance if by nothing else.

On the other hand, work for ends in themselves desirable is the highest kind of work, the culmination of all work. It is left to individual freedom and genius only; no one can be compelled to take up a profession; no one can be compelled to do the best kind of work, to live a self-complete life. Hence all this work is done by free initiative absolutely; the individual makes a complete life of his own and "takes the risk."

Because this is the "highest work" (for it makes man an end in himself), all work aspires towards it; most men want to be "in a profession," "professions are looked up to," and their members "look down on" other kinds of work, can afford to do so because the professional life is "complete in itself." Hence the attempt on the part of so many people to describe their work as a "profession."

Again, because work for its own sake is self-complete, there is a "leisure" about it not found in the other kinds of work, a detachment, a freedom from "sordid care" not found in the other kinds. It must be so, for its ideal is not of the moment but for ever. Hence it tends to take the form, in non-serious minds, of an amusement, a play—in that case it is "amateurish." When it is serious, professed and followed, it is a "noble task" and a "high toil"—in fact not only a profession in the ordinary sense of the word, but a profession of belief in an ideal which must be seriously and wholeheartedly pursued.

**6**  We sometimes look on polygamy as incidental to a certain type of society or a certain type of civilization. That may be true, but it is really due to a certain conception of marriage. If marriage is looked on simply as a manifestation of *sensuous* satisfaction, whether negative or positive, then, since the life of sense is essentially variable and manifold, the ways of obtaining that satisfaction must necessarily be varied and manifold. Its essence consists in change and variety of *sensuous* content. But in the case of marriage this can only be obtained through different organisms, different bodies of different beings. Hence a plurality of wives is the logical consequence of placing marriage on the basis merely of sensuous gratification. It is just the life of mere animal activity become self-conscious; there is a single self, a single unity throughout—viz. the man's life; its content is varied by different women. On the other hand, when marriage is regarded not as the mere satisfaction of sense but as the realization of a permanent spiritual experience, its constitution is different. There is one self to be satisfied in all the complexity of its interests and ideas and feelings, and all these ideas, etc., are referred to a single self which is the one universal throughout all. What is wanted is the unity of one life, and a *felt* unity: one ideal and one reality to be achieved. It is recognized that the mind at its highest only rests in *one* God, a Father Spirit who fills all and satisfies all; and in just the same way only one finite spirit is held to be necessary and sufficient to supply all the needs of union on the part of finite individuality. In fact this union with another finite spirit seems to be considered as the ectype of our union with the Infinite Spirit, and to provide the obvious formula for its interpretation; "God is love" means love of spirit as spirit.

Monogamous marriage thus rests on the spiritual conception of marriage and has its basis in the singleness of the ideal and unity of the life of spirit.

This is the dominant conception of marriage in "highly civilized" communities where man's spirit has free development as spirit.

We come to regard the cases of polygamy that do occur in such states of civilization as even criminal. They do occur in various forms because there are individuals in highly civilized communities who take a purely sensuous view of the relationship; and possibly more people would show this attitude practically "if they dared."

**7** There seems, looking at actual experience, a good deal of truth in Plato's abstract *a priori* reasoning regarding the division of functions in the State. It seems indeed to extend necessarily to *all* phases of life: even, as Plato suggested, to family life. Thus the higher refinement of the best citizens seems inconsistent with the perpetuation of species but admirably adapted to government and the cultivation of the arts of life. It would seem as if those who gained or attained the higher levels of realization of human ends reached such a completeness of spiritual existence that they had no need of the earthly satisfactions provided by the manifold life of a complex family whole. It would seem as if the manifold variety of life in a large family circle were a kind of compensation for the absence of free spiritual life and insight such as are possessed by the higher spirits of society; as if the want of extent or greatness of intelligence in ordinary people were made up to them by being spread out or distributed over a number of individuals! (Much as in the old view children were born for the sake of their parents, to enrich them even materially, a kind of interest given by God for the capital of affection possessed by the parents!)

After all, what human life aims at is self-completeness and self-sufficiency; and if this is gained, or not gained, by one way, it is sought by another. Hence, if people of high spiritual activity and equipment do not possess or do not have the desire for increase, it is largely because they really do not need it for their fulfilment of life. "Nature" seems to agree with this; and Plato says not merely that they *do* not need it, but that they should not need it. And perhaps he is right.

**8**  The "voice of the people" is, no doubt, in a sense the "voice of God": but we must distinguish between the voice of the people and the roar of the multitude.

**9**  It is sometimes said that there is not much to choose between marriages arranged by third parties (parents and guardians) and marriages brought about primarily and solely by the mutual choice of the individuals directly concerned. From the point of view of the State and the maintenance of species, this remark is perhaps true; and even from the point of view of consequences, it is largely true: people are unhappy and happy in both kinds of marriage. But the significance of the relationship from the point of view of individuality is vastly different in the two cases; and this comes out in a curious way in crucial circumstances. In the first kind of marriage, a woman would not much hesitate to leave her husband for another man whom she loves; at any rate, she sees little wrong in it and longs to do it even if she does not actually take the step: the call of individual love seems the call of the higher destiny. But in the second kind, the right-minded woman would not answer to the call of another man's love even though she "felt the attraction"; for to do so would be an admission that her original choice was a wrong one: and she knows that the choice was bound up with her whole individual life, and thus connected with her own destiny in this world. The last thing a reasonable person will admit is that she (or he) could have been mistaken on an issue of the profoundest and most vital importance; hence the sense that her primary love was her destiny, her fate, comes to her support in the day of temptation, and she submits to her destiny and regards any regret or loss or pain, which may arise from setting this other love aside, as part of her destiny too. She will rather believe that she was mistaken in the second case than suppose that destiny speaks twice and speaks differently the second time. She will regard the new suggestion as a "temptation" to be resisted, not a choice to be made: and will be reconciled to her fate in such a way as to bring peace even through pain. So it is that normally when the institution of marriage is left to the free play of individual choice and feeling, there is less chance of it being invaded and destroyed by the later history of the individuals concerned than there is when individual choice and feeling were suppressed or ignored at the start. And at the same time the value to the individual of the institution as a social factor vastly increases.

This is a good illustration of how the free development of individual life tends to the stability and the elevation of social life.

**10**  People speak of peace as if somehow it rendered war unnecessary and unthinkable. But if peace is such a supreme benefit, it must be kept and protected against its enemies. Arms and armies are thus the indispensable condition and guarantee of peace. Peace is not self-protective; and if unprotected, it is at the mercy of the destroyer. No virtue is secure if it relies merely on its own intrinsic merit; it needs other virtues for its support. Every virtue is a limitation, and limitation undefended is weakness. The weakness of peace alone is its powerlessness to defend itself, and this weakness unrelieved is a source of danger to peace itself. If, recognizing this, we fail to take measures on behalf of peace, we encourage its enemies to come on; and so, by courting the danger which threatens it, we become its enemies ourselves.

**11**  Civilization works largely on the assumption that those who speak most and speak best will have most recognition in the final summing up of humanity. This seems little more than the apotheosis of self-advertisement.

**12**  Democracy means morality with bad manners. Aristocracy has often meant immorality with good manners.

**13**  Much is said nowadays for and against the expropriation of individual wealth of the rich. It is not a legal question. It is at bottom a moral question. Expropriation, communism, socialism, etc., are ways in which many men, doubtless erroneously in method, are seeking to emphasize the moral necessity for individuals to own and use property. Nothing, it is felt, gives moral stability and the sense of personality so much as the possession and transmission of property however small. In principle, this is sound.

**14** It is often difficult to understand the intense passion which animates men for such forms of association as a nation state or a church or freemasonry. They seem to be held in greater esteem than the natural association of the family. This is probably because they are more the result of deliberate and free untrammelled choice on the part of the individuals comprising them: they are freely created and freely accepted in a way that natural associations are not. Men always cherish most highly what springs from or expresses their own sense of liberty. May it not be that there are degrees of naturalness in human association; or from another point of view degrees of freedom in the forms of association, and that the higher the sense of freedom in a social grouping, the more it seems to express and fulfil the ideal aims of man and to enable him to feel that he belongs to it. On this view it is quite intelligible that man should be more passionately devoted to a "church" than to any other form of human association based on instinctive or natural wants; or to an ideal form of association like a "Kingdom of God" than to any form of human association whatsoever.

It may be that secular forms of association are the training-ground for purely spiritual forms of fellowship.

**15** People in safe places are aghast at the internationalism of the "labour movement." That is because they will only see one thing at a time. They seem to think nothing at all about the internationalism of science, or even the internationalism of religion, at least of a religion like Western Christianity. Who has taught labour to internationalize its labour policy? The scientific internationals. According to these gentlemen, anything that savours of nationalism and patriotism is little better than either crime or folly: crime if they divide men asunder, folly if they are supposed to preserve anything worth having. For evidently if science is the greatest achievement of man's life, and if science is international, the cultivation of anything national must be the cultivation of what is not worth keeping in the long run.

What seems so strange at the present time is that this internationalism should have pervaded thought—economic, political, scientific—precisely after a war which was supposed to have been fought for the "rights of nationality," and even for the rights of small nations.

**16** The reason why poets and philosophers can never be expected to govern their fellow-men is that they cannot form a coherent society amongst themselves. They all depend upon their individual inspiration and are guided by that alone. And when the pentecostal spirit of inspiration seizes man, it produces not unanimity of utterance but a babel of tongues: they all speak the wonderful works of God doubtless; but they speak of them in different languages and have nothing else in common.

This is the salvation of the spirit of truth amongst mankind. Nothing could be worse for man than that inspired people should all agree with one another and unanimously lay down the law for the uninspired and for future generations of possible inspired persons. Inspiration is the vitality and spontaneity of the human mind at its best and should not be controlled, as in fact it cannot be controlled.

Social institutions on the other hand require a certain amount of dogmatic fixity in opinion and belief and method. That is their strength and their weakness, their privilege and their limitation. The more important the institution, the greater the need for fixity and order of conviction and procedure. This is illustrated by the State and the Church: the first in its establishment and maintenance of rights, the second in its establishment and defence of beliefs, holding alike for all within its bounds.

But no institution, not even the greatest, can entirely escape the incursions, however occasional, of inspiration amongst its members: for dogmatism is but a part of man's requirements, and there is no absolute separation of dogmatism and inspiration in the mind of man. When inspiration, with its individual initiative, seizes a member of a compact social institution the result is sure to be a tragedy for the individual in the first instance. He is expelled, despised, imprisoned or crucified. But what is a tragedy for the individual will in course of time, if his inspiration is sound, become a "divine comedy" for the institution: though it may have expelled him as a scapegoat, it will be imbued with a higher insight into the truth as a result of his teaching, and will welcome him back, at least in memory, as a lost sheep which has at last been found.

**17** The State cannot supply the highest things nor can it guarantee them. Beauty, religion, science, conscience—these are beyond the power of the State to provide or produce: it can only provide conditions which make them possible and give them free play. They derive their vitality and importance from the inner and higher life of the mind when freely exercising its powers to reach its ideal ends. They create and supply goods of the highest kind and of the utmost concern for humanity. Those who lay primary emphasis on the importance of the State and its operations for human welfare, tend to regard everything it cannot control or supply as inferior and relatively unimportant. What cannot fall within the recognition of the State becomes a matter of indifference: what the State cannot regulate is not worth regulating and is, therefore, a matter of choice or chance of the individual. Such a view impoverishes human life and in the long run lowers humanity.

And as there are goods which the State cannot provide by positive action, so there are evils which it cannot touch by punishment, e.g. jealousy, envy, lies of the soul, evil desires and intentions. The fact that the State cannot touch them does not, however, show that they are of little account, but rather that they are of supreme account. From the highest point of view a feeling of hatred may be much worse than any crimes which are committed in action.

**18** In the long run the justification for preserving as completely as possible the records of human history is that they enable us to make life intelligible in the present. The search for the continuity of man's life with his own past is just as much an intellectual need as to try to establish his continuity with nature.

**19** The establishment of corporate self-governing institutions and societies within the community of the State is the surest guarantee of freedom. And the more of them there are in a community the better. For they keep each other in check, in such a way that none of them can occupy a dominating position; and at the same time they can and will combine against a common oppression.

Valuable as they are in the interests of freedom, they have one disadvantage or defect which may increase as they get older: they tend to cherish their purposes as privileges of their own members, instead of, or at the cost of, recognizing their responsibilities to the community as a whole; they pile up their rights as capital and lose interest in their duties; they enjoy the exclusiveness of their own societies and ignore the inclusiveness of the larger society within which they subsist; they may even create mannerisms peculiar to themselves which prevent others from intimate contact with them. When these peculiarities become very prominent, the institution is in need of "reformation" from within or from without; and the time comes when the judgment of the world is brought to bear on its corporate life.

These dangers naturally vary from age to age. Since the conduct of an institution depends on the members who carry it on at a given time, they will be chiefly felt at times when people are narrowly conservative and fail to adapt their institutions to new situations and to the larger demands of the community.

The history of a great institution like the Christian Church has illustrated the defects of institutional life at different epochs of its development. The older universities in this country have revealed, and perhaps still reveal, the same kind of disadvantages inherent in all institutions. The attitude of the older universities towards reform in the middle of the last century was typical of old institutions strong enough to be financially independent and important enough to be indispensable in spite of their defects.

**20** There was a sound human instinct behind the distrust of machinery when it first gained a footing in industrial production. It was the instinct of self-preservation; and at its core was the need to preserve mankind from the forces of Nature. For though machines are usually invented as a way of controlling Nature, they are not so unnatural as they look: in fact they are only the forces of Nature consciously directed. They never cease to be Nature's forces, even when used by man for his ends.

Nature, if not hostile to man, is at least independent of him and regardless of him. It is possible, therefore, that the more Nature is mechanized for man's service, the more power will Nature have over the welfare of man. Machines may produce more than man needs and make men as individuals unnecessary. It is as if Nature said, "You want to utilize my resources to the utmost? Here I give you all you seek, which is all I have, and it is more than you want." What can it profit man to gain all that Nature gives or can give? He can only gain it at the expense of his own life. Such is the irony and tragedy at the heart of Nature. And we seem to be in sight of this at the present time in our history.

**21** There seems a dramatic necessity in the politically subordinate and dependent position characteristic of the Jewish community everywhere in the world. The "law" under which and by which they live is incompatible with the very nature of a political

State and of political government. A State is an organization of human beings, which is self-contained and self-regulated, recognizing no law above that which is devised by itself and adapting this self-devised law to meet changing conditions and varying earthly circumstances. Government is the art of framing, modifying and altering laws to meet variable historical situations. The Jewish "law" is absolute from the first, is divinely prescribed and, therefore, does not and cannot change: it does not arise out of circumstances, it rather makes circumstances conform to itself: it does not grow and it cannot be abrogated: and those who obey it reckon themselves to be under the leadership and protection of a non-earthly authority—the God whom the Jews worship, and who is above all political conditions.

A political society could be said to "discover" its laws, and its government to put them into language. But the Jewish society has laws which were given once and for all, and are handed down as a tradition: they are ready made and not discovered. A people which takes up this attitude towards its laws obviously cannot form a political community or appreciate the essential character of political government in the world.

The only kind of community which a people of this kind can form is a religious community resting on two unchanging facts—those of race and religion. This is exactly what has happened throughout Jewish history since the dispersion. But since the Jews cannot of themselves form a political society, and yet must exist as a community, their only possible course is to place themselves within and under an alien political society where State conditions and political government are found. Thereby they become at once dependent, subordinate and in a sense parasitic. It does not matter under what government or in what State they live, as long as they are allowed (and of course they can only be allowed as a favour) to carry on their own community life. Hence they are equally willing to live, and equally happy, under any political State when they are given their freedom of ritual and practice. They are always and necessarily "aliens" ethically, even though for legal purposes naturalized. They never become really incorporated: they are merely attached to and associated with the other citizens and the State. In a sense, they are always citizens on sufferance; and they tend to alienate sympathy, because they do not need anything more than bare protection. They are strangers and pilgrims, as were all their fathers. But they are content to be so, and do not need pity because they are satisfied to be members of their own religious community. Their subordinate position in the State is inevitable, not incidental: and this is responsible for many of their characteristic qualities.

It is a mistake to suppose that the Jews are subordinate simply because they have never practised the arts of government or formed a State. The essential point is that they are incapable of forming a State and incapable of exercising the arts of government: they would produce social chaos for themselves if they tried to do so. For the same reason, they cannot appreciate the necessity for power behind the law of a community, the exercise of which in certain circumstances may lead to and necessitate war. Hence it is that they are essentially pacific, quietist; and this may make many of them even pacifist. They rarely in everyday experience use force, for as a result of their religion they do not understand the need for force: Jehovah is their buckler and defender. They rely on suasion, persuasion and the cunning of reason and mental strategy to gain their ends.

The only kind of government which the Jews ever attempted was a theocracy, the failure of which was inevitable from the start.

The nomadic character of the Jew, his exclusive interest in business of a certain kind, his cultivation of certain of the arts and sciences, his occupation with certain professions and not others—all these confirm and illustrate the fundamental quality of his mind just described.

**22** The weakest defence of any institution is to say that it was founded long ago.

**23** The British aristocracy care for nothing so much as the stability and security of family life. All else, politics, religion, art, is a means to that end. And there is much to be said for this view.

**24** The average Englishman does not really believe that a fundamental change of character is possible for any man. He believes in men changing their opinions and improving their habits, but nothing more. Transformation or individuality in a life-time, by spiritual or any other means, he regards with scepticism or at least suspicion. He believes in the methods of the stock-breeder to effect radical change, and leaves it to Nature and three generations to form a gentleman. The mixture of this naturalistic fatalism with official Christianity gives the impression of hypocrisy to the onlooker, and produces practical insincerity in the average mind.

**25** A common danger will create a democracy amongst human beings quite as much as common aspirations.

**26** English civilization will last as long as the coalfields, but not longer: it is centred round the hearth and the home and these are inseparably associated with an open fire.

**27** In some ways health, or at least a healthy race, might be preserved better in a community without the services of a medical profession. The unfit and unhealthy would simply be eliminated by Nature's processes. Would this in the long run elevate or degrade mankind?

**28** There is an exhilaration in a just war, like nothing else. It gives men an opportunity to act like devils in the name of God: and in some form or other that is a state of mind which many enjoy.

**29**  There are those who seem to suppose that right should and will justify itself, as if so to say it had some supernatural force within it to control men's wills and minds. This has been the folly of the so-called peaceful nations after a war. The result is they are at the mercy of all those who challenge existing rights by the sword. If right is to prevail it cannot be separated from might, any more than truth can prevail unless it is proclaimed and defended.

If might without right is brutal, right without might is just futile. Both are folly, and it is difficult to say which is the more foolish and dangerous.

**30**  Men often criticize modern warfare on the ground that the opposing armies now fight at a distance from each other, and do not meet face to face, man against man from the first encounter, as in the "old days." Fighting in earlier wars, it is said, was a real test of courage of the individual soldier: now it is a test of armaments and not men. This criticism overlooks the brutal savagery of individual encounters between the combatants which was characteristic of pre-mechanized warfare: hate and a murderous instinct were almost essential in the soldier of those days. Mechanized warfare has the great advantage and merit of being impersonal, almost as impersonal as science or machinery itself. There is no call, or less call, for violent hate: success depends on cool skill and scientific precision in the use of weapons which destroy at a distance. This is surely less brutalizing and inhuman.

## IX

**1**  Noise in the world there is in plenty, but of music very little; yet both are produced by the same physical agencies, the difference is in the amount of intellect in each, in the arrangement of such agencies.

**2** If there is any element in our nature beyond argument and instruction, and having its sole value in its pure spontaneity, it is humour. And the appreciation of it is more spontaneous than the framing of it. Yet if it could be taught, what an acquisition to a college curriculum!

**3** The final and supreme destiny of the scholar is to unite wisdom with kindness, knowledge with love, care for truth with love of man—and without reverence that is not possible.

**4** Nothing is so valuable and welcome and, at the same time, so dangerous as "new" ideas. New ideas, just because new, are so apt to remain merely ideas. They seek to act as if they had the warm life of truth within them; but it is fever heat not blood heat which warms them. Too often they are the mere fairy-tales of a mind which would fain regard them as history or fact, but is rational enough to know that they are incapable of standing the ordeal of contact with reality.

**5** Bookish men and narrow specialists are like safety matches—they scratch only on their own box.

**6** Nature is not art, and art alone gives us what is beautiful. When we say Nature is beautiful, we mean detached and unified portions of Nature, i.e. Nature subjected to artistic construction. Nature as it stands is too confused, is an indefinite wealth of form and arrangement. Beauty must be limited and determinate, both in form and content.

**7** A "cultured" person is just a person with a sense of values. He may not have a great deal of knowledge; he will try to have this, but he will always feel strong in the certainty of things worth knowing, and will not easily be misled by any ready-made theories.

**8**   Men have often sought to express the essential peculiarity of human beings as distinct from other animals. Perhaps the most characteristic and indisputable peculiarity of man is that he is an actor, that he can wear a mask of personality and put himself in the position of another individual of his own kind. No other animal seems capable of this. No other animal can detach itself from its own character and put on the character of another of its species. Man can. This is an extraordinary feat, and no man can do it except for a limited period of time without threatening the destruction of his own personality.

(Hence it is that actors who act the same character day after day for a very long period "lose their reason," lose the sense of their own personality altogether.)

**9**   The contempt for ceremony has often been looked upon as a sign of virile honesty, of the sense of "reality" against "shows." It is no doubt important to be "virile" to this extent. But greater "virility" and "honesty" are seen in the man who knows how to use ceremony as a means of expression and a form of intercourse between men.

Just as there are men who put all the stress of the moral life on the elementary virtues, and ignore all the others which give richness and adornment to moral behaviour, so there are men who "see nothing in" (i.e. regard as nothing) the ceremonial and decorous pageantry of high institutions. For them the "simple reality" is enough. And it *is* enough for them; but this merely proves their natures to be rudimentary and elementary, and not that the ceremonial is valueless or insignificant. These people, in their crude sense of reality, are all unintentionally quite superficial in their view of things. The surface seems to them to be "merely surface"—"show"; they *can* see no connection between the foundations and the cupola, the invisible and the visible, the reality and the expression. The ceremony is all on the outside, and there is no inside to it. In this respect, they have precisely the same kind of intelligence as those who, seeing *only* the surface, take the surface to be everything, who are so taken with the mere ceremony that the ceremony is all in all to them—the formalists, the ceremonialists. So the man with the crude sense of reality, who disregards the necessity for outward expression, and the man with no sense for the underlying reality at all, but only for the surface, have precisely the same onesidedness of intelligence; the difference is merely that they see different sides, neither sees the whole.

The fuller mind and the richer nature see and feel the value of both, of the basis as well as the surface, the reality as well as the appearance, the bare walls as well as the ornate architectural perfection of the structure, the truth as well as the expression. The fuller mind is found in the artist, the dramatist, the poet.

**10** The criteria of a cultivated mind are a capacity for the free manipulation of one's own mental resources, and a capacity for readily understanding the mental outlook of another mind.

**11** It is the habit of almost all people who make much of elementary moral principles to regard the artistic aspect of human activity as irrelevant or as an external ornament of life. Very few indeed realize the truth that art is just the perfection of human activity, and that no human activity can rightly dispense with the finish which art alone can give. In a true sense one may say that to ignore the artistic element is to be less than human. There is an art in speech, in gait and in bodily action; there is an art in moral conduct, in the graces of fellowship with our kind and in the subtle control of the nuances of social communion; there is an art in controlling and guiding all emotion—the fine sarcasm which concentrates effectually the passion of hate, the terrifying irony that makes antipathy, dislike and irritation something to be feared, the well-turned retort which proves the excellent weapon of defence against the enemy; there is an art in religious life, the worship which achieves the beauty of holiness, the imperturbable peace which greets the trivial obstacles of life with genial humour, the joy of spirit which feels the life of God in the flowers of the field as well as in the stars in heaven. Art is indeed the basis of all that is best in the world.

**12** There is essentially a great healing power in art; perhaps that is its greatest value for human life—as the earthly reconciler of man to his destiny in a complex and competitive world. In the light of drama, tragedy or comedy, the moral discords of humanity are seen in a pattern and a plan of action. Forgiveness of wrong is then made unnecessary, and the wrong loses its sting: or forgiveness may itself be the means of linking the elements which form the drama. So of pain and even death; the dramatic outlook, taking the larger view, sees life larger and sees it whole, and this brings the peace of reconcilement and submissive acceptance. The "spirits of beauty and of grace" check the "stern judgment" on individual action and bring joy in which "thoughts" are no longer with "better thoughts at strife."

**13** It will make all the difference in the world to a nation whether its highest institutions of learning are conceived to be factories for producing and warehousing information or are regarded as mansions where the human mind can expand in the free atmosphere of truth and enjoy unrestrained fellowship with kindred spirits.

**14** For success in public life it is necessary for a man to have some of the qualities of an actor. He must be able to put himself at the point of view of the public as if it were his own interest for the time being and embodied his own conviction—in a word, as if he personified the public. That is acting: no man can without vanity or exaggeration regard the public welfare as his own intimate good, the public requirements as his own necessity, the course of public life as the direction of his own destiny. But the acting is of a peculiar kind: on the stage a man acts to interest the public, on the platform a man acts in the interest of the public: in the one case the audience consists of spectators, in the other of agents, potential or actual. If, therefore, the actor on the stage shows too great individual enthusiasm and not enough detachment, he is not a good actor: if the actor on the platform betrays indifference or detachment, he will not create confidence and so will fail. The man who can combine the right amount of enthusiasm for the public point of view with the controlled detachment from the particular topic which enables him to handle it freely and independently—that is the kind of acting the public wants in its leaders, and that is the kind which makes a successful leader.

**15** Probably the time may come in the history of Western civilization when men and women will see what a very limited amount of good is to be had from book-learning and the so-called education of the intellect. At present the whole trend of prejudice in national life is in the direction of cultivation by means of books, leisure to read books, money to buy books, etc.; and naturally the publishing businesses, which live by book-readers, and scholastic institutions, which train the youthful mind, support the prejudice with all their strength and with all the enthusiasm which self-interest can supply. But this prejudice may pass and give place to another—the prejudice in favour of educating the sentiments and emotions, and training the senses to accurate manipulation of the objects of Nature—to handicraftsmanship of all kinds. Men may come to see that working with hand and brain for the production of complex and intricate objects of artistic interest and social usefulness will do more for social life and for the satisfaction of the individual than the study of complicated schemes of scientific ideas or the perusal of imaginative literature. They may come, in short, to restore the lost aptitudes for life without literature which existed before the invention of printing.

**16** It seems ironical to offer education as a solace to poverty. It is like trying to make rags comfortable by sprinkling them with rose water.

**17**  All embodiments of tradition are as precious as the gifts of the dead, and if they have to be destroyed after reflection, should be buried with regret. Wanton destruction of them, especially of the best of them, is treachery to humanity. Hence our feelings in confronting the reckless ruin of great buildings. It is as if humanity had committed suicide.

**18**  There was a profound antithesis between the life of the scholars and priests of the Middle Ages, and the secular life of that epoch: the former high, transcendental, refined; the latter crude, barbaric, mundane, uncouth.

That contrast was due to the former having imported the ideas and achievements of nations which had reached a superb level of civilization and then been overthrown—Rome, Greece and the East. The thought and literature of these past nations were not indigenous to the West and consequently stood out in relief against the primitive life of the Western peoples; they belonged to a higher level of civilization and consequently condemned the barbarism around; they were cultivated by the select few who possessed and cherished them in the interests of a higher humanity and consequently separated off the scholar's life and the life of the priesthood from the secular life of the time.

It was a peculiar instance of the perennial contrast between the "spirit" and the "world."

**19**  A good deal of scholarship seems to consist in clever men picking holes in the work of men of genius.

**20**  Education in a sense is superimposed upon life. It lifts man out of the natural world and places him in touch with the spiritual world. Hence the effect of discontinuity often seen in the case of educated men between their everyday world and the world of ideas in which they feel at home; an effect which is unfortunate and which wisdom alone can get rid of. The same sort of effect also appears when educated people try to regard themselves as a class apart, creating a kind of mental aristocracy of their own.

**21** There is one important function fulfilled by novels and imaginative literature of similar kinds; they do help, as hardly any other literature can, to liberate the mind from the burthensome pressure of the day's work: they detach the mind completely from the day's details; they give the mind both release and relief from a world which can be, and for most busy people is, too much with us; they restore the mind to itself, and that is always a refreshment and a renewal of life.

**22** The longer one lives the more one sees the importance of form in human affairs: form in speech, form in thought, form in action, form in feeling. The material world of the senses seems merely the basis or the medium for the display of forms which are grasped by the mind—a very old doctrine.

**23** It is bad art to put everything down. Art should suggest, touch the imagination, not strike it dumb, hint and not explain, stimulate and not satiate. The spirit of beauty cannot be confined within the medium of expression; it breaks through and uses the medium as a means of permanent and repeated enlightenment.

If our life be a work of art there should be no need for a demonstration of immortality. It would be enough if there is a hint of a suggestion, if the end of the curtain be raised without the curtain being drawn aside. There are such hints and suggestions; and they serve to keep alive man's interest in an inexhaustible future.

**24** Some people would have us believe that work is the basis of civilization. It is no paradox to say that leisure is the basis of civilization. Liberation from the constraining necessities of nature can alone give free opportunity for the development of the higher interests of the human spirit; and in the full expression of the spiritual life lies the end and achievement of civilization. Leisure is only possible when such liberation has been attained, and with the acquisition of leisure the higher life can begin.

**25**  The best that can be taught is the proper way to learn. Nothing else matters so much, and nothing is so lasting in its effects.

**26**  It is one of the paradoxes of education that while its aim is to enable people to understand one another better by understanding the world about them, the more an individual knows the fewer are the individuals with whom he can communicate intelligently and fully.

**27**  Increased refinement makes a greater demand on the resourcefulness of the mind. Otherwise it becomes a limitation and not an expansion of the spirit. Hence it is that refined people are often so dull, reserved and uncommunicative.

**28**  Education is an attempt to help people to live in better company than most of them are fit for. That is why so much education has so little effect, and why it seems to be thrown aside after the scholastic period is over.

**29**  The higher education has not so far brought people together. It has separated them by new class distinctions.

**30**  A scholar is very often one who has been curious for so long about so much that he has himself become a curiosity.

**31**  It is doubtful whether half the people who go to school and college are worth educating. But it is necessary to give them all a chance in order to find out which half are worth the trouble.

**32**  Education is often looked on as a way of gaining the upper hand by knowledge instead of by wealth. The motive is bad in both cases.

**33**  There is folly and cant in the academic attitude, as well as in the aristocratic attitude, of condescension towards and contempt for riches and money-making. It is the past acquisition of wealth, and the inheritance of riches, which have made possible the leisure and freedom from secular cares which are characteristic of the academic life and of the privileged position of the aristocracy.

**34** It is a mistake to speak of the madness of Hamlet. His change from his ordinary frame of mind after seeing the ghost of his father was the normal change which might be expected in any man who discovers by experience that the "dead" are in another world, active and real, and in communication with this world. The vivid realization of this discovery alters a man's attitude to the present world: the everyday world comes to seem rather trivial in many respects, an appearance in all respects, a show revealed to the senses, but insubstantial because subject to mutability and extinction. A man who feels this rises above the present world, treats it as a mere means, a jest (sad or cheerful), feels exalted above its incidents and reluctant to be tied to its necessities (like love, friendship, laws, etc.)—and this of itself requires some adjustment and at first produces a shock. Hamlet's behaviour confirms all this.

Hamlet's tragedy therefore lay in his inability to adopt with absolute confidence the assurance his father gave him and, consequently, to reconcile his attitude to the other world with his attitude to everyday life. He was torn between the two, the two loyalties, and he set himself by one method and another to test the truth of his father's statement, i.e. he questioned the reality of the ghost's existence. This cleavage in his mind was his ruin, when it should have been his inspiration, as it would have been had he once for all accepted his father's appearance as authentic and acted accordingly. The wonder is he did *not* go mad, instead of merely blundering into the murder of his uncle and bringing about his own destruction.

**35** The ecstasy of an experience, mental or physical, is necessarily beyond expression in speech, and can never be reproduced in speech. It is the concentrated absorption of the whole resources of the individual into a short interval of experience: it cannot be sustained for long at a time without exhaustion. Speech, on the other hand, since words have some degree of universality, can give permanence to the content of experience, but at the cost of being able to express only what is general. No description can reproduce the concentrated experience of a moment; nor can it revive or recreate such an experience, since the experience depends on the convergence of factors from different sources and their harmonious co-operation. Ecstasy is thus not below speech but above it, and reveals the limitation of speech as a medium of expression of experience. This comes out clearly in the higher experiences of music and religion, as well as in human affection.

**36** The influence of a refined and finished classical education—in the widest and best sense of the term, an education in the appreciation of classical models of excellence—is of incalculable importance to the mind. It supplies permanent standards to which the individual comes instinctively to conform his thought and action, and by which he can judge the thought and conduct of others without fear of challenge, for these standards are the creation and expression of human life at its best.

**37** Civilization should mean liberation of personality. But in spite of all achievements, civilized peoples are not yet free, and do not seem to know how to become so. They seem even half afraid of freedom.

# III
# THE WORLD AND OUR KNOWLEDGE OF IT

### I

**1** All philosophy must be a "transcendental deduction" in some form or other. We cannot philosophize to show that philosophy is impossible; we cannot have a theory of knowledge which will tell us there is no knowledge; we cannot have a science of phenomena which will show us there are no phenomena, and so no science.

**2** May we not accept it as a principle that any system which not only does not account for or justify our present beliefs and ideals and wants and instincts, but shows them to be futile or meaningless is assuredly false or wrong? Further, since reality must satisfy us (unless indeed the world is essentially irrational), may we not be at liberty to reject any theory, the adoption of which would not lead us higher than at present we are or can be by the system we do hold?

**3** Singular that, while Kant was writing his *Critique of Pure Reason*, a savage was eating his fellow on an island in the Pacific—and both extremes in one world!

**4** Unquestionably there is mystery in the world, but there need not, and should not, be any mystery in our statements regarding what we take to be the meaning of certain facts in it; "mystery" in this respect implies both obscurity of expression and confusion of thought. And this applies to all doctrines, for they are simply expressions of our interpretations of the meaning of certain facts.

5   To most people philosophy appears at first as a sympathetic, kindly, easy companion, with whom it is possible to have just what acquaintance they please and when they please, and at last it presents itself as a commander whose behests are recognized as both necessary and intolerable.

6   It seems doubtful at times if a deepening of our knowledge of the world would be entirely tolerable. If everything in heaven and earth were full of meaning to the human intellect—and if the intellect were always alive to the meaning of the world—the conscious presence of inexhaustible interest, the very richness of all-pervading knowledge, the continuous intensity of all-suffusing light, would oppress the intellect and involve it in unending restless activity. What, then, in such a case, becomes of the aim of science, which is nothing less than omniscience? What becomes of the satisfactions of the truth? It would be a misfortune if men became omniscient; they would cease to wonder, and that would be disastrous.

7   It is sometimes said that a philosophy is the last stage in the experience of an epoch—the reflection on an epoch which can only be reflected on if it has come to an end—and consequently (as Hegel supposed) a kind of palinode or epitaph. But is there any more truth in this than there would be in saying that poetry as the expression in elegant form of ripe emotion, or religion when explicit in the expression of a deepened experience, are the last stages of the experience in question, that those arise simply on the ruins of experience and are the symbols of its decay? Does it follow that an experience has come to an end simply because we are now able to say precisely and fully what that experience is? We

should expect that the statement of the experience would simply strengthen and enlarge the experience and make its continuance more possible, indeed deeper, in future. Hegel's view suggests how philosophy develops, how each philosophy, therefore, is finite and the history of philosophy a process. But is a philosophy something with no value or significance for future generations?

**8** It can be said in philosophy, as is said in religious experience, that, after we have done all in our power to understand and spell the truth, "we are unprofitable servants." The riches of truth can only be appreciated by those who have toiled terribly to acquire them; and yet the attainments shown in acquiring them seem so insignificant and fragmentary that the natural and inevitable reflection is "inadequate," "unworthy," "poor," even "contemptible"! This line of reflection should prove quite sufficient to arrest the absurd notion that progress and courageous persistence in the pursuit and acquisition of all knowledge would lead either to intellectual conceit of any kind, or to some manifestation of the wrath of the gods against those who have come to know so much of truth, and have developed so great a pride in their knowledge, as to feel themselves to be "like unto gods." The knowledge of the truth only leads to readier willingness to receive it; this very attitude of willingness is an attitude of humility, and the truth itself will support those who can receive it.

**9** It seems, after all, doubtful whether the so-called "practical" interest in philosophy is not in reality a mistake, a mistake due simply to a confusion of thought. This "practical" interest in philosophy rests on the assumption that it is absolutely necessary to come to some conclusion or understanding about ethics and religion and in some cases even about the universe itself before we can find ourselves at home in the universe; that, until we can tell what religion, etc., "mean," we are simply astray and have really nothing to hold by and believe in except what doubt suggests may turn out to be a fiction. The source of such an attitude is in reality not a true and genuine interest in philosophy but a religious need, the desire for some "reconciliation" with the world and with its purposes—with God in fact. But, instead of seeking this satisfaction where alone it should be found, in religion, we attempt to satisfy our emotional and spiritual demands by an intellectual interpretation of the meaning of that which is demanded, and thus confounds the intellectual craving for truth and system with the emotional and really practical life of religion. And this confusion is maintained all through; for whatever cannot fit into some intellectual scheme, whatever will not satisfy an intellectual need, is rejected as untenable; religion is not allowed to speak for itself, its own cravings are not listened to, still less is it allowed to act quite independently; and the discovery of the meaning, the interpretation of what is "sought" by the religious instincts, is taken as a substitute for the actual life and experience of religion. Hence a double error; on the one hand in the exaggerated zeal and moral earnestness with which philosophy is pursued and in the importance attached to its claims, on the other in the inadequate satisfaction which is offered to the religious needs of man—the satisfaction, namely, of understanding and seeing clearly the ultimate ends of human life and the meaning of human destiny. This confusion of mind is very common; a significant and familiar illustration of it is provided by the importance commonly attached to the supposed religious implications of scientific discovery—i.e. that man must have originated from a non-human species and morality from a non-moral way of life. But the whole point of view is plainly erroneous. It may be perfectly true that reality is rational, and that philosophy as a system of reason is a rational statement of the rational-real; but philosophy is emphatically not the same as reality. No matter how close may be the connection and relation of philosophy with its object, to attempt to identify philosophy with its object, so as to say "the one just *is* the other," is a sheer absurdity. Nobody supposes that science can substitute its conclusions for the object about which the conclusions are made; and philosophy in this matter is certainly not capable of more than science. In fact we might just as well say that we cannot live till we have discovered what life means.

It is doubtless true that philosophy lies closer to religion and the subject-matter of religion than it does, say, to physical science or mathematics and, consequently, the discussion of the supreme topics of philosophy may very directly affect religious claims and needs; and how close that relation between philosophy and religion is would have to be determined by philosophy itself. But certain it is that in no case does philosophy try to do duty for religion or even attempt to interfere very markedly with religious aims and objects; for, on any such interference, religion is quite at liberty to reject and defy the conclusions of philosophy regarding what affects it directly. If it is not at liberty to do so, it most assuredly cannot claim an independent being and life of its own which even philosophy assumes that it actually has. And if it has a life of its own, it is as much at liberty to reject the decisions of philosophy as morality for example is. For if the moral judgment, or the moral instincts, disapprove or reject, on moral grounds, the conclusions of a philosophy of morals and refuse to admit the principle of conduct suggested by such a philosophy, the philosophy dare not insist on its conclusions, nor dare the individual accept them; for if he did, he would thereby declare himself to be an immoral man; and to be an immoral man and a good philosopher at one and the same time is in the last resort impossible.

There is of course no need to deny that if philosophy is to be pursued as a science, it must be pursued as earnestly as possible; indeed it probably does attempt to give a more final and complete truth than any particular science. But the business of the philosopher is to learn and not to teach, to understand and not to legislate, to be a man and not an abstraction. One of the gravest difficulties and dangers, and really one of the greatest obstacles to philosophy itself, is the substitution of a finding in philosophy for a guide to conduct, the attempt to make a philosophic conclusion do duty for the reality itself. That is a fatal error. From this position most important conclusions follow, both for philosophy itself (its origin, significance, methods, etc.) and for the various realities discussed by it, ethics, religion, the sciences.

**10** "Science," says Hegel, "is the crown of spirit." Yes! but a crown of thorns!

**11** There is nothing like a theory for blinding the eyes of a wise man.

**12** The great problem for the philosophy of the future is to unite and do justice to the positions established so securely by Copernicus (more particularly in the "New Astronomy") on the one hand, and by the great German philosophers on the other. There seems little doubt that the fundamental contention of each position taken by itself is valid, and yet it seems equally clear that the two positions stand in direct opposition to each other. The Copernican theory has made it plain that this earth is a satellite of the sun and dependent on it, and that man, who is so dependent on the earth, is consequently of remote insignificance in the plan of the physical universe, an insignificance which becomes the more manifest when we have to take account of the other important fact established by the new astronomy, namely, that there are other suns and millions of planets similarly situated to our own and, in highest probability, inhabited by creatures like ourselves. Unquestionably all this flashes a searchlight on the ultimate value of those ideas, ideals and conceptions which have hitherto governed man and his history.

The great German philosophers, on the other hand, have made it equally plain that the focus of the light which lightens the whirling confusion of details, facts and circumstances which make up the aggregate of the world (physical and other) is to be found solely and simply in man's intelligence, in man's mind, in self-consciousness; the pivot on which the whole system of knowledge turns is man's own spirit; all his knowledge, all the truth he establishes regarding the world, without or within him (and the Copernican theory is nothing if it is not knowledge, truth, systematized fact) comes from, is the expression of, is in a sense created solely by, his own intellectual and spiritual effort. And this doctrine seems not only to contradict the other one, but actually to turn the tables against it; man now becomes all important in the scheme of the universe, the fire that would burn him to cinders is of his own making, the searchlight that is to make him ashamed of himself is cast upon him by his own desire and will. Our two doctrines, then, stand directly opposed to each other and neither can be denied without making shipwreck of human experience. How to justify both—that is the problem.

Much the same problem may be put in another way from the point of view of biology. The problem here is to unite the two counter-posed views that man was made a little lower than the angels, and that man was made a little higher than the monkeys!

**13** Philosophy is like marriage, let it be never so commonplace it is none the less necessary and none the less interesting—would that it were as joyous!

**14** All philosophy is a way of saying your prayers by teaching you to do without them.

**15** The best exposure to which any system can be subjected is an accurate exposition of it.

**16** An important part of the business of a philosopher is the knowledge of his own business, of what philosophy itself means. It is the fatal and fatuous error of many philosophers to suppose that the actual nature and intelligibility of the world depend upon their understanding it. If they do not grasp its principles, the world is said to have no meaning; while if they do, there is nothing further to know, or worth knowing! The absurdity of this position is seen even in the very simple fact that the existence of another generation of thinkers gives the lie to both assertions. Into such perversions the thinkers in the various fields of science never fall; they never suppose that ignorance signifies meaninglessness, nor even that knowledge of a part is incapable of re-interpretation.

The error of the philosopher is due to his attitude towards the problem of knowledge. Because he deals with the whole of experience, he supposes that the meaning of experience waits upon him and upon his enquiry; because he stands at the point of view of the absolute, he supposes that his statements all have the solemnity of absoluteness. He forgets altogether to notice that his own enquiry is itself only a part of his own experience and, indeed, grows out of his experience and presupposes it, and cannot therefore be something by itself, still less something over and above ordinary experience. To take it, therefore, so out of focus, so "seriously," as to proceed as if the existence and stability of experience wait for the result of his enquiry, is a distortion which perverts reverent acquiescence in the truth into solemn responsibility for the reasonableness of the world, and transforms joyous eagerness in the discovery of light and truth into the melancholy oppression of a burden too great to be borne because never intended to be carried by man at all.

Philosophy, like every form of purposive activity, is a means for the elevation and strengthening and dignifying of man's spirit; unless it be directed by reverence and love, its end will never be attained. It is a completion of experience (as Hegel put it "the crown of the life of mind") and, in that sense, something of an inevitable luxury of the human mind. It can be joyfully, as well as reverently, accepted and realized by those whose spiritual development makes them capable or desirous of it; but other people can really do without it.

**17** The reason why physical science can be "abstract" and *is* abstract is that its material can be *abstracted*, and yet be unaffected by the process. Physical things are just what can be translated from space to space, from one position to another, can be taken to pieces and looked at separately or put together again, and *all the while* retain their own properties. This, again, is another way of saying that physical things are inherently *spatial*. Whether they can be abstracted because they are spatial, or are spatial because they can be abstracted, does not affect the fact of connection between the two.

Now in other subject-matters, for example life or mind, the parts and elements cannot be abstracted and transposed from place to place indifferently. They have an inherent activity of their own; and this must be considered. Since abstraction of such material is so difficult, or even impossible, the science of life or mind is just on that account *not* abstract in character. For this reason, too, its difficulties are greater than those of a natural science like physics. In natural science, things have to be compared, related, separated, in order to establish differences and identities; and so if abstraction is possible to any extent, the science can be readily prosecuted. But these things are in the nature of the case impossible in dealing with life and mind. The difficulties of abstraction in dealing with life and mind lie, not only in the fact that forms and parts of life and mind cannot be isolated indefinitely and indifferently, but that life as such (and still more mind as such), cannot be isolated from other things, for example, from physical nature. That makes the difficulty enormous.

The same is true of physical science and the sciences of life and mind in regard to time. The former takes its facts apart from any particular *concrete* time (history), looks at them from the point of view of *abstract* time. The latter must consider concrete (actual) time, cannot shift from one time to another indifferently; things have a time of their own making, not what we give them.

**18** In a cynical moment, one may very well say that metaphysics is the science of framing legitimate questions and the art of concealing illegitimate answers.

**19** It is a mistake to suppose that philosophy is not the highest form of experience merely because it is confined to a few individuals, and realized by these for a comparatively brief period of life—and even then only intermittently. The highest is none the less the highest because it is rare, and because it is brief in duration of experience.

After all, we do not refuse to regard the higher mathematics as higher because most people are concerned with the simpler processes of arithmetic and the simple relations of space. As a matter of experience there are only a few years or a few days or a few hours of our life that are really worth living; and we would not renounce those hours for all the rest, but would rather give up all the rest for them. So, too, we cannot always philosophize: a period of strenuous vision is exhausting and we retreat to a lower level, but we do not on that account think this level better than philosophy. No doubt religion is a more constant support and fulfilment of life than philosophy; but this only means that our normal life is more emotional and practical than intelligent and speculative. As we know, too, even the purely religious life fails to give us always all we want, and we fall back on the social relations of family and friendly fellowships, which are more normal, more elementary, than religion. But, again, we do not on that account regard religion as lower than social life.

**20** The objection to philosophy that it cannot use terms technical enough to be of unvarying significance and universally intelligible, is not an objection of any importance: it indicates how clearly philosophy is bound up with human life and how inseparable it is from living individuality. To put philosophy in technical language would mean a marriage of death and life, darkness and light. This is the danger of German philosophy, especially in the hands of men like Kant. It is not a danger that seriously threatens, or has ever threatened, English or French philosophy. The Teutonic and the Saxon and Celtic strains in European philosophy thus check each others' faults.

**21**  Abstract theorists, and propagandists of all sorts, are always more or less egotists. Only in the whole truth can the soul expand and be cheerfully and joyfully at rest, and only there are the selfish egoisms of life dissipated.

**22**  Metaphysics is too much a process of un-doing or *un*-making your own mind instead of making it up. This turns thinking into a kind of self-consumption.

**23**  One aim of philosophy is to cut down questions to a minimum—and answers, too.

**24**  Most philosophers are philosophers only in their studies: they are very common fellows outside.

**25**  A system of philosophy is curiously unsatisfying. It is too much like an elaborate funeral of the Absolute without the hope of a resurrection.

**26**  To speak to the Absolute (in religion) and to speak about it (in philosophy) both imply the same contrast of man to the Absolute. "Absorption" is as impossible in the one case as in the other.

**27**  A man who lives inside a system has locked the door of his intelligence.

**28**  If pure scepticism is intellectual suicide, an absolute system is the sarcophagus of the intelligence. And so far as life is concerned there is not much to choose between suicide and a sarcophagus.

**29**  Philosophy is man's opportunity to show whether he is or is not a fool.

**30** Theories can only be constructed by the application of consistency: and experience is not consistent.

**31** We appeal to philosophy to remove the difficulties created by the sciences; and sometimes pursue philosophy for its own sake as a more satisfying intellectual undertaking than science, and one which enables us to escape from the limitations of science.

But it seems vain to expect philosophy to clear up the difficulties of the sciences, when all it seems able to do is to create new difficulties of its own, which are merely added to those which the sciences bring about.

And it is equally vain to suppose that philosophy will satisfy the mind if science fails to do so; for philosophy must finally appeal to a faith in the human intellect. Science can surely do as much as that. And science has this advantage, that whereas philosophy gives no knowledge of the world different from science, and has only faith to offer in the end, by pursuing science men do acquire definite knowledge and they can rest in the faith which underlies all knowledge without the labour of learning this from philosophy.

**32** Metaphysics is a method of watering the capital of human knowledge.

**33** Poetry can penetrate to secrets which philosophy cannot approach. Faith and love and hope can reach heights of experience which philosophy can neither define nor defend.

**34** Science and philosophy are no more substitutes for the real world than history is a substitute for human experience, or poetry for the love of life. Science, at its best, is but a voice, an utterance, not the whole of man's mind.

**35** The philosophical spirit may perhaps be better realized in trying to see the whole of *a* thing than in trying to see the whole of things. This is more becoming to the modest limitations of man's mind, and in the long run will lead to more satisfactory results. It is difficult enough to see all round any subject of everyday life. It seems almost pretence to imagine we are able to see all round all subjects whether separately or together.

# II

**1** Popular relativity must necessarily be at bottom *hypothetical*. It assumes, to start with, the opposite natures of beings, i.e. the opposite nature of the knowing subject and the known object. Hence its position is "*if* things in themselves are different in being from us who know them, then we cannot know things in themselves"; for it is evident that, if they are the same in being with us who know them, then to translate them into terms of our being (which is *knowing* them) does not in any way express differently their nature, i.e. knowing does not for the knower alter the nature, the peculiar nature, of the things known. Popular relativity, however, breaks through this peculiar hypothetical position and makes it categorical. It says: "knower and known *are* different beings in their nature, in their essence." But how does it *know* this? It cannot speak in this way from the viewpoint of relativity, for that would be too obvious a circle. And yet it cannot do anything else without altering its whole attitude. The blunt duality of knower and known does not as such (as immediately given to our conscious nature) give any warrant for any assertion regarding the nature and essence of the being known. This can only come as an afterthought. Hence, if all afterthoughts (reflective knowledge) are darkened by "relativity," any assertion regarding our knowledge of anything must be tainted with relativity; hence, cannot be absolute, cannot be categorical; hence must rest on the above hypothetical *assumption* regarding the nature of things in themselves. The peculiar untenableness of this position is that there is no ground in knowledge at all—and no ground in us who know or in the thing known, or anywhere —for this assumption, still less for the presumed nature of the thing or things about which the assumption is made. For relativists, relativity-philosophers, there is no escape, so far as I see, from this dilemma. If on the other hand they assume that any of our knowledge is of the real (e.g. our knowledge of qualities, etc.) and is utterly valid, then either they have no right to talk of the complete relativity of our knowledge at all, or else no right to admit the *thorough* validity of *any* knowledge whatever. And from this dilemma equally there is no escape. At bottom they really demand that "like shall be and can only be known by like." The fact is, however, that all knowledge is really hypothetical, but so far true because resting on a categorical basis of fact. And just because it is hypothetical, it is absurd to talk of knowing or not knowing things in themselves. Knowledge is *our* attitude to other-being, being over against us, our conscious life in a particular mode of activity. Everything must start there just because it can start nowhere else and *is* nowhere else. All reference to the real is *our reference* to the real over-against us. But if we are a focus of being, of the universe, then our knowledge of it must be accurate enough, so far as it is knowledge and so far as we bear in mind what knowledge really is. Does this imply that the only important and significant fact in our knowing is *consistency*?

**2** Is there not a difference between saying "the real is (the) rational" and "the real is the *reasonable*"? Is it because people do not recognize this difference that they object to the Hegelian dictum "the rational is real, etc."? Yet there is a point of great importance in the second statement. You might show, e.g. the causes, sources of a certain evil action, and in that way you might explain it—make it intelligible (i.e. rationalize it), but that would not prove it to be "reasonable."

**3** Significant that in Epictetus, rather than in Marcus Aurelius, we find the strongest sense of the majesty of man.

**4** If knowing and being are so utterly opposed to one another, each so uniquely *sui generis* and independent of the other and indifferent to the other (as some thinkers, e.g. Lotze, seem to suppose), then it matters not what you believe, nor what you think. Whether you know a "thing" or do not know it, that thing will act in its own way; your knowledge will not make any difference to it, nor its relation to you, and your not knowing will be equally unimportant. Knowledge will thus be a passive luxury, a pleasant toy for the possession or loss or absence of which you are not responsible in the long run; it is useful to have, perhaps, but has no assured objectivity or importance *in rerum natura*.

**5** Granting that all the aspects of reality (as well as reality itself as a whole) are simply pulsations of the notion, manifestations of thought, still there seems to remain the grave question: what is it that constitutes the difference among those details of reality? What makes one thing what it is, as distinct from another which it is not? The fact that all things are pulses of the notion would unquestionably suggest a fundamental identity of the whole series of phenomena. But such a theory only accounts for half the facts: it still remains a question what makes the phenomena different from each other. Yet it might still be urged that why red is red and not black, why grass is green and not blue, why wood is not stone, are questions that cannot really be asked nor answered; they are simply an affair for the universe itself to settle and not for us who are parts of the Universe. This would not nullify the Hegelian conception; in fact both Lotze and Hegel could exist side by side—and mutually supplement each other.

**6**  Is it not more true to say that a man's ideals are determined for him than that his actions are determined? Certainly a man did not create the moral law for himself nor the ideal which the moral law subserves.

**7**  It is a mistake to suppose that a complete understanding of Hegel's Philosophy can save a man the trouble of learning piecemeal for himself the facts and details of the world and the special principles of the special sciences. Hegel's Logic simply works, and can only work, with the facts of the world before it. The movement of the Notion in its triple manifestation is simply the ground form, the ultimate principle, *the* character *par excellence* of what is. But the special mode in which it manifests itself we must find out by experience. We can of course regard it as the most general method of interpreting and rationalizing experience; and we are assured that facts will reveal themselves in accordance with it. But how in particular any given set of facts (e.g. of psychology) shall in their special sphere operate, we must learn by a patient analysis, etc., of those facts as presented to us. This seems to have been how Hegel himself set to work. His principle seems an ultimate generalization, a vast induction won by patient labour in the special sciences. But in addition to the induction, the completion of his scheme obviously required a systematic Deduction. And it is with this deduction that his works are mainly occupied; and the fact that they are mainly occupied with it seems to be the chief ground of objection against them. But of course the deduction presupposes and must presuppose a prior induction. And since this is more a process than a final complete result, Hegel does not show it in his work. He gives his final result, and "burns his bridges." But this does not mean that he had no bridges: it only means that he seems to have thought them his own and not the world's affair, and so he does not give them. So, too, Kant. Indeed, who not?

**8**  Empiricism is so true that the closer one keeps to it—without becoming an empiricist!—the better. Just as, on the contrary,

Idealism is so questionable that the farther one keeps from it—without ceasing to be an idealist!—the truer will one's view of reality be.

**9** Singular how Kant's philosophical question directly affected his whole problem and the sort of solution he was to offer. He did not start primarily with a doubt regarding all knowledge, but only with a doubt regarding metaphysical knowledge. Scientific knowledge is a fact, but is metaphysic science? In this distinction lies concealed that presupposition which governs his whole view that things are real, that they exist, but need not, in consequence of this, be known by us as they are. Metaphysic, as dealing with things as they are in themselves, is therefore a doubtful science. Hence noumena and phenomena, etc. But had he widened his question into how is any knowledge possible at all, and what are the conditions, not of the knowledge which is known as science, but of any knowledge whatsoever and without limitation, his problem would have been very much larger and more comprehensive, and there would have been no prejudice in favour of one form of knowledge more than another, and consequently no presupposition regarding the nature and existence of things in themselves. And this is really the problem for any theory of knowledge. The possibility of metaphysic stands or falls with the possibility of any knowledge. If one knowledge is possible then all knowledge is possible.

**10** Kant may be regarded as having attempted to establish scientifically the crude philosophical opinions of the practical man of the world. The latter also says "beware of metaphysic, of going 'beyond experience,' keep to 'plain facts' and do your duty and let the rest go."

**11** We sometimes speak as if in philosophy there were nothing new to learn. We have but to compare the fundamental conceptions at work and dominant in the seventeenth and eighteenth centuries to see that this is not true. The meaning of organic unity, purpose, end, hardly seems to have dawned on the minds of these epochs. To us, however, these are precisely the notions which are being used most fruitfully at the present day.

The next generation, or even the next century or two, may find itself occupied simply with the effort to understand and work out the meaning of these notions in all their bearings. Certainly, as yet, they are not so much not understood as barely more than admitted.

**12** Idealism may be described as a theory which seeks to make the universe stand on its end: and this in the long run means that it must stand on its head.

**13** People often think that, in saying the Absolute is entirely beyond our grasp, they are paying it a great compliment and doing it honour. They do not see that, in saying so little of it, they are treating it to condemnation or contempt. That whose highest attribute is beyond our ken is next door to being nothing for us at all. To establish its existence on the basis of our incapacity is not the best kind of honour to bestow on it.

There is a certain conscious or unconscious hypocrisy in producing with one hand the conception of an Absolute, and then with the other taking away all attributes from it on the assumption that the one hand does not know what the other is doing.

**14** The quarrel which the finite individual has with necessity (whatever be its form) is that he objects to being compelled or carried along by powers alien to, and beyond, the plan of his own purposes, powers which are not continuous in their nature and operation with the powers inherent in individual life. No one would care even to think correctly if he were merely the channel through which some other being were thinking its thoughts. What we want is that the scheme of things should be joyful in our activity and should support us in our efforts, not that its success should be secured merely by using us as means or instruments. Any form of necessity is tolerable if we have a share in securing it and directing its processes. The relation of our individual effort to the necessity—which surely must work in the world—must, in some way, be akin to the relation between the individual will and the systematic working of the State. There we have necessity, but at the same time our spontaneity counts from first to last. This is why the conception of God as spirit seems so important and sympathetic to man's nature.

**15** The insistence on the social importance of heredity, innate qualities, sound constitution, etc., of which biology makes so much at the present time, rests on a very familiar principle. It has long been held that "out of the heart proceed evil thoughts": it has long been maintained that the environment is not the fundamental fact in human life, that *caelum non animum mutant* and that, for reformation of social life, what is required is "a change of heart," a "new heart and a right spirit." The whole question turns on how this "change of nature" is to be brought about.

It is remarkable to find religion of the most spiritual type, and naturalism of the extreme type, insisting on the same principle—the necessity for a transformed constitution in the individual if social transformation is to be brought about, that environment is not primary but secondary in the process. But, whereas naturalism insists that the change of nature is to be brought about by breeding, religion insists that it must be brought about by baptism of the spirit, baptism in fire and water. Naturalism appeals to genetics, religion to grace.

**16** An immense tract of our thinking on the world has been influenced by the mere physical facts of weight and mass. These are not the most important facts either of the world or of experience. The tension between forces, and the indivisible continuity of fields of energy, are much more potent factors in our experience. Mass and weight are clumsy embodiments of cosmic reality; and, were it not for the fact that they impress our senses so vividly, they would not occupy our minds so seriously.

**17** It is remarkable that the most valuable things are not always the most enduring—perhaps it is true that nothing that is valuable is made so by enduring, or made more precious by lasting. Love, joy, peace are by no means lasting, and they constantly come and go: a gracious act dies in the doing and would be made ungracious by an attempted repetition: a song, a poem, a true utterance passes with the breath of the speaker: and what is more changeable, instable, than a thought in the mind whose nuance alters with every change of attention?

If this is so, why should Reality be looked on as necessarily one and unchangeable and abiding?

**18** It may be said that at the beginning of modern philosophy consciousness of self was used almost exclusively in the sense of consciousness of isolated separate existence—which is consciousness of self in the poorest and weakest sense: at the end of the modern period we find consciousness of self used primarily in the sense of consciousness of the union of self with all reality, and thus as the clue to the meaning of reality—which is consciousness of self in the fullest and richest sense. Between these two interpretations lies the whole history of modern philosophy—the logical evolution of the first interpretation found its final expression in Hume's well-known negations—the logical evolution of the second has found its final outcome in the disappearance of the substantial reality of the individual, the result which is arrived at in Hegel and his successors. Perhaps it might be well to regard this movement, from self-consciousness in the first sense to self-consciousness in the second, as finally closed.

**19** If, as is highly probable, man becomes more fully aware of himself in communion with his fellows (in social life) than in his relation to anything else, it is but natural that he should take his social (i.e. moral) life to be the key to his reality, and indeed to the meaning of reality as a whole. He supposes in fact that reality must respond and reciprocate with him as he responds to his fellows, that his relation to the world should be like that of a social fellowship. And this view is easily distorted in such a way as to suggest that moral experience is the primary reality (even that it is the only reality) and that all other experiences are secondary.

The objection to any such interpretation of the Universe in moral terms is that it ignores the essential fact in the moral (social) situation. In morality, an individual does expressly commune with another, reply, reciprocate and the like. But in regard to reality as a whole or other things, for example in nature, there is no such explicit response of self to self, communion of mind with mind. The communion is one-sided: the thing does not respond as a self, but as either less or more than a self. The "fellowship with reality" is thus at best an anthropomorphic construction.

But this failure of reality as a whole to enter into fellowship with man does not necessarily mean that reality is less than a self, or that our relation to it is unintelligible or unsatisfying. Rather all that follows from the want of real "social communion" between mind and things is that, after all, moral experience cannot be the final key to the solution of the problem of man's relation to the world, nor the final clue to the meaning of reality. Reality must be (or may be) more than a self and all the more valuable to us on that account.

**20** It is certainly impossible to prove that the human individual is the highest or the most valuable or the most important creature on the globe, for every such argument must move in a circle; and every creature might equally prove a similar conclusion by the same circular process.

All we can do is to take it for granted that we are the most important species on the globe, act accordingly and see what happens: which amounts to saying that we should act so as to fulfil our own being to the utmost, mind our own business, and leave the rest of the world to do the same.

We cannot prove we are superior because we make other beings serve us, e.g. sheep, horses, cattle, etc., for the animals might just as well say *they* are superior because we serve them—we provide them with food and shelter, etc.! Nor can we say that we are superior because we feed on other forms of life and use them for our sustenance, for other forms of life, very lowly forms even, feed on us, and can eat us up! Nor can we say that we have all the powers of other beings and something over; for we do not know all the powers of other beings and we have lost (or have never possessed) many powers which they obviously have! It looks as if the supposed superiority of human beings was after all a mere assumption.

**21** Chance, which plays so large a part in the history of man's life, is sometimes regarded as the opportunity for the display of freedom of will. But if human affairs are at the mercy of chance, freedom can only be itself a happy or unhappy accident; and one feels that a species which is so much in the hands of chance can really not be such an important part of reality as humanity takes itself to be.

**22** The elementary distinctions made by the primitive mind seem to survive all the changes of developed thought. They are accepted as assumptions, and then control later thought as prejudices. One of the most important is the division of the world into two separate regions which are external to each other —mind and the physical "natural" realm of things. The problem of "uniting" these two has occupied some of the most capable of human intellects, who never seem to have asked whether the separation was justifiable to begin with, or whether there might not be more regions in the real world than just these two.

To maturer reflection it seems evident that the world of the real is not divisible into parts at all. It consists rather of a series of planes or levels of energy, from the lowest which is merely the physical energy of matter to the highest which is the energy of mind at its best. Between these lie the energy of chemical processes, the energy of living processes, the energy of barely conscious activity such as we find in animals, and higher still the energy of the lower kinds of mentality (sub-conscious, etc.). All these forms of energy interact and interpenetrate in ways we can hardly even pretend to grasp. The higher assume and subsume the lower; and the highest of all is only possible by utilizing all the others, by implying their co-operation: it is the highest because it can use and direct them all. *Mens agitat molem.* That which co-ordinates, animates and directs all to a single unity is all and is in and through all, thus forming a single system of the complex universe. It is in fact what we call God: not pure thought alone, and not pure spirit alone, but thought which pervades and unifies all other forms of energy, spirit which controls and concentrates into itself all other levels of the world's forces or energies. Man focuses in his individuality a certain range, very limited and very incomplete, of most or all of the other energies: hence his power to communicate with and to "resemble," to be "in the image of," God: but his finiteness makes him at the same time completely dependent on God. He can, therefore, never "understand" God; never grasp God's being except through a narrow perspective, and thus only imperfectly at the best. What he does not know he has, therefore, to supplement; and he can supplement by what he chooses to call Faith, a faith whose object is one in substance with what he knows in his own realm and in his own imperfect degree.

It is in some such way as this that man must try to approach the problem of the unity of his "mind" with "nature." An initial opposition of the two makes the problem unintelligible and insoluble.

**23** Hegel was one of the few men in the world's history who ventured to be on speaking terms with the Absolute Mind. But was the result a monologue by Hegel or a revelation by the Absolute? Who knows?

**24** Much of the opposition to materialism is due to sentiment and not to reason. Many people dislike "materialism," and nothing will make it attractive to them: any reason is a good reason against it. And even those who rely on reasons to refute or criticize materialism, almost invariably make an appeal to the emotions in considering its consequences and effects.

This is curious. Even religious people should surely recognize that matter is capable of exquisite beauty and magnificence of form and arrangement, and that the creation of matter and of its conditions falls within a divine purpose. Why should that purpose not be exhaustively expressed in the stuff and form of matter? Need materialism mean more than this?

The reason for our emotional hostility to materialism is of course our instinctive sense that we are distinct from nature and superior to it.

**25** The theory of organic evolution, in the sense of the struggle for existence and the survival of the fittest, is not logically defensible, unless we assume that the theory of evolution is itself the result (the final result) of the course of evolution of the human mind. Even this makes the defence of evolution depend on a circular argument, and at the same time it contradicts the other assumption of evolution—that the process of evolution is still going on and has by no means come to an end nor will come to an end in any calculable time.

But a stronger case can be made out against the doctrine when we look at the so-called "highest" outcome of evolution—man. If there is sound reasoning and evidence in favour of the theory, we should have expected that the highest creature would have been the creature most fitted and adapted to its total environment, and that the lowest creatures would be less fitted. This is a fair expectation, since the highest creature has a longer life history behind it—the whole course of life on the planet in short, and, therefore, trial and error have been engaged in the formation of this creature for the longest time. What, however, do we find? That the lower creatures are better adapted to their respective environments than man is to his environment; that man is out of harmony with his environment at every point, is even in opposition to and conflict with his environment; and that throughout the whole course of his known history he has shown no greater adaptation at one time than another. Huxley pointed out the disharmony between moral values and the conditions of natural evolution. But this is only a part of the discordance. Compared with the remarkable adaptation to their environment of birds, fish or bees, man is a stranger to his environment from the first. He has no reliable instincts, which he can follow with safety to a precise purposive result; he can do nothing without instruction from his elders, cannot even walk or feed himself without guidance; he cannot think or feel or act with safety when left to his own resources, is haunted by fears, and blocked by failures at every turn, is stupid, blind and incompetent from one generation to another. Is this the best that evolution can do? It looks as if evolution did the opposite of what is claimed for it—as if it consisted in making the lower creatures more fit for their environment than the higher. All this would seem to mean that evolution is tenable when read backwards, but not when read forwards. Though human life should provide more evidence than anything else of the success of evolution, man is of all creatures the least explicable in evolutionary terms. It is useless to say evolution has failed only in the case of man; failure there is failure everywhere—if the theory is to apply to organic life as a whole. Maladaptation to environment cannot, without paradox, be regarded as the outcome of progressive adaptation.

It may be said that man has the *conception* of perfect adaptation to his environment in the form of his ideals of good and truth and beauty, and that these, though to be realized in the future, are the outcome of mental evolution in the past. But if we say that, we must admit that evolution has not only produced a creature ill-adapted to its environment, but has made him even more at odds with his environment than he would otherwise be.

**26**   Our knowledge of man is curiously different from our knowledge of nature. We know why man acts and thinks and feels as he does; we know the purposes he has in mind; but we can hardly be said to know how man acts, and how he thinks or how he feels as he does. In the case of natural objects we claim to and seek to know how they are what they are, and how they operate; but we do not even pretend to know why they are what they are, or why they act as they do. This is the profound difference between spiritual and natural beings, and creates many of our problems.

**27**   The more one sees of human life the more evident it becomes that man is a creature independent of mere nature and natural conditions. There is too great a discrepancy between man's aims and nature's processes to permit of an explanation of man's life in terms of these processes alone. Man has never been able to accommodate himself completely, or even adequately, to nature, as lower organisms, plants and animals, seem able to do. He is uncomfortable in its presence, is either at odds with it or seeking to bring it into subjection to himself in a way other organic creatures do not do. Not only that; but, from the first, he has been at odds with his own fellow creatures, in a way that animals are not. It may even be that he is at odds with his fellow-creatures because he is at odds with nature.

It must, however, be admitted that this is in large part due to the fact that they have never been able completely to love and understand one another: the fear of man for man is almost greater than his fear of nature. This estrangement of man from nature is at once the paradox and the main problem of man's existence.

## III

**1** In the close scrutiny of an object, a man's knowledge of it will depend on whether he is actually studying it or merely staring at it. How much apparent study is just *staring*!

**2** Individual conviction, individual perception of the existence of certain particular facts, is often taken (e.g. by such persons as theosophists, "spiritualists," ghost-seers, etc.) to be an impregnable security against any attacks on the certainty of the belief in these facts. The argument is that "if you don't see it, why then that does not hinder me from seeing it, and you are unable by your own confession to deny the truth of what I assert." But it is forgotten that these facts—the knowledge of which is essentially private property and incommunicable—are precisely the least important, the least true, the least real, the least valuable in all senses. Those facts are the most stable and significant which are capable of, and which secure, universal assent and acknowledgement. It is no advantage whatever to appeal to private conviction regarding the truth of given beliefs—in fact rather a disadvantage, because in the nature of the case private conviction does not possess the universality and necessity and compulsion which are characteristic of all truth. These facts may exist, they may be. But what of that? Private possession of reality is a misfortune in every sense; for the security (not to speak of the intellectual and moral satisfaction) which comes from feeling that our awareness of the world is shared by our fellow-men is absent from it; and it leaves us alone and solitary in the isolated ownership of unenviable, insignificant fragments of reality. To rejoice in such a private property is at once an idiosyncracy and a self-contradiction. One might even say that individual certainty, the insistence on private undoubted assurance regarding the "truth" of particular facts and of all details and steps of the intellectual and moral life, is the demand for the abolition of all faith from the intellectual life of man. It is a kind of intellectual miserliness and greed.

**3**  It is curious how personal and private men's desire and love of the truth will show itself to be. For example, men sigh for the truth, "will be satisfied with nothing less," and yet so little do they expect to find it that, should anyone profess to offer enlightenment, the first impulse of the "seekers after truth" is to doubt and distrust what is offered to them. Again, those who cry aloud for the truth are often those who will take least trouble to discover it or make plain to themselves the truth which lies at their very hands. The fact seems to be that much "yearning for truth" is in reality yearning for something much less solid, and will be satisfied either with vacuity or with some temporary triviality. Most people who profess to feel it are indifferent to every truth which brings no personal advantage, incapable of appreciating any other truth, and idle even in the pursuit of such truth as they can appreciate, with the result that they distrust truth in general and are dissatisfied with every truth in particular. It is by this general attitude towards the truth that most people are influenced in their regard for what profess to be systems of the truth. There are, probably, very few men living at any time who could honestly say that they loved the truth for its own sake only.

**4**  To praise the notion of Lessing that it is more desirable to seek truth than to have it, is to admit the paradox, indeed the absurdity, that to make a fortune is better than to possess one, or that courtship is preferable to marriage. The truth emphasized in Lessing's statement is that to accept truth means too often merely to swallow it without digestion; to admit it without the travail and experience necessary to appreciate it, and thus to miss in the main its meaning.

**5** It is sometimes said that poetry is anthropomorphic, while science seeks to get rid of anthropomorphism. This is hardly accurate. Finding the laws of our mind in the world is as much anthropomorphism as finding our emotions and feelings there. If we "prescribe laws to nature" in any way, we are not going beyond the demands of our own spirits, our own purposes.

And if "nature" guarantees and justifies the laws, why should she not equally guarantee and justify our motives and feelings? When the poet finds his moods in nature or imparts his feelings to it, shall these be rejected? We seem as much entitled to find "nature" answering to our emotions as to our thoughts. And if so, then part of the religious attitude of mind is justified in precisely the same sense, or for the same reason, as the scientific.

**6** It is a mistake to say we must have faith because we cannot know. The truth, rather, is that we must have faith because there is so much to know, and we cannot know it all at once. If we did, we would be confused by its very complexity.

**7** There is a certain sanity in disbelief: it is the critical attitude towards fixed dogmas, which rests on the fundamental claim that life is much richer than any particular statement about it.

**8** We do not discern the rise and fall of the floods by watching the main stream but by observing its gradual encroachment on the land: nor do we discern the rise of a new truth except by observing the gradual disappearance of the old landmarks of experience.

**9** There are some men who take the possession of truth to be so much of a personal affair that they stake their sanity on winning every argument.

**10** Many men mistake the power to think clearly for the power to think the truth: that is confusing the art of the draftsman with the art of the designer, the washerwoman with the tailor. A statement may be clear because it is true, but it need not be true because it is clear.

11   Take your stand anywhere on the truth and the whole system of it will rally to your support. It is the whole material universe which keeps a tower in position, not the few feet of ground on which it rests.

12   One of the unexplored domains of the problem of human knowledge is that of the *imagination*. Sense-perception is important, memory is important, so is judgment: and all of these have been, at least in part, discussed in their bearings on knowledge. But the function and operation of imagination have so far remained practically untouched. There is more in Kant's suggestion about the "schematism" of the imagination than has yet been recognized—even by Kant himself.

13   The "convictions" and "beliefs" of some thinkers are so much stronger than their reasons for holding them that one is left wondering why they ever took the trouble to seek any reasons at all.

14   Suppose all knowledge be of no more (and no less) significance than the work of the artist? The artist paints his picture, composes his poem, or his music, to fulfil his own cravings for self-expression. His result may be based in the nature of things; it is at least based on his own nature. But is he complementing or reproducing the world? Or is he merely satisfying himself? Does knowledge do any more than accomplish one or other of those ends? Does it reproduce the world? That is very like the artist's business, and equally "superfluous" to the course of things. Does the knower satisfy himself? So does the artist. Are

we compelled to know and understand the world on pain of being damned? Why should we be, any more than we are compelled to paint the colours of nature, or construct its sounds into music?

**15** In our apprehension of the world, there is intellectual photography and there is also high intellectual art: the first is merely reproduction of the "facts"; the second is constructive of a scheme of understanding the facts: the first is repetition, the second creation. May it not well be that the higher science and philosophy bear the same relation to everyday knowledge that painting does to mere photography or poetry to speech? We commonly hear scientists contend that "science reproduces reality as it is" and is true "if and because science agrees with reality." This may be true of the elementary levels of knowledge; but there is as much difference between these and the high constructive results of scientific thought as there is between a copy of nature and a painting by Turner. Both kinds of knowledge may be "true"; but the "truest" will be that which most thoroughly fulfils the demands of intellectual activity. Intellectual activity, like artistic activity, has an ideal of its own demanding satisfaction in its own sphere: and, in the attainment of its end, individuality (i.e. imagination, insight and perspective) counts as much as in the case of a work of art.

**16** The process of logical thinking is at best an articulation of the concentrated vision of reality found in intuition or imaginative insight. The step by step procedure of articulate thought is due to the exigencies of language, attention and communication. There is no special merit in this connecting process nor in the terms connected: nor is truth any "truer"—any more a conscious fulfilment of reality in mental form—for being laid out and exposed bit by bit. We do not have a better hold of reality that way than by the living realization of it in imaginative insight. Logical thinking is to insight or vision what the letter of speech is to the spirit, words to a sentence, letters to a word. Insight is the germ and vital centre of the whole process: it must already be present in us before it can grow into articulations and become "logical," i.e. connected unified thinking.

**17**  The only reality we can speak of in the sphere of knowledge is the energizing mind: ideas are not real by themselves nor do they by themselves "give" reality to anything else. They are functions or specific operations of the mind as a centre of mental force. We might as well talk of colour being real "by itself," apart from things coloured, as of ideas being real as ideas.

**18**  Philosophers and scientists are apt to regard truth as something (a thought for example) which has to be embodied in written words, and is completely communicable when the words are accurately framed into written sentences. But this attitude ignores the vast range of our emotional appreciation of the world about us. It also ignores the fact that a great deal of the meaning which seems to be expressed in words or other outward symbols is really conveyed by the tone of voice, by the accent, intonation and inflexion given to the words by a speaker. Written words do not and cannot convey such suggestions of the truth: and yet such nuances are inseparable from the mind of the speaker and are a completer expression of the truth he wants to convey than a bare written statement.

**19**  Probably our knowledge of the world proceeds on much the same plan as the artistic representation of external nature: external nature is a suggestion which stimulates the artistic activity of man for the satisfaction of his sense of beauty rather than an object which he just reproduces. Why should he "reproduce" it anyway? Not merely is it beautiful as it stands, it would give him all the satisfaction he wanted if he attained through it the satisfaction of his sense of beauty. But as a matter of empirical fact it stimulates him to activity; and we naturally suppose that the activity stimulated by it must be different from the mere contemplation of it, and must serve a different end than the production of a "second copy" of it. So with knowledge. We do not in knowing merely have the object over again; the object just stimulates our mind to create for itself a satisfaction of its own desire—the desire for co-ordinated thinking.

**20**  It is possible to be intoxicated by the truth: but the worst form of intoxication is that produced by a half-truth.

**21**  There is a communion of the mind with the Real through the channels of the senses as genuine and important as its communion through the channel of ideas or imagination. It is mere prejudice and want of experience which induces philosophers and "thinkers" to suppose that only by our thoughts, and more particularly by our articulate thoughts, do we get a genuine consciousness of the Real. Such people are primarily interested in thoughts and in expressing thoughts, and hence take this to be the most important or the only permissible avenue to Reality: and, as they are more voluble than other people, they are apt to think their views beyond dispute, because to dispute them involves using their weapons and thereby indirectly confirming their point of view.

All this, however, is rather like a dog chasing its tail in order to make progress. For it should be obvious that there are experiences which are beyond argument and where argument is sometimes irrelevant, sometimes an impertinence. Indeed, in the handling, the touching, the seeing, and the hearing the things of this world, the Real reaches the innermost of the mind of man in a manner which no thinking can displace, replace or supplant. We commune with the Real through the throbbings of sensation, the upheavals and the quiet passiveness of emotion, the energy of our moving bodies, and not alone through ideal formulae. That is why the vast multitude of human beings can live their lives intensely with only the minimum of intellectual interests. Living human beings do not need formulae to enjoy and strive with one another, or to enjoy and strive with the hard things of the senses, or to find their minds throbbing with the communications of eye or ear. To look down on all this with pity and disdain, as "bondage to the life of sense," in the way many philosophers have done, and as so many abstract religious people have done, implies mere want of experience and lopsidedness of mental equipment. If that means bondage to the senses, then these philosophers are equally suffering from another bondage—the bondage to ideas; and bondage for bondage, one is as good or as bad as the other.

There is a "language" of the senses quite as valuable as the language which conveys thoughts; and the senses convey the multitudinous meaning of the Real to the mind of man in a manner entirely unique and irreplaceable. From the religious point of view this appears in the best religious life as the sacramental attitude of the spirit, the attitude in which every act is a sacrament, an embodiment of the Real Presence of God, in which every pulse of sense is a revelation of the most High, the attitude by which in seeing we are seeing God and seeing in God's light, in handling things we are touching an "incarnation" or materialization of the Divine, the attitude in which, in short, we eat and drink and do all things not merely "*to* the Glory of God" but as an expression of God's glory in the world.

Detachment from sense is no doubt a condition of the activity of thought. But it involves the abandonment of the channel of sense through which man is equally able to commune with Reality; and is thereby responsible for the abstractions which are the most obvious defect of thought as ordinarily understood. In any case to make a condition of thinking a ground for despising sense experience and for speaking of "bondage to the senses" is not merely a misunderstanding of the nature of thinking itself but a misunderstanding of the resources of the mind's life and the mind's powers. It is just as foolish for "thinkers" to despise the senses, as for the "man of sense" to despise thinking.

**22** It is just possible that we are as restricted in the number and variety of concepts we can employ for the purpose of thinking as we are in the number of our senses. This suggestion may be at the back of the minds of those who speak of the "impossibility" of knowing certain objects.

**23** If truth be the union of the mind with its object in terms of the intellect, the union of the whole mind with the real, wherever found, may be called "the Truth." But truth in this wide sense need not be found only in one way. In the case of intellectual activity, and especially in science, it is found by effort, selection, abstraction, generalization. In the case of religion, it is found by giving up effort of our own, by submission and acceptance, which together and at their best we call Love of the Highest.

**24** Faith is necessary to mental life not only (as is so often supposed) in order to support the mind in the pursuit of truth, but because we know so little, and what we know is so imperfectly known. Faith is not simply demanded as a supplement or substitute for defective knowledge, as if it were a second-best, which will disappear as knowledge advances. Faith is required even with knowledge, for all our knowledge cannot be present to the mind at once: it consists of a series of judgments of which we are aware separately and discontinuously. Knowledge is not only partial but is of parts: faith is an attitude to the whole, and the whole can never be resolved even into all the parts; it is more than the parts, it is the totality and unity of them.

For these reasons, faith is in a sense more necessary to the mind than any particular act of knowledge: it is a continuous attitude of confidence and trust in the stability of the foundations of our experience.

**25**   It is worthy of note that an emotional interest in a subject may be so transmuted as to render an interest in knowledge of the subject more effective. In the practice of medicine a doctor's anxiety and sympathy for his patient do not interfere with his strictly scientific interest in the case; they tend rather to intensify and stimulate the scientific resources and resourcefulness which he brings to bear on his patient. Thus the emotional concern on his patient's behalf puts him on his mettle to strive to win the victory over the disease. Humanity comes to the aid of the scientist; and science, by being suffused with human consideration, thereby becomes more efficient for its purpose.

This affords a curious illustration of the coincidence of scientific ideals with human welfare. Generalized, it should be true of all science. Science need not be inhuman because it is abstract, detached and impartial.

**26**   Behind credulity in mankind there is a pathetic sense of faith in larger purposes, and in the reasonableness of the world. Men are credulous because they wish to believe the truth, and because the truth means so much to them.

**27**   In regard to certain matters we should be glad that we need only believe, and are not asked or expected to understand.

**28**   We often wish we had the power to see the future, and feel it a deprivation that we cannot anticipate or forecast even the coming day. We forget that, if we are to know the future, we must know the whole of it or none of it; we cannot select. If we really knew the whole of it, we should lose interest in life: our going forward would look like the march of fate: the foresight of inevitable evil and pain would add an unbearable horror to life in the present: the mere consciousness of what is to come would burden the present beyond our powers, which are rarely enough to handle the actual present successfully. We should be grateful to the beneficent dispensation which entirely conceals the future from our eyes and focuses our attention on the vivid present. It is better to face the future with faith and hope; and these are enough to keep us steady and give us all the confidence we need and require. Knowledge would only undermine our peace and add to our anxiety.

**29** It requires a community of some sort to express a truth. It is often said that a truth can bring minds together. But the converse also holds: a truth only becomes a truth when an association of minds openly affirms it. In fact the full force and value of a truth are only realized by the individual when it is so affirmed.

**30** It is sometimes held that knowledge has as one of its aims to get rid of faith. Nothing could be more superficial. There are some spheres of experience where knowledge cannot possibly enter at all, and which can only be faced by faith. One of these is the experience of death: the great venture into that realm of complete silence can receive no help from human knowledge. Faith and hope alone can give the individual security and confidence.

We dispense with knowledge even when we commit ourselves to sleep.

**31** The cultivation of knowledge will not be carried on with the greatest zest, and will not give all the satisfaction to the mind of which it is capable, unless knowledge is regarded as a form of the spiritual life of man, unless in fact it is felt to be an element in the beauty of holiness. Thinking deals with the invisible world, knowledge is communion with the unseen, a spiritual function, an activity of the Divine Spirit incarnated in man. All the greatest thinkers have taken this view of knowledge —Aristotle and Plato, Spinoza and Hegel. And they are right.

Yet it is almost entirely ignored in the schools, even in those of higher learning. Knowledge is looked on as a kind of mental craft or even craftiness, a dodge or a game, an instrument of practical success in the worldly sense—anything, except a particular form of realizing the religious life.

**32**  Of faith you can never have too much: of knowledge you certainly may.

# APPENDIX

1   Mercurial opinions cannot be fixed or rendered permanent by any frost of examination or criticism.

2   Human endeavours and strivings seem often like a race for life with a precipice for a terminus.

3   Can a person who hates or despises the past and its movements love the present, or appreciate it?

4   Cynicism of the ordinary kind seems the easy refuge of disappointed incompetence: a sort of articulate envy.

5   It is symbolical of many forms of human experience that, when music is at a distance from us, we only hear the stronger, wilder notes.

6   It can hardly be said to be in a man's power to increase his life as regards its length, nor even as regards its breadth; there seems, therefore, nothing left but to increase its *depth*. And this each man can do.

7   How much has the simple perception of a starry or a moonlit night done to ennoble and beautify man's earthly life! Quite apart from anything it may suggest or imply, the mere vision of it, even by the most childlike observer, can have these effects. What had been man's lot had he been obliged to gaze for ever on an unchanging blackness of surrounding space, or even on a starless canopy?

8   As long as there is something to know there will always be something to do.

**9**  To tamper with truth at any point is to destroy one's belief in it and one's sincerity towards it, and that is the beginning—indeed, the kernel—of all shame, fear and cowardice.

**10**  To some people everything is so mysterious that mystery itself has become a commonplace.

**11**  The world is mysterious enough when we do understand it; it is only a good deal more so when we don't.

**12**  The only mystery is the truth, and the truth is not darkness but light.

**13**  There is a kind of optimist who wishes everyone well and yet feels surprised, and even slightly disappointed, when his wishes are realized because he is thereby robbed of the chance of showing pity for the misfortune which he really expects to occur.

**14**  If to be wealthy is insupportable to the vast mass of mankind, is it likely that men would know what to do with wisdom if they had it? If men find it difficult to regulate their possession of such a thing as wealth, would they find themselves able to control their ownership of the truth? Each man should seek no more truth than he would wish to find and keep.

**15**  We are all fearfully and wonderfully made, but that is no reason why we should make ourselves fearful and wonderful.

**16**  One of the most perplexing of men is the person of great earnestness but without insight and without humour: a very puzzling spiritual malformation.

**17**  Significant that the highest in man, his thought, his reason, is alone what is communicable between man and man.

## APPENDIX

**18**  Our contact with what is great will only enlarge our minds if we are bound to it by reverence or love; only so does it become part of our personality. The attitude of a critic or a spectator will still leave us in our littleness and feebleness.

**19**  To grow and know what one is growing towards—that is the source of all strength and confidence in life.

**20**  Amongst human beings, spirit is the principle of individuality, and not matter. It is not bodies which distinguish men and women or attract them to each other, so much as character.

**21**  It is very significant that the whole firmament of heaven has to be set ablaze to bring out the full glory of the dewdrop on the daisy.

**22**  It is notable that, though people mourn for their dead, they would generally be alarmed if they came to life again.

**23**  There is nothing worth dying for that it is not also worth living for.

**24**  Even truth can be too dearly bought—if it is purchased by the loss of the capacity to appreciate it.

**25**  So many people confuse a capacity to see all round a subject with an incapacity to make up their minds. The two are essentially distinct.

**26**  Some people take up with all beliefs and all faiths on the assumption apparently that some of them must be true: much as a man might swallow the contents of an apothecary's shop on the chance that some of it will cure his disease.

**27**  A man's suspicions of evil in others are the reflection of his own temptations: a man's judgments on others bear the stamp of his own ideal of himself.

**28**  It is foolish to be in a hurry to be good, for nobody can be good in a hurry.

**29**  When streams are low we may alter the river bed; in flood they deepen their own water-courses.

**30**  The "inspiration" which inspires the reader is the only kind of inspiration which any document need lay claim to.

**31**  Two things are supremely worth having—the love of knowledge and the knowledge of love.

**32**  There are, perhaps, not many things that are more valuable when second-hand than when new, but there are some: one is old furniture, another is flattery.

**33**  A sidereal perspective and a parochial perspective are both essential to the proper appreciation of life.

**34**  If we are to live bravely and well, we must be prepared to risk all the capital of the past in the venture of the future. We must not hoard our capital, that is cowardice: we must not face the future without capital, that is foolhardiness; we must invest it—and all of it—in the future, that alone is the courage that makes a true life.

**35**  It is an important rule never to think of the broken eggs when you are making your omelette.

**36**  For the security and level prosperity of everyday life the average nature of man requires three things: good health, good sense and peace of mind. For the average individual nothing else matters.

## APPENDIX

**37** The only use some men have for their intellect is to disagree with their neighbours.

**38** It is often easier to displace one vice or evil tendency by another vice or evil inclination than it is to displace an evil inclination by a good one!

**39** The world can be divided along many lines: and one line separates those people who grow on the sunny side of God's providence from those who grow in the shade.

**40** It is interesting to notice how the controlling inspiration of life varies with age: in youth it is hope, in middle age faith, in later life the charity that tolerates and comprehends.

**41** In the lower levels of experience men can herd together and share experience: in the higher levels we must be prepared to stand alone—like summits of the hills ranging together and running into the plains.

**42** It would be worth while knowing just how much influence has been exerted over the imagination and the thought of man by the mere fact of his living under the dome-shaped form of the sky and looking at it every day.

**43** Only the man who finds the whole earth to be a temple is really at home in the world. For such a man churches are little better than caves.

**44** Laughter and joy will hold people together much better and much longer than logic and argument.

**45** If it is wise to forgive our enemies, men should begin by forgiving themselves, for they are often their own worst enemies.

46   We should never suppose that passing by an obstacle is the same thing as surmounting it.

47   A man who has made up his mind about everything has probably not had a mind worth making up on anything. He has merely put his prejudices into pigeonholes and labelled them principles.

48   We must learn the purpose of our destiny by our mistakes and by our defeats as well as by wisdom and success.

49   A new suit of clothes acts on some people like a fresh moral start.

50   Put into the execution of your purpose the energy of passion you will certainly feel, if you fail to realize your purpose. There will then be less passion to spend on regrets.

51   It needs as strong a heart to carry gladness with safety as to carry grief.

52   Wild oats do not make good porridge. Those who sow wild oats must expect to be asked to eat them.

53   The worldliness of the poor is quite as deep-seated as the worldliness of the rich: just as the pride of the poor can be as strong as that of the rich.

54   Most of the maxims about human life have been discovered by making mistakes. That is why so many of them are expressed in a negative form.

55   If virtues were more lovely, morality would be much easier.

## APPENDIX

**56** Youth is naturally conservative. It is only, or mainly, manhood that has the capacity to be original.

**57** All the forces of the world are on the side of the brave man: they all seem to work against the coward.

**58** There are no rules for winning a game: there are only rules for playing it. Rules for winning a game would spoil the game. Rules are made to restrain or direct a person when he plays. To win, the player depends on two things of an entirely different kind—luck and the weakness of his adversary. So in the game of life.

**59** Family pride and self-respect will do more to keep people straight than all the rules of any decalogue.

**60** It may be possible at all times and on all occasions to love God: it is certainly not possible on all occasions to love man.

**61** What if all kinds of moral and social reform be but a species of moral quixotism, tilting against the ineradicable follies and weaknesses and vices of mankind?

**62** With many desires, life may be difficult; without desires, it is impossible.

**63** It is curious how in old age men tend to become avaricious. Probably their uncertain hold of life makes them uncertain of their hold over wealth; and their weakness leads to fear that they may lose what they have, and thus to greed for more. Greed is all that is left when their own powers have gone.

**64** It is a good rule never to shut a door so that you cannot open it again.

**65**  People do not always like to be looked at from the dramatic point of view: but very many like to look at themselves in this way.

**66**  There are some men whose time seems so occupied looking after the whole universe that they have no time to mind their own business.

**67**  It is a good rule to trust your loves and to distrust your hates.

**68**  More hopes are destroyed through cowardice than abandoned through failure.

**69**  People who aim at being like gods usually repeat in their moral experience the story of the "fall of man." To be fully human is as much as any man can be, and more than most can attain to.

**70**  The worst sign of age is to forget you have grown old.

**71**  If a nation has to choose between stagnation and storm, it is better to have the storm.

**72**  Forgive the dead: it is one of the few things you can do for them.

**73**  Many people announce their theories with the big drum. But true wisdom always seems to prefer the still small voice.

**74**  Posthumously born wisdom is better than none: but wisdom should also be the companion of experience; experience should not die when wisdom is born.

**75**  Most people seem to prefer to carry their knowledge in their hands—in books or otherwise: few carry it in their heads: fewer still in their hearts.

## APPENDIX

**76** There is no sense in selling the coat off your back to buy a hat for your head.

**77** Too much light produces the same effect as darkness to the eye of man, and to the mind of man. Faith relieves us from the danger of both.

**78** In the moral life it is a safe rule—when in doubt, do not act: let circumstances prove later on whether action would have been good or the reverse.

**79** Good manners seem always to be the outcome of traditional behaviour of long standing, whether the tradition be that of a family or a whole civilization. Manners by rule seem artificial even when "correct."

**80** People who counsel themselves against fear are already afraid.

**81** The virtues cost nothing: vices have always to be paid for.

**82** There are men who mistake the phosphorescence of an excited brain for the light of an intelligent mind, incessant effervescence for plenary inspiration.

**83** There is a consistency which is as barren as a mere arithmetical formula.

**84** It is never wise to create a deficit in your business in anticipation of an act of God to square your accounts.

**85** The important thing about opinions is not that they should be right but that there should be many of them.

**86**  A layman is a man who is prepared to lay down the law on matters which he does not profess to understand.

**87**  In England there is a close connection between property and the proprieties.

**88**  Common sense is the wisdom of the passing hour: mysticism is the wisdom of the eternal.

**89**  The last sin of all is the pride which will not accept forgiveness.

**90**  Many people seem to think that the possession of strong convictions is better than having a conscience.

**91**  It seems very difficult to discover the will of God in matters of finance. It looks as if finance were the devil's own field.

**92**  The desire for the millennium is often nothing more than a form of anxiety for the morrow. It is wanting the Kingdom of God in a hurry. God is never in a hurry.

**93**  The best that can be said for an action in many cases is that it is a better mistake than usual.

**94**  Man is the only animal that can make a fool of itself.

**95**  Self-made men so often are gratified by the flattery of their contemporaries because they feel the want of the approval of their ancestors. Men with a tradition behind them look to the approval of their forefathers to release them from the need to seek any favours from their contemporaries.

**96**  It is good to be backed by your grandfathers: it is better to be backed by your grandchildren.

## APPENDIX

**97** Most people prefer to be standardized rather than to have standards of their own.

**98** A religion *de luxe* is merely worldliness masquerading as other-worldliness. It ignores the warning that it is impossible to serve both God and Mammon.

**99** He is a wise man who knows how to appreciate the value of the second best.

**100** One fool may make a comedy: two fools may make a tragedy.

**101** The conceit of ignorance is as common as the conceit of knowledge and far more dangerous.

**102** Where is leadership to be found? In the songs of a few obscure poets, in the hymns of some poor saints, in the lives of a few heroic souls.

**103** Death should not take us by surprise. We are waiting for it all our life.

**104** A great part of a good life consists in avoiding mistakes. This is perhaps the only part of conduct that the young can learn from the old.

**105** Miracles have been objected to because they upset the laws of nature. Why trouble about that? That nature has laws is merely another kind of miracle.

**106** It would make an immense difference to the interest and value of each day if the individual could live it in full view of his death. But this is perhaps too difficult for most men, even though it is the only true attitude to adopt. Most people live in the illusion that they are going to live on indefinitely in this world; and the illusion probably helps them to live.

**107**  It is a good rule followed by all peoples not to abandon your own religion till you find a better.

**108**  Independence without dignity is the travesty of self-respect, the freedom of the tramp and the social alien.

**109**  Much as we may be disappointed with men and even with mankind, that is no reason for dealing with them "as they deserve." After all, the Almighty has tolerated with Divine compassion the foolishness and the errors and the wickedness of man for so long that the best we can do is to share His magnanimity instead of taking our revenge.

**110**  No doubt people are mostly fools, or at least largely foolish. But men were probably intended to be friendly and kind rather than clever or even wise. Certainly they very quickly show and respond to friendliness towards one another.

**111**  One of the difficult arts of life is to do and take disagreeable things in an agreeable way.

**112**  Self-depreciation is generally a form of inverted vanity.

**113**  The amateur loves the object, the specialist loves the knowledge of the object. On the whole the amateur gains most and has the more interesting type of mind.

**114**  There are men who cultivate humility in order to satisfy spiritual pride.

**115**  The Englishman takes anything seriously if you try to deprive him of it, and nothing seriously if you do not.

# INDEX

In references to subsections the Roman numeral indicates the number of the section, the Arabic that of the subsection. All other Arabic numerals refer to pages

Absolute, the, 79, 247, 254, 259 f.
Acting, *see* Drama
Agnosticism, 82, 90
Altruism, 198
Anthropomorphism, 23, 65, 79, 82, 265
Architecture, *see* Religion and Architecture
Aristotle, 108, 191, 210, 293
Art, 147, 150, 159, 161, 227, 229 f., 233, 266 ff., *see also* Religion and Art
Atheism, 40, 49, 83 f.
Atonement, 18, 56, 63, 74, 135 f., 190
Aurelius, Marcus, 251

Beauty. *See* Art
Buddhism, 62

Catholicism, 27, 58 ff., 69, 108, 110 f., 123
Ceremonial, 115, 228 f.
Charity, 63
Christianity, I. 4, *passim*, 42, 87, 90, 94 f. 125 f., 43. *See also* Church
Church, the (and Churches), I. 7, *passim*, 55, 57, 60, 134, 218. *See also* Christianity, Catholicism, Protestantism
Clergy, the. *See* Church, the
Comte, 26, 94
Conversation, 199 ff., 207
Copernicus, 292 f.
Crucifixion, 66 ff., 75 ff.

Deism, 24
Democracy, 113, 209, 211 f., 217
Drama, 154, 196, 228, 230-1

Education, 230 ff., 234, 236
Emotion. *See* Feeling
English, the, 186, 195, 225, 284, 286
Epictetus, 251
Evil, II. 3, 4, *passim*, 30, 39, 47, 127. *See also* Sin
Evolution, 140, 260 ff.

Faith, 34, 40 f., 42 f., 44 f., 70, 72 f., 265, 271 f., 273 f.
Feeling, II. 5, *passim*, 146, 156 f. *See also* Religion and Feeling

Freedom, 146, 182, 189, 221, 236, 254 f., 258
Forgiveness, 19, 56, 135 f., 138 ff., 170, 182, 196

God—
and the Absolute, 79 f., 91 f.
communion with, II., *passim*, 39, 41, 58 ff., 90 ff., 94 ff., 103, 108, 259, 269 f. *See also* Atonement, Faith, Prayer, Forgiveness
Fear of, 20, I. 2, *passim*
Knowledge of, 17 f., 22, 29, 44, 57, 82 f., 84, 91, 108
Love of, I. 2, *passim*, 72, 108, 143, 198, 214
Goodness (Moral), II. 2 and 4, *passim*, 50, 145, 164, 167 f., 186, 190 ff., 205 f. *See also* Religion and Morality, Forgiveness, Sin
Gratitude, 43, 52, 161
Greeks, the, 20, 95, 133

Habit, 131, 184 ff., 188
Hamlet, 235
Happiness, II., *passim*, 45, 129 ff.
Hebrews. *See* Jews
Hegel, 238 f., 242, 244, 250 ff., 256, 259, 273
Hume, 256
Humour, 48, 227

Immortality, I. 6, *passim*
Incarnation, 65, 67 ff., 71, 90
Individuality, 100 ff., 106, 122, 183. *See also* Personality
Inspiration, 219 f., 278

Jews, the, 17, 20, 61 f., 95 f., 133, 135, 162 f., 222 ff.

Kant, 160, 237, 253, 266
Keats, 126

Lessing, 264
Lotze, 251
Love, 36, 42, 105, 125 f., 196, 197 f., 189 f., 204, 206, 214. *See also* God, Love of
Luther, 59

287

# INDEX

Marriage, 121 f., 214 ff.
Mediation, 20, 69
Miracles, 35, 54, 71 f., 85, 88, 106, 285
Mohammedanism, 27, 62
Morality. *See* Goodness
Mysticism, 21, 82, 177

Nature, 25 f., 99, 126, 222, 227, 261 f, 265, 285. *See also* Religion and Nature

Pacifism (and Peace), 127 f., 217
Paul, St., 61 f., 68, 74, 90, 114, 121 f., 138
Personality, II. 6, *passim*, 79 f., 106
Pessimism, 143
Philosophy, III, *passim*, 160, 253 f., 256. *See also* Religion and Philosophy
Plato, 191, 215, 273
Pleasure, 148 ff., 152, 155 ff.
Polytheism, 24
Prayer, I. 3, *passim*
Pre-existence, 97
Protestantism, 27, 69, 110 f., 115 f., 119
Providence, 27, 36, 52, 81

Reformation, 59 f., 115 f.
Relativity—
    in Knowledge, 249 f.
    in Morality, 158
Religion—
    and Architecture, 29 ff.
    and Art, 36 f., 94 f., 161
    and Feeling, 80 f., 130 f., 183 f., 269 ff.,

Religion—*continued*
    and History, 55 f., 58 ff., 60 ff., 63, 66, 70, 73, 87, 95, 133. *See also* Christianity
    and Morality, I. 8 and 9, *passim*, 20, 25, 56, 161, 175, 180. *See also* Sin, Forgiveness
    and Nature, 31 f., 58, 88, 93 ff., 126 f., 255
    Natural Religion, 21, 65, 93, 132
    and Philosophy, 80 ff., 83 f., 89, 91 ff., 239 ff., 246
    and Science, 20, 25, 36, 88, 92 ff., 128
    and Society, 110 f., 114, 207
Resurrection, 54, 68, 70, 74, 78, 103

Sacrament, 37 f., 270
Science, 161, 240 ff., 244 f., 248, 265 ff., 272. *See also* Religion and Science.
Self-consciousness, 192 f., 104, 202 f., 204 f., 207, 256
Self-realization, 138, 191 f., 194, 214 ff.
Self-sacrifice, 197
Sin, I. 10, *passim*, 164, 166, 172
Shakespeare, 138
Spencer, 26
Spinoza, 26, 108, 273
State, the, 111 f., 117, 220 f.
Suffering, 96, 136 f., 145, 149, 152
Superstition, 17

War, 127, 217, 225 f.
Wealth, 165 f.
Worldliness, 170 ff., 280
Work, 147, 208 ff., 212 f.

For Product Safety Concerns and Information please contact our EU representative GPSR@taylorandfrancis.com
Taylor & Francis Verlag GmbH, Kaufingerstraße 24, 80331 München, Germany